Selected Essays and Dialogues
by Gianni Celati

Literature and Translation

Series Editors: Timothy Mathews, Geraldine Brodie and Ana Cláudia Suriani da Silva

Literature and Translation is a series for books of literary translation as well as about literary translation. Its emphasis is on diversity of genre, culture, period and approach. The series uses the UCL Press open-access publishing model widely to disseminate developments in both the theory and practice of translation. Translations into English are welcomed of literature from around the world.

Timothy Mathews is Emeritus Professor of French and Comparative Criticism, UCL.

Geraldine Brodie is Professor of Translation Theory and Theatre Translation, UCL.

Ana Cláudia Suriani da Silva is Associate Professor of Brazilian Studies, UCL.

Selected Essays and Dialogues by Gianni Celati

Adventures into the errant familiar

Edited and Translated by Patrick Barron

First published in 2024 by
UCL Press
University College London
Gower Street
London WC1E 6BT

Available to download free: www.uclpress.co.uk

A CIP catalogue record for this book is available from The British Library.

ISBN: 978-1-80008-641-8 (Hbk)
ISBN: 978-1-80008-640-1 (Pbk)
ISBN: 978-1-80008-639-5 (PDF)
ISBN: 978-1-80008-642-5 (epub)
DOI: https://doi.org/10.14324/111.9781800086395

Contents

List of figures

Acknowledgements

After long wandering through Gianni Celati's fascinating, kindred webs of thought, and though loathe to come to an end, at least on this particular journey, I am also thankful to see at last the publication of *Selected Essays and Dialogues: Adventures into the errant familiar*, begun in Bologna in 2018 as I was finishing the translation of *Verso la foce* (*Towards the River's Mouth*). I am grateful to Celati for his trust in me and his encouragement. I wish that he was still here with us, but in many ways he still is, his voice continuing to weave its way through. My special thanks to Gillian Haley for her granting permission both to translate many of Celati's writings that appear in this collection and to reprint a number of photographs of him. I deeply appreciate her support of the project and her assistance. My thanks, too, to Quodlibet Press for granting permission to translate many other of Celati's writings that appear here. I must also acknowledge my debt to the main collections of his essays published in Italy and variously edited by Marco Belpoliti, Nunzia Palmieri, Marco Sironi, Anna Stefi, Jean Talon, Ermanno Cavazzoni and Gianni Celati himself.[1] Most of the essays that appear here are drawn from these earlier books. Additional thanks go to the National Endowment for the Humanities and to the University of Massachusetts, Boston, for their support; to Nida Caselli for her patient and generous help in revisiting tricky passages in the translation; to Adele Ghirri, Maria Fontana and the Luigi Ghirri Foundation for their help in locating and for granting permission to reprint a number of Luigi Ghirri's photographs of Celati; to George Tatge and Vincenzo Cottinelli for granting permission to reprint their photographs of Celati; to Jim Hicks and *The Massachusetts Review* for publishing work both by and about Celati, including a three-part colloquy shortly after his death in 2022;[2] and to the many other people who have given me encouragement and guidance along the way, including Rebecca West, Marina Spunta, Nunzia Palmieri, Andrea Cortellessa, Robert Elliot, Serenella Iovino, Jonathan Skinner, Christopher Johnson, Manuela Mariani, Piero Barron and Giacomo Barron.

Notes

1 See Gianni Celati, *Finzioni Occidentali* (Turin: Einaudi, 2001 [1975]); Gianni Celati, *Alice disambientata: Materiali collettivi (su Alice) per un manuale di sopravvivenza* (Florence: Le Lettere, 2007); *Riga 28: Gianni Celati*, eds. Marco Belpoliti and Marco Sironi (Milan: Marcos y Marcos, 2008); *Documentari imprevedibili come i sogni: Il cinema di Gianni Celati*, ed. Nunzia Palmieri (Rome: Fandango, 2011); Gianni Celati, *Conversazioni del vento volatore* (Macerata: Quodlibet, 2011); Gianni Celati, *Studi d'affezione per amici e altri* (Macerata: Quodlibet, 2016); Gianni Celati, *Celati: Romanzi, cronoche e raccconti*, eds. Marco Belpoliti and Nunzia Palmieri (Milan: Mondadori, 2016); Gianni Celati and Carlo Gajani, *Animazioni e incantamenti*, ed. Nunzia Palmieri (Rome: L'Orma, 2017); *Riga 40: Gianni Celati*, eds. Marco Belpoliti, Marco Sironi and Anna Stefi (Macerata: Quodlibet, 2019); Gianni Celati, *Narrative in fuga*, ed. Jean Talon (Macerata: Quodlibet, 2019); and Gianni Celati, *Il transito mite delle parole: Conversazioni e interviste 1974–2014*, eds. Marco Belpoliti and Anna Stefi (Macerata: Quodlibet, 2022).
2 See 'The Writer as Meditative Thinker', *The Massachusetts Review*, https://www.massreview.org/node/10278.

1
Introduction

I came to know Gianni Celati's writings in the late 1990s when I found his *Narratori delle pianure* (*Voices from the Plains*) in a bookshop in Ferrara, a town in northern Emilia Romagna, not far from the Po River, where I was living at the time and working as an English teacher.[1] On the cover is a photograph by Luigi Ghirri showing Celati as a lone figure facing away from the camera and standing on a muddy road that curves to the left across a vague expanse of snowy land; he is slightly crooked and bent over something immediately at hand (see fig. 13.1). I imagine that Celati is taking notes, trying to describe his surroundings – the seemingly nondescript expanse of wintry plain that envelops him – as Ghirri describes him and his location, a photographic frame around the frame of words Celati is writing. None of this was apparent to me at the time, but I found Ghirri's image haunting, strangely inviting yet also difficult to interpret, and the title of the book promised insights into the same plains on which I was living and attempting to know, yet finding somewhat inscrutable.

As I read this book and others by Celati, I became increasingly drawn down tangled paths through literature, film, photography, the visual arts, theatre, everyday stories, other people, other places, a seemingly endless series of adventures of the mind and body, always infused with a great sensitivity for an encompassing collective imagination not restricted to the so-called high arts or letters, but very much also engaged with the everyday lives, places and tales we all constantly share. One feels in good company reading his work, as if the topics and texts at hand, however foreign or far-flung they may seem, are also of some personal, familiar relevance. No matter how challenging or bewildering the notions he at times entertains, Celati puts readers at ease while whisking them off on some wild goose chase or stroll around the neighbourhood. Reading his work indeed often feels like going for a walk with him to parts at once unknown and known. One of the few times I met Celati was in Cork, Ireland, in 2016. His health had started to decline a bit, but he still had a slightly impish air about him, sauntering around the city with a sense of joy at simply being there, at one point crooking his arm around a light post and swinging slowly around to look back at me, the street, and us, smiling with wonder, a smile the vestiges of which I feel now on my own face.

Celati was born in 1937 in Sondrio and moved soon after with his family to Trapani and Belluno, and then, a few years following the end of World War II, to Ferrara and later Bologna, a town and a city less than an hour apart by train in the Po River Valley, the manifold site of assorted perceptual and physical adventures as recounted in many of his books and films.[2] Widely recognized as one of the most important contemporary Italian writers, he first became known for fiction associated with the neo-avant-garde of the late 1960s that focused on unstable identities and the socially marginalized in books noted for their disjointed, experimental language. His writing later became somewhat leaner, demonstrating a wariness of institutions while compassionately examining contemporary society and everyday cultural landscapes, among much else. Scholarly interest in his work has continued to grow, both in Italian and other languages, including in English, with an expanding body of monographs and articles.[3] Celati taught at the University of Bologna, had visiting professorships at the University of Caen, Cornell University, the University of Chicago and Brown University, and spent extended periods travelling across the US, West Africa and Europe, including England, where he moved in the mid-1980s with his wife Gillian Haley. He died in January 2022.

This short biographical description, necessary or *pro forma* as it may be, is to be taken with a grain of salt, as all such summaries should. It is particularly difficult to categorize or summarize Celati's work. His writings, moving in concentrated flurries from narration to translation to commentary to poetry to screenplays, are hard to pin down because they are driven by adventurous imaginaries and drawn always on and into the beyond of some small or large homeland of the mind (without monuments or patriotisms) instead of bogged down by a compulsion to follow rules, literary or otherwise. His books and films move across others, other ideas, other places and other texts, wandering into unknowns that are also familiars, rethinking and reinventing as a way, as Celati puts it, of 'prolonging the state of non-fixation that exists in imaginative gusts'.[4] Wandering and re-wandering, whether across places once known or not, invites adventure – however minimal or exaggerated matters little. Celati's adventures range from the 'expository adventure of archaeological discourse', or a peripatetic and 'uninterrupted encounter with the molecular places of a heterotopic city where residues of extraneity float to infinity', to 'swerves of intensity' or 'new ways of wandering with one's head', to the 'adventures of ordinary humans', or 'micro-histories that play out in dimensions to which no one pays much attention because they are not sensational'.[5]

The selection of his variously theoretical, musing and scholarly work translated here into English, ranging from the late 1960s to recent times, gives but a taste of these errant, ever-shifting interests and should not be taken as representative, especially considering how prolific Celati was, publishing myriad essays and over 20 books, from *Comiche* (1971) [Slapstick silent films] and *Le avventure di Guizzardi* (1972) [The adventures of Guizzardi] to *Quattro novelle sulle apparanze* (1987) (*Appearances*), *Cinema Naturale* (2001) [Natural cinema], and *Selve d'amore* (2013) [Amorous thickets], and producing four films: *Strada provinciale delle anime* (1991) [Provincial road of the souls], *Il mondo di Luigi Ghirri* (1999) [The world of Luigi Ghirri], *Case sparse – Visioni di case che crollano* (2002) [Scattered houses: visions of collapsing houses], and *Diol Kadd* (2011). He also translated many books from French and English into Italian – from Honoré de Balzac's *Droll Stories* (1967), Roland Barthes' *Roland Barthes by Roland Barthes* (1980), Herman Melville's *Bartleby the Scrivener* (1991), Stendhal's *The Charterhouse of Parma* (1993) and Jonathan Swift's *Gulliver's Travels* (1997), to James Joyce's *Ulysses* (2013). Most of these translations include fascinating and extensive introductions that engage with various intricacies of the texts as well as the translation process. In 2016, his collected narrative works, *Romanzi, cronache e racconti* [Novels, accounts and stories], was published in Mondadori's Meridiani series. And, just as I was completing this book, an over 600-page collection of his conversations and interviews was published: *Il transito mite delle parole: Conversazioni e interviste 1974–2014* (Macerata: Quodlibet, 2022) [The gentle passage of words: Conversations and interviews 1974–2014]. The selection of his work presented here clearly only scratches the surface.

The title of the book in hand, *Selected Essays and Dialogues: Adventures into the errant familiar*, does, however, indicate qualities inherent to all Celati's output, his daringness as a thinker and fondness for the unexpected ordinary. Indeed, a genial adventurousness can be found within Celati's many and varied writings, collaborations and dialogues, which are driven by an affectionate and light-hearted engagement with the surrounding world, embracing both what he is and is not, as well as what he might be. Key is the idea that all writing can be viewed as a form of translation understood as a process of surrendering, transforming, being transformed, and passing on and through a changeling interplay of relational indices with the awareness that any one place, one meaning, one phrase is never the same as itself, always subject to change. Translation implies always being nowhere, as if in no place, being by definition in multiple places, neither entirely here nor there linguistically or culturally or otherwise, but both here and there.

For Celati the reading, writing, rewriting, translating and retelling of texts overlap in a sort of overlay map or palimpsest of the everyday in which interrelated fragments are constantly brought into relation, and one that resists the 'tendency to write in a way that can be passed off as acceptable to anyone – because in reality no book is acceptable to everyone'.[6] Writing for Celati is never stable but, rather, always in transit and undergoing shifts, with writing implying rewriting, and all literary genres better understood 'as collective modes of storytelling, of writing poetry, of imagining life', or as 'a collective flux of words'.[7] Awareness of this flux depends on tapping into a certain sort of *allegria* (mirth, lightheartedness) that he calls 'a vital and basic way to go beyond the self, towards an exteriority of everything that we are not: things, stones, trees, animals, the spirits in the air and the darkness inside our bodies'.[8]

After the playful and condensed 'One-page autobiography', *Adventures into the errant familiar* begins with the 1968 essay 'Speech as spectacle' in which Celati draws overlapping parallels between everyday speech, performative and silent reading, music and spectacle, focusing on what he calls the 'gestural sense of words' in an extended analysis of the transcription of speech in Louis-Ferdinand Céline's writings.[9] Next is Italo Calvino's note on Celati's first book, *Comiche*, and Celati's accompanying extended reply in which he explains 'why I don't recognize myself in your little portrait', emphasizing, among much else, that 'we must always die in order to write something that reaches that other world. And everything we write comes from the other world: whether heaven or as others say Hades'.[10] Celati's relationship with Calvino, as a mentor, collaborator and friend, is referenced in several pieces in the collection, including his account of Calvino's death and funeral in 'Italo's death'. Close on the heels of this correspondence is the 1973 'Surface stories', an attempt to identify and analyse then-recent work by Giorgio Manganelli, Edoardo Sanguinetti and Calvino (in particular *Invisible Cities*) characterized by a delimiting of space that causes 'the intangible universe of [each] book's depths to be reduced and carried to the surface of its material space as a paper artefact', a type of writing that Celati calls 'a surface story in as much as it is a story of what occurs on a surface, and a rejection of the old depth of discourse'.[11]

Other pieces from the 1970s include 'The virtues of the gorilla', an account of a group of theatre students from the University of Bologna, notably Remo Melloni, who with Giuliano Scabia revived and (re-)enacted 'Il Gorilla Quadrumàno', a piece of collaborative theatre based on an early twentieth-century farcical play written in local dialect about a 'tall and ferocious simian' who is variously a monkey, a human and a magician, brought to life by the students who created a giant gorilla puppet and performed the play in the open air, inspired by in part by literature (Boiardo, Pulci and Ariosto), and in part by carnival folk models from small villages in the countryside near Reggio Emilia.[12] The next essay, 'The archaeological bazaar', which originated in part from discussions with Calvino, Carlo Ginzburg, Enzo Melandri and Guido Neri, argues for an archaeological conception of historical knowledge, guided by the idea that

> there is no reason to make of history a temporal field rather than a spatial one, when the search for individual identity is substituted with the recognition of pure exteriority in relation to ourselves and our origins. It is exactly in those spaces that are marginalized or simply ignored by memory-tradition, that there resides that difference without which history is tautology.[13]

Moving to silent film, 'The comic body in space', drawing on Maurice Merleau-Ponty's theories of phenomenology and perception, is a roving mediation on early comic theatre and cinema, part of a long-enduring and evolving search for a type of writing capable of reproducing the effects of everyday, often colloquial or dialectal speech, as well as leading to a repertoire of syntactic constructions and rhythmical movements disruptive of codified narrative schemes. After a short meditation on Foucault's *Discipline and Punish*, two excerpts then follow from the book *Displaced Alice: Collective materials on Alice for a survival manual*, a collaborative work that grew out of an experimental course Celati taught on nonsense literature at the University of Bologna during the 1976–1977 student protests. Rounding out the 1970s is 'Soft objects', a mediation on Claes Oldenburg, including *Store Days* and various works of soft sculpture.

'Adventure at the end of the twentieth century', based on a conversation in 1982 with Luca Torrealta and Mario Zanzani on shifting notions of adventure in literature and film, as well as the relationship between narration and experience, is one of a number of writings that I call 'dialogues', musings of various sorts that grew from discussions with others and interviews, many of which that appear here are collected in *Conversazioni del vento volatore* (2011) [Conversations with the gusting wind]. Celati writes in the foreword to the book that 'writing is a conversation with whoever will read us, and conversations carry us like the wind – we never really know in what direction. Here "gusting wind" can be taken to mean that atmospheric force that words take on, scattering them across various topics, from cinema to autobiography'.[14]

Collaboration with others and openness to variously lissom and unpredictable flights of thought underlie all Celati's work, which, beginning in the 1980s, in part thanks to his friendship with photographer Luigi Ghirri, turned increasingly to how we perceive, shape and inhabit our surroundings. 'Fictions to believe in: an example', which appeared in the 1984 *Paesaggio italiano/Italian landscape*, a collection of Ghirri's photographs and writings, is a declaration of a new poetics inspired partly by Ghirri and other photographers engaged with describing the everyday world and with loosening and reattuning ingrained habits of spatial (landscape) perception. As Celati puts it in his opening note to *Verso la foce* (*Towards the River's Mouth*, 1989), written during this same period,

> every observation needs to liberate itself from the familiar codes it carries, to go adrift in the middle of all things not understood, in order to arrive at an outlet, where it must feel lost. As a natural tendency that absorbs us, every intense observation of the external world carries us closer to our death – and perhaps also lessens our separation from ourselves.[15]

Another roughly then-contemporaneous essay is 'A system of stories about the external world', which focuses on everyday descriptions and storytelling, especially as practiced in conversation, and how we might imagine what could be called 'an ordinary representation of the external world'.[16] 'Desert crossings', which appeared in a 1986 collection of photographs and essays on the Adriatic Coast, is a related meditation on what Celati refers to in *Towards the River's Mouth* as a 'variety of countryside where one breathes an air of urban solitude', which also becomes 'the path to rediscover and follow, the silence to cross in order to once again speak with others'.[17] 'The frontal view: Antonioni, *L'Avventura* and waiting' is similarly interested in spatial perception, what Celati calls a 'reopening' of environmental awareness in Michelangelo Antonioni's films in their many 'still moments, lingering aimless gazes and gestures, the steadiness of the frontal views'.[18] He argues that with this sense of sustained outward perception, 'all places become observable', beautiful and ugly alike, with the very act of pausing to linger in places becoming a sign of 'our inhabiting the earth, in the realm of the indeterminate'.[19]

The remaining pieces that follow range from a dialogue on varying approaches to narration over time ('In praise of the tale') and an auto-biographical musing on earlier collaborations and writings ('Two years of study at the British Museum'), to essays drawn from introductions to a few of Celati's many translations, such as Jack London's *The Call of the Wild*, Jonathan Swift's *A Tale of a Tub*, and James Joyce's *Ulysses*. There are two additional essays on Ghirri ('Comments on a natural theatre of images' and 'Threshold for Luigi Ghirri: how to think in images'), notes on a collective interchange of storytelling that relies on what he calls 'ways to rediscover reserves of things to read by way of writing, always with the sense of something already experienced or felt, or in other words, not revealed for the first time' (Introduction to *Narrators of the reserves*), and a reflection on the intersections of Celati's work as a writer and translator ('Rewriting, retelling, translating').

There were many other writings that I had hoped to include, but only so much can be included in a single book. My difficult selection choices were guided by a desire for a variety of writings, both formal and informal, and spread as evenly as possible from the late 1960s to recent years. Various fascinating longer essays on diverse topics, from theories of space and place in narrative writing to photography and the visual arts, and on writers such as Herman Melville, Stendahl, Miguel de Cervantes, Daniel Defoe, Samuel Beckett, Mikhail Bakhtin, François Rabelais, Mark Twain, Henri Michaux, George Perec and Flann O'Brien, simply did not fit.[20] With what is offered here, I hope that readers leave with a renewed or reinvigorated sense for ordinary (textual, environmental, social, artistic) adventure, perhaps even increased affection or least light-hearted tolerance for wherever they happen to inhabit, believing, as Celati puts it,

> that everything that people do from morning to night is an effort to come up with a credible account of the outside world, one that will make it bearable at least to some extent. We also think that this is a fiction, but a fiction in which it is necessary to believe. There are whole worlds of narrative at every point of space, appearances that alter at every blink of the eyes, infinite disorientations that require

above all a way of thinking and imagining that is not paralyzed by contempt for everything around us.[21]

I hope, too, that in translating Celati's work to have rendered some sense of its heady daring, coupled with its absorption in the thoughts, works and places of others, its mutable and unpredictable adventurousness, its urge to wander who-knows-where in search of both the ordinary and the extraordinary (the two becoming in the process hard to tell apart). As Celati writes,

> producing a translation that 'objectively' corresponds to the original of course will not do. There is no easy path forward in any translation. But perhaps there is a way to approach the linguistic bent from which a book is born by keenly pursuing its words to eliminate from the text purely functional readings and instead to restore to it an unpredictability that it had in the beginning, as a single, singular thing.[22]

Though Celati wrote this in relation to his translation of Jack London's *The Call of the Wild*, the embracing of unpredictability, especially as it relates to adventure and wandering, can be applied to much of Celati's writings in the various forms in which they appear. For instance, in the novella 'Condizioni di luce sulla via Emilia' ('Conditions of light on the Via Emilia') from *Quattro novelle sulle apparenze*, the philosophical sign painter-phenomenologist Emanuele Menini asks 'why do we never see immobility? We think of it only after having seen it, when the tremor is about to come over it and everything begins to move once more.'[23]

Such a question is in the same spirit as Alberto Giacometti's decision to stop making surrealist objects and instead dedicate himself to representing a head, his point being, as Celati puts it, 'the virtual impossibility of depicting a head exactly as we perceive it', or how

> it is possible to depict something surreal, imaginary, dreamlike or realistic, anything already officially assigned to a more or less codified category, but not the common appearance of something in plain view. The desire to depict a head exactly as someone sees it in space presents a difficult problem: not 'how we look' but 'how something appears to our perception'.[24]

Shifting attention to these ambiguous and evanescent appearances, focusing on the vividness and active inaction of an object instead of on the act of looking, is akin to breathing instead of attempting to grasp the air, embracing the poet Badalucco's notions on the (im)permanent atmosphere as expressed at the end of his sixteenth sonnet dedicated to the open air, as slyly transcribed by Celati:

> Certezze effimere, permanenza incerta,
> questa è la mia canzone all'aria aperta.[25]

> (Ephemeral certainties, unsteady intransience,
> this is my song to the uncluttered air.)

As we attempt however futilely to glean some fleeting sense, either from the gusting open wind or (in)stable, (im)mobile objects (whether people, places, or things) all around us, one circuitous path forward lies in what Celati terms 'documentaries as unpredictable as dreams' – pseudo-documentaries based on what we cannot see or seek out intentionally (but rather encounter haphazardly and without a clear plan) and capable of recounting or demonstrating how any comprehensive sense of the 'reality' of the external world is ultimately un-documentable.[26] As he puts it, 'encounters with places are always unpredictable, attracting us to something we don't know, to something we don't know what to call'.[27] Key to this is what Celati calls 'il disponibile quotidiano' (the accessible everyday) – everything in landscapes, welcoming and unwelcoming alike, that passes on around us.[28]

Menini's interest in the hyper- and hypo-local – in what is over and constantly runs above, as well as what is beneath and runs under any given ordinary place – stems from the unpredictability and imperceptibility of what often seems should be predictable and perceptible because it is either routinely encountered or seems unmoving. Menini describes his quest to understand the unease that afflicts people unable to appreciate, much less tolerate, things that do not seem to move:

> I think we have to ask ourselves what is light and what is shadow so as not to leave things alone in their sorry state. I'll come to the point: you'll see lots of people going about who become furious if they happen to see something that doesn't move. For them it's normal for the light to be splintered, since it goes with the tremor and then everything moves and one must always be busy. Well, what can we say about those people who find no peace in the immobility of things?[29]

This question is one that Celati too shares, both in his own restlessness as a thinker and traveller, as well as his attraction to the vibrating interstices between objects, the edges that would appear to belong to all things that seem stationary but in fact are always in transition and transitory, whether places, people, objects or texts and languages.

Menini's obsession with the impossible urge to observe immobility in a world of rushing and impatient human consciousnesses is related to Celati's recurrent interest in flux, whether James Joyce's (and Dziga Vertov's) keen ability to perceive 'a general sense of discontinuous yet collective motion located everywhere' or 'the idea of a space' as evident in certain comic slapstick films 'entirely full and without voids in which the void is nothing but a momentary effect of movements, of gestures, that then suddenly disappears amid other movements and gestures', or for that matter a conception of literature as 'a collective flux of words' as opposed to the 'old humanistic pretence' of believing that there exist 'static monuments of classic literature'.[30]

It is somewhere between these two related notions of continual flux and impossible yet essential immobility that we can momentarily locate Celati's approach to writing (and translating and filmmaking), as always from an angle and angling across, in search of nothing in particular and yet certainly searching, with an affection for the ordinary and an anticipation for the unexpected. As Celati writes in his introduction to a collection of stories by Antonio Delfini that he edited:

> excluding the notion of a perfect correspondence between the thing to be said and its expression, writing transforms into an activity that moves ahead by swerves and approximations. From here, there arises the need to orient oneself by way of an intuitive under-standing through those signs which Delfini calls primitive. In place of the ideals of professional bravura, there arises in importance 'the ignorance of signs', a 'lack of distain', and all that which loosens the tension of expressive schemes. Imaginative intuition isn't born of schemes, but by way of intensive irradiations in the dust of moments; it is thus necessary to disengage thought, to liberate it from the pillory of expression, to give space to the points in which the armour of the self lets pass a bit of air, out of distraction by the world.[31]

These 'intensive irradiations in the dust of moments' that arise out of a loosening of the self, a sloughing off of our own skins, a letting-go of accepted means of thought, are related to Celati's shifting of perception to the external world, of becoming used to small, scattered attentions in such a way that there is also the substitution of one form of listening with another, in which there also entered seeing, no longer disconnected from listening. We see voices and listen to things; in narrative work there isn't the dividing up of the senses.[32]

These intense practices of observing are closely tied up with a sort of dual clear-headedness and distance characteristic of not belonging to a country and its people that Celati, in the introduction to his translation of Swift's *Gulliver's Travels*, associates with

> someone not immersed in the perceptive habits of a place, the lucidity of an outsider who reconstructs everything from afar and in isolation from his contemporaries. [...] This detached gaze catapults us into a state of complete estrangement, in which the most normal things, the most ordinary habits, become new and surprising objects of study.[33]

Celati's many translations, from the work of William Gerhardie and Friedrich Hölderlin to Swift and Stendhal, are inseparable from his other writings over time, whether it be the pared-down descriptive accounts of ordinary, often isolated people and places in books such as *Narratori delle pianure* and *Verso la foce*, or his playful earlier work, such as the three books – *La banda dei sospiri* [The gang of sighs], *Le avventure di Guizzardi*, and (completely rewritten) *Lunario del paradiso* [Paradise almanac] – collected in *Parlamenti buffi* [Droll parleys] that he refers to as 'tellings', 'games of speech', and 'games for all' with 'variations and outbursts and cadences and shiftings of voice to follow with the ear, a dance of the tongue in the mouth and a loss of breath'.[34] All Celati's meandering writings and other output, including his films, in one way or another pay heed to the belief that 'if someone tells me a story, it becomes an event that drags me out of myself, an event in which certain strange turns of phrase continually arise, because "to fabulate is to fabricate"'.[35]

To concoct is indeed to patch together, to imagine is to partake of and in an imaginary, to write is to rewrite, reverse, revert, relate and translate. To shed one's skin and assume another, then another, with each passing appearance and its corresponding mode of speech that together reaffirm our essential if all too often (in)tangible humanity, its myriad swarming consciousnesses and bodies in and out of place, amid an immense and paradoxically serene mêlée. To adventure with Celati means not only entering the fray but becoming part of it, zigzagging across textual and extra-textual realms, both here and there, never quite home but always on the edge of the familiar.

Notes

1   This introductory chapter draws in part from a number of articles and shorter pieces that I have written on Celati's work, including 'Gianni Celati's *Verso la foce*: "An Intense Observation of the World"', *Forum Italicum* 2 (Autumn, 2005): 481–97; 'Gianni Celati's Poetic Prose: Physical, Marginal, Spatial', *Italica* 84, no. 2–3 (Summer–Autumn, 2007): 323–44; 'Gianni Celati's Voicing of Unpredictable Places', in *Italy and the Environmental Humanities: Landscapes, Natures, Ecologies*, eds. Serenella Iovino, Enrico Cesaretti and Elena Past (Charlottesville: University of Virginia Press, 2018), 17–27; Gianni Celati, 'Introduction', *Towards the River's Mouth (Verso la foce)*, ed. and trans. Patrick Barron (Lanham: Lexington, 2018), xi–xxv; 'In Memoriam, Gianni Celati (1937–2022)', *The Massachusetts Review* (19 February 2022), https://www.massreview.org/node/10282; and 'Celati's Transverse Adventures into the Errant Familiar', *Elephant & Castle: Laboratorio dell'immaginario* 29 (2023): 150–5.
2   Nunzia Palmieri, 'Gianni Celati: Due o tre cose che so di lui (e dei suoi film)', in *Documentari imprevedibili come i sogni: Il cinema di Gianni Celati*, ed. Nunzia Palmieri (Rome: Fandango, 2011), 86–7.
3   Some of the key scholarly publications in English on Celati include Rebecca West's *Gianni Celati: The craft of everyday storytelling* (Toronto: Toronto University Press, 2000), which also contains an extensive bibliography of primary and secondary sources; essays by Marina Spunta, Monica Seger, Matteo Gilebbi, Serenella Iovino, Michele Ronchi Stefanati, Damiano Benvegnù, Thomas Harrison, Massimo Rizzante and Franco Arminio that appear in the critical edition of Gianni Celati's *Towards the River's Mouth (Verso la foce)*, ed. and trans. Patrick Barron (Lanham: Lexington, 2018); and a range of recent scholarly essays, including the following: Pasquale Verdicchio, 'Authoring Images: Italo Calvino, Gianni Celati, and Photography as Literary Art', in *Enlightening Encounters: Photography in Italian Literature*, eds. Giorgia Alù and Nancy Pedri (Toronto: University of Toronto Press, 2015), 51–69; Monica Seger, *Landscapes in Between: Environmental change in modern Italian literature and film* (Toronto: University of Toronto Press, 2015); Charles Klopp, 'Elective Affinities: Gianni Celati Reading Antonio Delfini', *Italica* 91, no. 4 (2014): 735–47; Monica Francioso, 'Impegno and *Alì Babà*: Celati, Calvino, and the Debate on Literature in the 1970s', *Italian Studies* 64, no. 1 (2009): 105–19; Cynthia Hillman, 'Celati, Flaiano, and Bartleby, the Scrivener: Refusal as Self-Preservation', in *'Scrittori Inconvenienti': Essays on and by Pier Paolo Pasolini and Gianni Celati*, eds. Armando Maggi and Rebecca West (Ravenna, Italy: Angelo Longo, 2009), 187–98; and Marina Spunta, 'The New Italian Landscape: Between Ghirri's Photography and Celati's Fiction', in *Translation Practices: Through language to culture*, eds. Ashley Chantler, Carla Dente and Manfred Pfister (Amsterdam: Brill, 2009), 223–37. An important point of reference in Celati studies is the Panzini Library in Reggio Emilia which holds a vast archive of his manuscripts and printed material, as well as digital material by and on Celati.
4   Gianni Celati, 'Riscrivere, riraccontare, tradurre', *Riga 28: Gianni Celati*, ed. by Marco Belpoliti and Marco Sironi (Milan: Marcos y Marcos, 2008), 47.
5   Gianni Celati, *Finzioni occidentali: Fabulazione, comicità e scrittura* (Turin: Einaudi, 1975), 219; Gianni Celati, *Alice disambientata: Materiali collettivi (su Alice) per un manuale di sopravvivenza* (Florence: Le Lettere, 2007), 69; Gianni Celati, *Conversazioni del vento volatore* (Macerata: Quodlibet, 2011), 24.
6   Gianni Celati, 'Riscrivere', *Riga 28: Gianni Celati*, 49.
7   Celati, 'Riscrivere', *Riga 28: Gianni Celati*, 49.
8   Celati, 'Riscrivere', *Riga 28: Gianni Celati*, 46, 44.
9   Gianni Celati and Carlo Gajani, *Animazioni e incantamenti*, ed. Nunzia Palmieri (Rome: L'Orma, 2017), 282.
10 Gianni Celati, 'Gianni Celati e Italo Calvino, Corrispondenza [Comiche]', *Riga 28: Gianni Celati* (Extra), http://rigabooks.it/extra.php?idlanguage=1&id=404&idextra=539.

11   Gianni Celati, 'Il racconto di superficie', *Il verri* XVII (1973): 93–4.
12   Celati, *Animazioni*, 285.
13   Celati, *Finzioni*, 221.
14   Celati, *Conversazioni*, 9.
15   Gianni Celati, *Verso la foce* (Milan: Feltrinelli, 1989), xxx.
16   Gianni Celati, 'Un sistema di racconti sul mondo esterno', *Riga 40: Gianni Celati*, ed. by Marco Belpoliti, Marco Sironi and Anna Stefi (Macerata: Quodlibet, 2019), 196.
17   Celati, *Verso*, 9; Celati, *Conversazioni*, 15.
18   Gianni Celati, 'La veduta frontale. Antonioni, *L'avventura* e l'attesa', in *Documentari imprevedibili come i sogni: Il cinema di Gianni Celati*, ed. Nunzia Palmieri (Rome: Fandango, 2011), 31.
19   Celati, 'La veduta frontale', 31.
20   See for example Gianni Celati, *Finzioni Occidentali* (Turn: Einaudi, 2001 [1975]) and Gianni Celati, *Narrative in fuga*, ed. Jean Talon (Macerata: Quodlibet, 2019).
21   Gianni Celati, 'Finzioni a cui credere, un esempio', in Luigi Ghirri, *Paessagio italiano* (Milan: Electa, 1989), 33.
22   Gianni Celati, *Narrative in fuga* (Macerata: Quodlibet, 2019), 58.
23   Gianni Celati, *Quattro novelle sulle apparanze* (Milan: Feltrinelli, 1987), 56.
24   Celati, *Conversazioni*, 81–2.
25   Gianni Celati, *Sonetti del Badalucco nell'Italia odierna* (Milan: Feltrinelli, 2010), 43; Badalucco is the name of an enigmatic poet who has supposedly penned one Attilio Vecchiatto's pamphlets, a once famous actor whose writings Celati discovers and revivifies.
26   Gianni Celati, interview with Fabrizio Grosoli, in *Documentari imprevedibili come i sogni: Il cinema di Gianni Celati*, ed. Nunzia Palmieri (Rome: Fandango, 2011), 7.
27   Celati, Interview, 8.
28   Celati, Interview, 10.
29   Celati, *Quattro*, 49.
30   Gianni Celati, 'Introduzione', in James Joyce, *Ulysses*, trans. Gianni Celati (Turin: Einaudi, 2013), xii; Celati, *Animazioni*, 314; Celati, 'Riscrivere', *Riga 28: Gianni Celati*, 46.
31   Gianni Celati, 'Antonio Delfini ad alta voce', in Antonio Delfini, *Antonio Delfini: Autore ignoto presenta: Racconti scelti e introdotti da Gianni Celati* (Turin: Einaudi, 2008), xxviii–xxix.
32   Gianni Celati, 'Il narrare come attività pratica', in *Seminario sul racconto*, ed. Luigi Rustichelli (West Lafayette: Bordighera, 1998), 33.
33   Gianni Celati, 'Introduzione', in Jonathan Swift, *I viaggi di Gulliver*, trans. Gianni Celati (Milan: Feltrinelli, 1997), xix.
34   Gianni Celati, *Parlamenti buffi* (Milan: Feltrinelli, 1989), 7.
35   Gianni Celati, *Studi d'affezione per amici e altri* (Macerata: Quodlibet, 2016), 140.

Figure 1.1　Gianni Celati, in San Casciano, 1988, by George Tatge.
© George Tatge.

2
'One-page autobiography' ('Esercizio autobiografico in 2000 battute', 2008)

Born in 1937, in Sondrio, a stone's throw from Switzerland. – Six months of life in Sondrio. – Father a bank teller, who argues with his own director. – Father who is punished with a transfer from one end of the country to the other at his own expense. – Travelling family. – Three years in Trapani. – Seven years in Belluno. – Three years in Ferrara. – High school in Bologna. – End of family life. – Travels in Germany and almost marriage. – Return to Bologna, studies in linguistics. – Time passes. – Military service. – Time spent studying the writings of the mentally ill, thanks to a psychiatrist friend. – Neurosis, in miliary hospital. – Thesis on Joyce. – Viral hepatitis, in quarantine. – Euphoria of writing like a madman, driven by it. – Italo Calvino reads some of the writing in a magazine, suggests turning it into a book. – Time passes. – Life in Tunisia. – Marriage. –

First translations. – Record store clerk in Bologna. – Studies in logic with Enzo Melandri, for naught. – Scholarship in London 1968–70. – First book. – Departure for the US. – Two years at Cornell University. – A fake life, trying to pass things off as something else. – Time passes. – Teaching post at the University of Bologna. – I meet a certain Alberto Sironi who puts me to work writing films that are doomed at their inception. – Another book. – Translations. – Time passes. – Four months between California, Kansas and Queens. – The sense of never having my feet on the ground, as if I were floating in space. – Time passes. – Paris, rue Simon-le-Franc, a year convalescing. – Return to Bologna, once again at university. – Friendship with Luigi Ghirri, photographer. – Calming work with photographers. – Explorations of the Po River Valley. – Periods of writing and wandering. – Move to Normandy. – Translations. – Another book. –

Daniele Benati, Ermanno Cavazzoni, Ugo Cornia, Marianne Schneider, Jean Talon and I found the magazine *Il semplice, Almanacco delle prose*. – In the US, Rhode Island, teaching for six months. – Time passes. – Move to England. – First documentaries. – Trip in Africa with J. Talon. – Time passes. – Other documentaries. – All uphill, no hope, no fear. – Fulbright in Chicago. – In Senegal, Africa, to soothe my mind. – A year in Berlin on a DAAD scholarship.[1] – Film in Senegal, unable to finish it. – Since 1990 in Brighton, England with my wife, Gillian Haley.

Note

1   DAAD: Deutscher Akademischer Austauschdienst, or German Academic Exchange Service.

3
'Speech as spectacle' ('Parlato come spettacolo', 1968)

> Tâchez que vos démons vous inculquent la flûte! Flûte d'abord!
> Regardez Shakespeare, lycéen! 3/4 de flûte, 1/4 de sang …
> (Make sure your demons teach you to play the flute! Flute first!
> Look at Shakespeare, schoolboy! 3/4 flute, 1/4 blood)
> Céline, *A l'agité du bocal*

> … imaginez-vous la musique sans points de suspensions?
> (… can you imagine music without ellipses?)
> Céline, *Entretiens avec le Professeur* (1955) (*Conversations with Professor Y*)

To read and understand a text we must at times reproduce it mentally as if the words were being spoken, including the range of their sounds, accents, pauses and such. David Shillan, in a paper on the melodic analysis of language by way of certain *détecteurs de mélodie*, writes that even a reader of *The Times* may suddenly pause before an obscure passage, able to continue only after having sounded it out, evidence of the limited separation of the written from the spoken.[1] While reading silently we often use our experience as speakers in order to decipher a phrase, creating a form of kinaesthetic analogy that transmits the message to us. But there are other cases in which it is impossible to grasp the full sense of a discourse without introducing into our minds its corresponding corporeal mimetic representation, or, in other words, the expression of the character and gestures of the person reciting the discourse, however nebulous they may be. In such cases we must fall back upon our experiences as consumers of spectacle, creating a much wider series of kinaesthetic analogies. When we tell an anecdote to a listener who doesn't know the person described, we often add, 'You'd have to know her to understand'. In so doing, we inform listeners that they are unable to recreate the character and gestures of the person and therefore gather, by way of our linguistic portrayal, the gestural sense of the words. I say gestural and not visual for a precise reason: not only are the movements that a person may enact at stake, but the totality of their expressive actions of which it is impossible to fully distinguish gestures, ranges in tonality, emphases produced by a particular series of accents, and emotive intonations.

Only in these terms does it seem to me possible to define the spoken without necessarily identifying it with common linguistic practices, let alone their mimetic transcriptions that appear in old and new works of realism. Then again, these are the same terms that Elio Vittorini uses in order to grapple with the problem, arguing that speech is an enrichment of the 'reality of communication' by means of 'miming, gestures, pauses, glances and tones, instead of words'.[2] And yet it seems important to distinguish speech from oral discourse, taking up a distinction from Raymond Queneau, but reiterating the hierarchical order (in the sense of 'expressive possibility') implicitly established by the French writer; I would identify speech as a form of conventional rhetoric and oral discourse as nothing else but mimesis.[3] From this we can distinguish three different practices of literary speech and three corresponding traditions, with varying levels of recognition, acceptance, enjoyment and consistency:

1. The written word, regulated for the most part by particular conventions of a visual nature (for example the acrostic) not trans-latable through gestures, but not for this reason without melodic qualities, due to the limited separation of the written from the spoken. Eliot's comments on Milton's rhetoric – that of a blind man, with a swelling of the auditory imagination to the detriment of the other senses – I believe might be reread accordingly; Eliot even compares Milton to Shakespeare, whose work contains perhaps the most complete use of speech, that is to say one developed within the widest possible range of modes of linguistic expression.[4] This is literary speech par excellence; acquisition of it is mainly intellectual and its meaning refers exclusively to our linguistic consciousness.

2. The oralized written word, found for example in the dramatic parts (or dialogues) of a novel; you might say that it has occurred most frequently and significantly within the tradition of the English novel, in which dialogue often serves to introduce a vernacular lexicon or spoken syntax, whereas in other traditions it serves more often than

not to quote idioms (Balzac's work contains many such examples in which idiomatic terms and expressions always appear in italics). Among more recent writers, Queneau is one of the most interesting and expert to employ this type of literary language.

3. The spoken word as a performative element, because it suggests or demands (for reasons of comprehension) performative representation, true or imaginary, and comes equipped with mimesis, emotive intonations, pauses, emphases and an entire series of conventionalized emotive or psychological shadings, which belong to the character pronouncing them. Acquisition of it is fundamentally participatory, provoking a collective reaction (not limited to our linguistic consciousness) as caused, for example, by a cinematographic image.

It goes without saying that L.-F. Céline falls within this last tradition, reinventing it and proposing it as the sole alternative to the impasse in which the production of novels based on the written word finds itself. It is not my intention here to accept or discuss the theories of Céline, which are wilfully crude and divisive beliefs of an artificer alien to the nagging narcissistic doubts of cultured twentieth-century Europeans, but rather to attempt to assay Céline as one of the few 'highbrow' writers of our time who have warned of the decline of the participatory function of the literature of the elite and, instead of using the written word to annihilate from the inside a literary institution already undermined to the point of reaching the very limit of possible participation (that is, illegibility), have adopted expressive models that reactivate this function.[5] It is for this reason that speech becomes an ideal and favoured instrument, because, as previously mentioned, its acquisition is mainly participatory and its characteristics are the same as those of the spectacle.

It remains, however, to examine the practical aspect of the question. Speech, in the form of written discourse that feigns oral or recitative discourse, depends upon a particular conventional transcription that signals the 'supplementary forms of communication' supplied by the likes of mimesis, expressions and expressive intonations. In a culture such as that of Elizabethan England, in which the institution of the spectacle included every form of literary production, this did not constitute a problem, because everything that was written was destined to be recited.[6] That plays, songs and sonnets were also printed (and thus read as written texts) was of secondary importance, at least until the time of Ben Jonson. The word was naturally gestural and spoken, because it was born out of the necessity of the spectacle and the conventions of acting.

These conventions, as far as concerns both diction (voice) and mimesis (gesture), determined the interpretation of the word and its delivery by an actor-character, and facilitated its comprehension even to an uncultured audience, such as the famous groundlings; it was a fixed code (of which we can detect echoes in *Hamlet*) that aspired to mimic the keen evidence of a gesture or an action, and thus to an immediacy of comprehension. For this reason, it also allowed the author the most daring verbal wordplay. Keen evidence and immediacy of comprehension are the peculiar qualities of the spoken word and represent its optimal level – the 'dramatic meaning', often present in the writings of Chaucer and Dickens, defined by Carlo Izzo as 'the capacity to suggest through the written word the gestural and tonal sense with which the text should be imbued if spoken'.[7] Now the techniques of transcribing speech are similar to those of acting, serving to ensure the success of a performance – a strategy adopted by those who produce or emit a message in order to reach the optimal level of speech.

But, in cultures where theatre has gone into decline and literature (that is, the written word) dominates, precise conventions are lost for the 'delivery' of texts, real or imaginary as the case may be, similar to those that guided Elizabethan acting; silent reading, which is based on analogies with our experiences as speakers, has need of signals, in order to find its way. The written word supplies only a minimal series of signals regarding mimesis and intonation; indeed, the absolute uniformity of the printed page favours a mechanical understanding of the word that leads to the forgetting of the medium, that is, the particular type of writing, and the sense of more specific signals (such as lexical shadings or spoken syntax) that permit a more complete identification with the events described.[8] If, on one hand, the printed text allows a more direct relationship with the subjectivity of the reader, on the other it increasingly negates all auditory and oral aspects of the word, and thus also a possible code for 'acting'.

And it is with the writer and printer Samuel Richardson and his suggesting of the tone of an oral discourse by means of punctuation and other typographical measures that we find one of the first attempts to overcome this obstacle: words in upper case that invite a more emphatic pronunciation, dashes to indicate the irregularity of phrases typical of spoken language, explanation marks and parentheses that allow for the expression of a naïve gestural pathos and other virtuous feelings that made him famous. In the work of Richardson there is thus recreated a code of speech from which all can benefit, friends and enemies, relatives and successors alike. But the application of such a code on a vast scale, in a manner unthinkable in the period during which *Clarissa* was written, was carried out by Laurence Sterne, who brought it to play across every page and every line of his masterpiece, *Tristram Shandy*, making use of dashes to interrupt the discourse and capriciously shift the argument, creating a simultaneity of various narrative strands and above all intimating the bland and monotonous tone of drawing room conversation. In Dickens' *The Pickwick Papers* there appear both the transcription of the spoken word (in the discourses of Mr Alfred Jingle, with the use of the dash, but rendered ever more lively by a telegraphic rhythm and by an accumulation of amassed phrases that completely disrupt traditional syntax), and the transcription of the oral word (in the discourses of Sam Weller, with an orthography that that reproduces dialectal pronunciation and an expressive, common syntax, full of ready-made proverbial phrases). This comparison seems to me of interest because it reveals the conventional character of speech in contrast to the mimetic aspect of oral discourse, demonstrating that if recourse to interjection, to colourful metaphor and to colloquial syntax may be enough to 'oralize' written discourse, it isn't enough to distinguish this discourse as speech.

Céline seems to have been aware of such a distinction, considering that, after having departed from a very lively form of oralized written discourse, he arrived at a form of written speech, not so much (or not solely) through argotic aspects of language, but above all through an efficient system of signs of 'supplementary forms of communication', as mentioned above. My discussion up to this point serves to clarify the relationships that exist between Céline's work and the conventions of speech in English literature, and also to show that the characteristic appearance of his writings in print is not a bizarre stylistic feature of their typography, but the continuation of an arduous search to restore to the word its performative qualities, and thus to reactivate the participatory function of the literature of the elite.

Before delving into an analysis, however summary and provisional, of the transcription of speech in Céline's writings, it is worth making two premises. Firstly, analogy is the foundation on which a relationship is built between the signs present in a text and a 'supplemental form of communication' of a gestural nature; analogy is the mechanism that makes silent oral reading possible, and for this reason it is also the mechanism that makes silent gestural reading possible. Secondly, I will omit aspects of the oralization (that is, the mimesis of oral discourse) of the written word in Céline's work, given that these aspects are so integrally a part of speech therein and increasingly lose, from *Guignol's Band* onward, the character of mimesis. Céline himself says as much, specifying the difference between the two functions and speaking of his work as an attempt to 'transpose' oral language into written form, but not in imitation of common speech, thus underlining the artificiality of the resulting style.[9]

With a reminder of the distinction present in Elizabethan theatre between voice and gesture, we can divide Célanian signs into:

1. Signs of duration, indicative of an extended enunciation and thus the pause that determines it; these correspond analogously with signs of diction (voice) because the extended enunciation and the type of pause express the relative duration and thus the time of the phrasing;
2. Signs of intonation, indicative of expressive variations of the melodic curve of the phrasing; these generally refer to interjections, asides, questions and exclamations of various types, corresponding more exactly with the gestural aspects of the speech, because in these cases the gesture very often accompanies the word furnishing the so-called context of actualization. These are, however, mimetic signs (gesture).

For example, in a passage such as 'C'est juré la main dans mon sang! ... Nom de foutre! ...' (*Le Pont de Londres – Guignol's band II* (1964) [*London Bridge: Guignol's Band II*]), the signs indicating the time of phrasing correspond to the three ellipsis points, and the signs indicating the intonation correspond to the exclamation points, which together suggest conventional gestures recreated analogously, beginning with our experience as speakers and as spectators. It is not always possible to distinguish signs of duration from signs of intonation within a single enunciation; and yet, while signs of duration may appear without signs of intonation, the opposite is not possible. This is because if we have, for example, a series of exclamations (that is, signs of intonation – 'La Vigue annonce! fort! que ça résonne! toute la voûte!' [*Nord* (1960) [*North*]]) without signs of duration, the exclamations also serve to indicate the time of phrasing.

It is thus useful to describe the various signs in the context of their relative durational meanings. We can begin by distinguishing between '*silences de reprise*' ('pauses of recovery') and '*silences de dérive*' ('pauses of drifting'). These terms come from Jean Guenot, who, in analysing the recording of an interview with Céline and attempting to transcribe it while taking into account extralinguistic expressive aspects, discovered a number of key relational points of great interest for the study of Célinian speech.[10] He found that in the oral discourse of Céline there exist: 1) *'silences de reprise'*, which at are those: 'où l'intensité de la voix est soutenue jusqu'au bord du silence et indique que ce qui viendra après est relié syntaxiquement et sémantiquement à ce qui précède de façon intime' ('in which the intensity of the voice is sustained up to an edge of silence, indicating that what comes next is syntactically and semantically intimately linked to what precedes it'); 2) *'silences de dérive'*, thus described: 'au moment où la voix s'arrête, une partie de la signification continue selon la gamme des contextes vraisemblables, et puis le silence dure et on ne sait pas si elle reprendra dans le même mouvement de morphologie et de syntaxe' ('at the moment that the voice stops, part of the meaning continues according to the range of plausible contexts, with the silence carrying on, leaving us uncertain whether it will resume in the same movement of morphology and syntax').

With respect to *'silences de reprise'* in Céline's work, we can distinguish the following:

A. A normal use of the comma; the text which precedes it is syntactically correlated to the text that follows it: 'Je vous l'accorde, tout le monde peut reconnaître une fièvre, une toux, une colique, gros symptômes pout le vaste public' (*Nord*). In such cases, the pause carries out an ordering function, not an expressive one, typical of written discourse, and thus constitutes a base line as far as regards indications of duration and of gesture in the phrasing.

B. A repetitive use of the comma to develop a sinusoidal flow of the melodic curve: 'Dans le désespoir il se dépiaute, il se fout à poil rapidement, il grimpe après la Banque de France, le voilà juché sur l'Horloge' (*Mort à crédit* (1936) [*Death on the Installment Plan*]). The pause might correspond with a full stop (period), but the full stop in common use corresponds with a prolonged pause, while here after every phrasing an almost immediate continuation is necessary to push along the melodic curve.

C. A use of the repeated comma to sew together short fragments with a melodic flow unlike that in B: 'Affalés, vautrés, hoquetants, on se retrouve brandis, extirpés, rabougris, reprojetés à dame!' (*Guignol's Band* [1944]). In these cases, the close-range succession of strong accents has a percussive function and suggests a frenetic discourse.

D. The use of ellipsis points that function as a comma to suggest an uncertainty regarding what follows, as if the speaker were searching for the words to express himself: 'Tout arrivait à lui sourire: l'anneau … les Gémeaux … Saturne … Jupiter … Arturus et ses contours …' (*Mort à crédit*).

E. The use of the exclamation mark where normally one would expect a comma: 'Une fois cette grande langue rengloutie! dans le trou du ciel! d'autres avions, d'autres charges!' (*Normance*). Here the exclamation mark is employed in order to vary the expressive sense of the melodic curve and, without separating the pronouncements more than would a comma, suggests a gesture of surprise, of fear, of anger, as the case may be; in this example there is a clear suggestion of an ostentatious gesture. Of note is the fact that the suggested gesture is not particularly emphasized, out of the need for an immediate return to the continuing flow of the text: a strong emphasis has instead need of a certain echo and thus a prolonged pause. This sort of emphasis can be defined as being of medium intensity, distinguishing it from a minor emphasis (lacking signs of intonation as in A, B, C, D) and from a strong emphasis (with signs of intonation reinforced by pauses).

F. The use of an exclamation mark as described in E, but with a more closely spaced repetition: 'Tout! les viandes! la camelote! les chars!' (*Guignol's Band*). In this case a strong emphasis is evident, but not through an accentuation of gestures, but rather an intensification of their succession, giving the sense of chaotic and panicked gesturing.

With respect to '*silences de dérive*', we can distinguish the following:

A. The use of three ellipsis points to signal a pause that leads to an elucidation, a repetition or a comment on the preceding discourse: 'On n'aurait pas pu rue Lepic … oh, pas que je pensais que ça durerait! (*Nord*). In these cases the discourse is interrupted by a consideration more or less relevant, but then continues to develop; the three dots thus might be thought of as a parenthesis: they thus suggest a lowering of the tone of voice, as is common with asides.

B. The use of an exclamation mark and three ellipsis points. In this case the exclamation mark varies the expressive meaning of the normal melodic curve of the phrasing, but at the same time the three ellipsis points give space to the emphasis that arises within the prolonged pause in the form of an echo; it is pointless to quote an example, as all Céline's books are full of examples (with the exception of *Semmelweis* (1924) [*Semmelweis*] and certain parts of *Voyage au bout de la nuit* (1932) [*Journey to the End of the Night*] and *Mort à crédit*). This construction gives the sense of a repeated interjection even to statements that are softly denotative and relatively expansive. Of note is how the gestural effect is conversely proportionate to the expansiveness of the statement. The emphasis here is always strong.

C. The use of the construction described in B, applied in a series of brief statements: 'La revoilà … jamais n'expire! … C'est une affaire! … riguendonne! … Le monde halète! pâme! … se rend!... farceur d'ivoires!... façon frippone!... (*Guignol's Band*). In this case we have a strong emphasis with the intensification of gestural suggestions in a rhymical sequence articulated by the percussive use of strong accents.

D. The use of a question mark for rhetorical questions: 'Ah, Je partirais bien aussi … J'avais peut-être encore une minute? … Peut-être qu'ils étaient encore là?'... (*Le Pont de Londres*). In these cases, the same statement expressed in a non-interrogative form would not supply different linguistic information; the question mark and connected syntactical construction function to introduce a melodic variation and to signal a gesture with which we would tend to identify, however imprecisely and subjectively, a particular expression of the speaker. On the other hand, we know that questions carry with them wide ranges of gestural complements that vary among diverse cultural groups, different situations and associated rituals.

E. The use of the repeated question mark to express a dilemma: 'Ah! merde! c'était moi? … c'était elle?'... (*Le Pont de Londres*). Here the question mark cannot be substituted by another sign and is employed in a manner different from that in D. It should be noted that the conventional and rhetorical character of an expression of dilemma, and of the expression itself, is based on matters of intonation, and is thus extralinguistic. The emphasis is strong, but the suggested gesture varies according to the context, as in many other examples not discussed here: in *Le Pont de Londres* the gesture is always comic, with a certain harlequinesque doubt, and in *Nord* and *D'un château l'autre* (1957) [*Castle to Castle*], it is rather dramatic. In addition, I would associate with this construction the forms of obsessive repetition typical of interrogation, so frequent in *Nord*, because their sense of drama signals a similar type of emphasis.

This summarized list of uses constitutes the typographical rhetoric employed by Céline. Such a code permits a gestural interpretation of this rhetoric – to the extent that Célinian speech makes use of the resources of written discourse (with, for example, many references to classic rhetoric), as well as those of oralized written discourse (with a mimesis of common, colloquial language). The listed uses could be studied in combinatory fashion and thus organized into paradigms according to differing characteristics, such as 1) level of emphasis; 2) rhythm;

3) type of suggested gesture, and so on. The result would be a system based on extralinguistic values, able to reveal much more of Céline's style. We know, after all, that many types of language are at play in the creation of every spectacle, various codes and conventions; speech, in this spectacle, is no exception, and to consider it only from the point of view of articulated language is not sufficient. Like music, speech has a system that transcends the level of articulated speech, and like music it too has need, in order to be performed, of a score that indicates the range of notes (and levels of emphasis), and their relative lengths. For good reason Céline defines his speech as 'music', and when he says 'flûte', he also means music – that is, the essential quality of a spoken text. One of his merits consists of having reminded Sartre that spectacle is not possible without 'flûte': 'Regardez Shakespeare, lycéen ! 3/4 de flûte, 1/4 de sang …'.

Notes

1 David Shillan, 'Metodo e ragione per l'analisi melodica del linguaggio', *Delta* no. 6 (May 1967). See also David Shillan, *Spoken English: A short guide to English speech* (London: Longmans, Green, 1954).
2 Elio Vittorini, 'Parlato e metafora', in *Il menabò 1* (Turin: Einaudi, 1959), 125–7.
3 Raymond Queneau, cited in L. A. Gordon, *The Movement of English Prose* (London: Longman, 1966), chapter 16.
4 T. S. Eliot, 'Milton I' and 'Milton II', in Eliot *On Poetry and Poets* (London: Faber and Faber, 1957), 138–45; 146–61.
5 Louis-Ferdinand Céline, *Entretiens avec le Professeur Y* (Paris: Gallimard, 1955).
6 Reginald A. Foakes, 'The Player's Passion. Some Notes on Elizabethan Psychology and Acting', in *Essays and Studies 1954,* ed. Guy Boas, (London: John Murry, 1954), 62–77; B. L. Joseph, *Acting Shakespeare* (London: Theatre Art Books, 1960).
7 Carlo Izzo, 'Comicità, umorismo e nonsense', Handouts from a course on the monograph held from 1960 to 1961.
8 Ian Watt, *The Rise of the Novel* (London: Chatto & Windus, 1957).
9 See: correspondence between Louis-Ferdinand Céline and Milton Hindus, letters from April 16, 1947 and May 15, 1947: Louis-Ferdinand Céline, *L'Herne* (n.p.: Savernoises, 1972), 107–38.
10 Jean Guenot, 'Voyage au bout de la parole', in Louis-Ferdinand Céline, *L'Herne* (n.p.: Savernoises, 1972), 348–63.

4

'Gianni Celati and Italo Calvino: correspondence (*Comiche*)' ('Gianni Celati e Italo Calvino, corrispondenze (*Comiche*)', early 1970s)

Italo Calvino's note on *Comiche* [Slapstick silent films]

Celati's way of writing (and imagining) resembles Klee's world: a childlike landscape drawing in which a talking bomber appears and disappears, becoming by turns a boarding school, an asylum, a seaside hotel, within which there arises an extraordinary monologue performance concerning persecution mania – which unfolds across shifting phases and a sense of liberation – in a sublanguage of hilarious effects often based on minimal syntactic distortions. Celati's most identifiable trait, compared with all the other 'linguistic operators' of his generation, is to be rooted in a clearly recognizable geographic and sociological humus: a small Italy of the Po Valley that from now on we will recognize as 'Celati's world'.

Letter from Gianni Celati to Italo Calvino

Dear Italo,
A few passing thoughts on *Comiche* and why I don't recognize myself in your little portrait. Fixed, cartesian geometry is something I detest. Everything that I write comes from the desire to chase after or stir up a mêlée or bruhaha: nothing interests me more than a mêlée, when everyone is hitting everyone else, everything collapses and falls apart, roles are mixed up, the world shows itself for what it is, hysterical and paranoid, with an all-pervading sense of madness. I detest Klee-like poetics apart from when they appear by mistake, or when they are an oversight or slip-up.

Infantilism gets on my nerves because it presupposes that childhood is some sort of isolated zoo, but it is instead a matter of adaptation.

Writers for children are so adapted to language that they manage to imitate its deficiencies. I am interested in a language of pure deficiencies. This I started to understand when I used to teach middle school in the countryside. The kids wrote in their versions of Italian, their skilful (because an outgrowth of an experience centuries in the making) adaptations to Italian, with a talent for irony and tension what would astound me; hardly childish, their misunderstandings were, purposeful or not, extraordinary feats of resistance. Teachers of Italian would then intervene, correcting those turns of phrase in which the effects were most archaically pleasing, where a phrase would follow the twists of speech, extraordinarily elongated by a kind of affabulatory incontinence, or instances in which ellipses skipped over necessities that written Italian retains as atrophied forms. Their maladjustment to the language is a maladjustment to the world of raving and paranoid bureaucracies. You speak of humus; I don't know if it is the case that I should be so honoured, but if this is indeed the intended meaning, it is accurate. But when you speak of humus you must also speak of what is rejected, excluded, of everything that is constantly removed in a world in which everyone plays the game of correcting everyone else.

The figure of the professor at work writing, while always in fear of making a mistake, scolded by voices that point out various errors, is perhaps illustrative of this game. Humus then means an archaeology of speech, not the pedantic sort out of some Milanese bar or lousy film but the sort of speech that no one utters except when going to pot or losing their mind. Then and only then does spoken language mean language that reaches your ears as a spectre from some distant place, as a voice of something (a 'world') that doesn't exist; only the dead speak a spoken language. With these premises it seems to me that I have assembled something else: a way of speaking built entirely of arcane 'voices' that come to your ear whether you want or not; obsessive as a schizophrenic echolalia, uninhibited as the eloquence of indiscretion. In short, I attempted a way of speaking that could not be followed as a syntactical sequence but rather as a sequence of echoes. True speech, I believe, is a spectacle in and of itself because it necessarily takes you back to recitation (if you want to read the lines), then to a mask, then to a speaking individual on a stage and moving on a stage with appropriate gestures. Writers who take themselves to be writers never pull it off because the task is tantamount to putting on the mask of someone who doesn't get it, someone who suffers from such a blistering maladjustment that words do not come out clear and sound but wrong, made up of malapropisms, slips and missed acts. I wanted to make a voice speak so that its speech was equivalent to the motions of a deteriorating mask, so that the mimetic tics were verbal tics readable only in their acted form. Can such a voice be made to produce in writing the effect of a Stan Laurel grimace? Herein lies the point. I don't know if this helps as a *rappel*, but I would add that I think of comic craftsmanship as a progressive, even existential identification (with no residue left to the writer-intellectual) with one's own mask; Stan Laurel becoming Mr Laurel in the movies; Tristano Martinelli becoming Harlequin Martinelli. Here is natural speech; speaking without knowing what you mean. The jester reproduces gestures not knowing what they mean with the sole purpose of producing bodily effects in the listener. The culmination of the effects of the jester's craft is the mêlée; that is, I think, something that resembles the model of anarchy that Artaud described with the image of the plague. *Comiche* pulls this off a few times as a mêlée of 'voices'; that is, the arcane voices of the underworld that grab you, start to make messes in the ordered world, erase familiar paths and create a reality of pure echoes. Of course, as you so well put it: a sense of persecution; the dead haunt us, precisely to the extent that only through the sense of persecution do we find the ancestral echoes of human acts. We must always die in order to write something that reaches that other world. And everything we write comes from the other world: whether heaven or, as others say, Hades. It is the metaphor of the story written at the suggestion of an unknown hand; the metaphor of one's own story that can be told only after the dream has suggested its meaning to you; this, which is somewhat the narrative structure of the book, expresses, I won't say the conviction, but the feeling I have more and more that the shadow realm lives with us and in us; that spectres exist in earnest; that the dead are never silent. And therein lies the deepest vulgarity but also the only reason for interest in this false fiction that is living. I say false because it is always a fiction in bad faith.

Expect news soon and material for *Alì Babà*.
My best to you and Chichita,
Gianni

5
'Surface stories' ('Il racconto di superficie', 1973)

I begin with three examples. In *Giuoco dell'Oca* [Snakes and ladders], Edoardo Sanguineti works within precisely defined boxes, each of which reprises a design. His entombing story consists of decorating the boxes with graffiti, diagrams and writings that at times seem twisted and bent into letters. The result is a path through various spaces in which inscription assumes a figurative value, resembling the scratches on walls enclosing the writhing secret violence of language. In *Nuovo commento* [New comment], Giorgio Manganelli compiles a series of notes to an inexistent book, and notes to the notes to the notes, thus enacting a descent into a court of miracles of words, which, for what they are, little 'idle' signs put down on paper, acquire the role of main characters. Without metaphors, his adventure is a path of scriptural personifications of rhetorical figures that substitute actors in constantly changing scenes, predicaments, gags. The third example is Italo Calvino's *Castello dei destini incrociati* (*The Castle of Crossed Destinies*), in which tarot cards are emblematically used as spaces to be redrawn through writing. Each card is reproduced next to the text such that one can compare the two, detail by detail, looking for possible overlaps between the scriptural and the figurative. The entire story is not composed as a search for narrative meaning but as a construction of a combination of figures (of cards): an array of figures legible in all directions, from right to left, from top to bottom, or, in other words, spatially.

Key to these three examples seems to be a delimiting of space – as in children's games in which a circle is scratched on the ground that contains all the action – causing the intangible universe of each book's depths to be reduced and carried to the surface of its material space as a paper artifact. Sanguineti's snakes and ladders boxes, Manganelli's footnotes and Calvino's tarot cards – all three are clipped-out surfaces containing the localized game of inscribing on paper, the only game that can be expected being the only game one plays when one writes: a sort of literalism in which the act of writing loses its old metaphorical connotations. I would define this type of writing as a surface story in as much as it is a story of what occurs on a surface, and a rejection of the old depth of discourse. Here I am using a pair of terms borrowed from Gilles Deleuze's *The Logic of Sense* because they seem of particular help in explaining this phenomenon in the books at hand. For Deleuze sense is not a pure effect, which as such does not exist but rather persists and subsists in the surfaces of discourse, a space in which we suddenly land when we begin to speak. I summarize in haste in order to arrive at the point that most interests me: Lewis Carroll, according to Deleuze, 'explored and established a serial method in literature'.[1] Series for Deleuze can be conceived as the simultaneous crossing of a plane by certain chains of attribution of the state of things. Sense is produced at the frontier between series, 'following the border', as he says, or tracing two simultaneous chains with an eye on both.[2] I quote: 'Sense is never a principle or an origin, but a product. It is not something to discover, to restore, or to re-employ; it is something to produce by a new machinery (*machineries*). It belongs to no height or depth, but rather to a surface effect, being inseparable from the surface which is its proper dimension.'[3]

Lewis Carroll, according to Deleuze's anything-but-simple explanation, is an exemplary case of the conquest of surface. At the end of Alice's underground journey, when it becomes clear that the entire story was the story of a shuffling of cards, comes the announcement that no depth dominates discourse, but that there is rather only a process of 'sliding' across a discontinuous series (as with playing cards). At the beginning Alice 'seeks the secret of events and of the becoming unlimited which they imply, in the depths of the earth [...]. As one advances in the story, however, the digging and hiding gives way to a lateral sliding from right to left and left to right. The animals below ground become stationary, giving way to card figures which have no thickness. One could say that the old depth having been spread out became width.'[4] Put in these terms, Alice's conquest of surface is also a 'disavowal of false depth, her discovery that everything happens at the border'.[5] It is also the discovery that discourse is like a game, an ideal game, in which certain series determine the behaviour of the player within a space that is flat and without thickness, and thus lacking relationships with things – because things too are another series. There is also the sense that discourse, the incorporeal, is only a sliding over of the membranes of things, the surfaces of their worldly attributes: 'it is by following the border, by skirting the surface, that one passes from bodies to the incorporeal'.[6]

Italo Calvino's recent *Le città invisibili* (*Invisible Cities*) is of help in extending this discourse, in revealing additional facets. In it we have the same type of abstract construction as in *Castello dei destini incrociati*: story as a path across an atlas, here being Kubla Khan's empire that contains the various strange cities that Marco Polo describes but also the chessboard that Khan considers the model of his empire. *Le città invisibili* is indeed a work of marquetry, a chessboard with a limited number of squares within which, according to Khan, all his cities can be reduced. This reduction of all his cities to a few series of squares is also suggested by the order of the chapters. There are 11 categories of cities that recur according to certain kabbalistic calculations that I do not discuss here. The fact that the number of chapters (that is, of the cities described by Marco Polo) do not follow a linear progression, but rather diverge into a fragmented series, allows us to say at the outset that there is no path that leads to some revelation but many paths that intersect on a plane, subdividing it into squares. The overall story lies here, in the spatial order of a plane. But this plane is precisely delimited by another order of chapters, those not assigned numbers, in which Khan expounds on his cities. It is worth noting that within the faceting of the book it is the unnumbered chapters with Khan that frame the first numbered chapters and give them context. If there is a game of cities there is also another space in which to interpret this game. Marco Polo's chapters can be traced in style to the fragmentary didactic tradition of bestiaries and herbariums, of wonder books and the medieval travel accounts of Sir John Mandeville: sparkling miniatures built to amass details. The chapters with Khan have the tone of a sustained and opaque exposition, something between a decadent causerie reminiscent of Huysmans and an epistemological dialogue. The numbered chapters have the fixedness and admirable uniformity of an archaic illuminated manuscript; the unnumbered ones instead take the shape of a discursive itinerary directed towards the defining point of the model. Surface, in the elemental form of empty space accurately partitioned, is proposed as the model (the chessboard) together with the game rules. The game rules serve first of all to delimit the field of play in which to position oneself but also contain the underlying principle behind the game and the matrix of allowed moves. The allowed moves are to be read as a strategic application of the rules: for this reason the reading I will attempt of the numbered squares takes the form of commentary, a definition of the underlying rules of the strategy.

I begin with the first of the numbered squares about the city of Diomira. Diomira has the quality of making the traveller who visits it on a September evening and hears a woman's cry come 'to envy those who now believe they have once before lived an evening identical to this and who think they were happy, that time'.[7] The space of the few lines that make up this initial fragment carries with it the realization that the writing itself moves within a syntactic tangle (described mostly as a tangle of streets) searching for an (apparent) aphoristic fullness. An aphorism, like a Delphic saying, is something whose sense retreats from discourse's surface (pronounced words) to another space where there seems to reside a more basic sense to be captured. The text, however, functions as a parable on the retreat from the surfaces of the fullness of writing. For example: there is a series that features a traveller who hears a woman's cry. There is another series, suggested as a possible referent of the cry, in which past life and happiness are discussed. Nothing could be more classic than this referential supposition: the relationship between memory and past life is something that usually characterizes depth effects in metaphorical literature. And yet the hinge between the two series is composed of verbs that manifest this very supposition. The traveller envies those who believe that they have already lived a similar evening; that is, he thinks that others think this supposition. The retreat from the surface is described as an act of presuming a retreat from the surface. The manifestation of the metaphorical series as an effect of discourse carries with it the loss of every latency.

What generally characterizes these squares is a movement towards the surfaces of series that seem to promise fullness. The city of Isaura 'is said to rise over a deep, subterranean lake'.[8] All that is above repeats what is underneath in as much as 'everything that moves in the sunlight is driven by the lapping wave enclosed beneath the rock's calcareous sky'.[9] Two hypotheses can be drawn from this: that Isaura's gods live in its depths, or that they live in the buckets drawn forth from the wells by a sprawling, complicated mechanical system that defines Isaura as 'a city that moves entirely upward'.[10]

This story recalls another comic devaluation: Manganelli's 'Discorso sulla dificultà di comunicare coi morti' [Discourse on the difficulty of communicating with the dead]. The analogy lies in the same procedure of translating a metaphor of penetrating depths in a description of mechanisms, or devices (material or verbal), in order to bring something back from the depths to the surface of a discourse. The following paradox arises: the depths are a discursive series to which surface devices apply – or they are a metaphoric series whose ambiguity becomes an object of play, transforming in the process into non-metaphoric hypotheses (the devices). The devices that Calvino lists so scrupulously have the following semantic property: they are objects without latency. At its heart is the same punning game that Humpty Dumpty plays in his explanation of the 'Jabberwocky'. 'Pun' as an esoteric word has metaphorical values that are diluted if explained, rendering its components literal. That the explanation is arbitrary, as in the case of Humpty Dumpty or Manganelli, doesn't matter: every device is arbitrary. Of note too is how in Calvino's work the first hypothesis about the gods inhabiting the deep is undivided, totalizing or non-analytical, whereas the second is fragmented in the list of devices. There is a clear opposition between metaphor and device, and between the two relative images of the literary product: a) that of depth, based on its metaphorical values as an undivided unity, a global and continuous metaphor; b) that of surface as fragmentation – a mechanism is a set of parts that all work together but between which there is discontinuity, disjunction and dislocation. We can choose these two series of metaphorical depth and of surface devices as the central concerns of our commentary. But bringing the two series together as Calvino and Manganelli do has further consequences to explore. The first comes from the fact that depth entails the illusion of an original, non-derivative, immediate and spontaneous sense of what is said. Writing seems to resuscitate an originary word carried within itself. To associate this with the image of the device is not only to reveal the illusion at the very moment it is produced, it is also to offer the word carried by the writing not as original but as reconstructed. This seems to me to be related to the tendency of surface stories to use recycled materials that indicate the non-original character of the discourse. Sanguineti, for example, in *Giuoco dell'Oca* uses clippings and passages clearly lifted from comic strips, magazines and other forms of mass media. This is directly reminiscent of the type of frame introduced by many examples of pop art that, especially with Lichtenstein and Warhol, have the merit of fixing surfaces wherein every visual metaphor appears as mechanically reproduced material, already in itself an element of a series lacking an origin. But to return to Lewis Carroll, this too is already part of his discovery: Martin Gardner's 1960 *Annotated Alice* makes it clear that a large part of the two volumes of Alice's adventures are composed of recycled materials. Calvino's rewriting of Marco Polo, like that of the tarot cards or of the Count of Monte Cristo in *Ti con zero* (*T Zero*), are all closely related. The distinction between play and literature is present throughout, in the fact that the game uses the previously discussed object of manipulation, while literature is supposed to use original-originary materials.

Elizabeth Sewell in *The Field of Nonsense* has, to my knowledge, made the most extensive cataloguing of the characteristics of a literature-game, as distinct from literature-literature: this would be 'nonsense' for her. She insists that to have a game it is necessary to have previously supplied components to manipulate, but components capable of retaining their integrity at every step: metaphorical transformation is not allowed for the components of the game. The components of the game must be taken at literal value. The permitted transformation is that of the rearrangement of a series based on disorder into a new order. This is the type of reconstruction carried out by the game-device: previously supplied components are manipulated until they rearrange themselves into a new series, with the 'Nonsense universe', as Sewell writes, consisting of 'the sum of its parts and nothing more'.[11]

The other side of the issue concerns the mechanisms with which to manipulate what has already been said. Mechanisms can be understood as operations that produce effects that conform to the rules or predictions of a programme. The past is the fundamental narrative effect, being not only the very subject of narration but the index of a transformation from something that precedes the passage from text to text. In metaphorical literature, the past is the event that gives rise to the text and the act of narrating. Calvino's towns and cities carry out a whole discourse on the past that coincides with an interrogation of the possibilities of narration. In Maurilia, for example, the traveller is shown certain old postcards of the town and is expected to comment – but only by following 'precise rules'. The following passages reveal something of the nature of the mechanism that produces the effect of the past: a) the traveller must say that 'the magnificence and prosperity of Maurilia [...] cannot compensate for a certain lost grace, which, however, can be enjoyed only now in old postcards'; b) in any case, Maurilia, now transformed into a metropolis, 'has this added attraction that, through what it has become, one can look back with nostalgia at what it was'; c) as for the postcards, they bear no relation to the present town of Maurilia – 'they do not depict Maurilia as it was, but a different city which, by chance, was called Maurilia, like this one'.[12] The series of this effect are as follows: a) the signs of a cut or discontinuity (lost grace); b) the signs of a continuity (the growth into a metropolis); c) an arbitrary object that isolates the two previous series in its space and causes their contiguity and succession to appear. This generates the effect of a transition from one series to the other, and precisely that effect which is the epic or historical past: the transformation of a discontinuity into continuity through words. The postcards, with their arbitrariness, come to indicate that the past is nothing but the spacing of two series in a certain clipping of the surface. But the same mechanism, used for other effects, works equally well for the two cities that make up Aglaura, the two levels of Argia, the city of the living and the dead of Eusapia, the two prophecies of Morazia, the stories of the animals and the animals of the stories of Theodora, the just and the unjust of Berenice and so on. In short, it is the fundamental mechanism by which the writing of the book develops.

As is often explicitly stated, the two series are actually two aspects of a single series that pass into each other, as in a Mobius strip where the inner and outer surfaces cannot be distinguished because one slides into the other. We read, for example, of Moriana: 'From one part to the other, the city seems to continue, in perspective, multiplying its repertory of images: but instead it has no thickness, it consists only of a face and an obverse, like a sheet of paper, with a figure on either side, which neither be separated nor look at each other.'[13] This can be compared with what Deleuze says: 'The continuity between reverse and right side replaces all the layers of depth, and the surface effects […] bring to language becoming and its paradoxes.'[14] Becoming and the paradoxes of becoming are the specifications of the effect described, the result of the procedure used by Calvino to bring metaphorical residues to the surface by showing them in their literal guise: figures without depth. Let us dwell on the transformation of the metaphorical into the literal. In *Alice in Wonderland* and *Alice through the Looking-Glass* almost all speech effects are literal explications of metaphors or metaphorical uses of language. This is one of the reasons that led Elizabeth Sewell to conclude that nonsense is a genre distinct from literature, or as she puts it, from poetry – a genre from which those components called dream and imagination are strictly excluded, because in nonsense, objects and words are kept distinct in their literal value and do not give rise to meta-phorical condensations or symbolic shifts. Symbolic shifts are replaced by literal transformations. One can see, for example, the game practised by Lewis Carroll in 'Doublets', as the passing from one word into another, letter by letter, yet maintaining the basic meaning of a sentence. For example: 'Make Wheat into Bread' becomes: 'Wheat/ cheat/ creep/ creed/ bred/ bread'. The rule of these games is: move from one series to the next in such a way that the transitions keep the series distinct (in other words, do not confuse them with metaphorical or semantic trans-formations), but put them in a circle by sliding one into the other on the written surface. The written surface is nothing more than the literal value of words: words as purely syntactic or equi-referential signs. The conclusion is that writing can implement all possible transformations between series. Writing is like Alice's reality, a space of perpetual meta-morphosis. But this essentially stems from the fact that nothing actually transforms – words and series are all the same, like numbers, if taken from the literal side. This is the absence of depth.

There remains much to say about the effects of the mechanism: the becoming and its paradoxes. In Theodora, the past is characterized by a series of animal exterminations. Each exterminated species leaves room for another invasive species, until the animals are completely exter-minated. The animals are consigned to books in the library to preserve their memory. But at this point another invasion arises: the fauna of the books, the 'sphinxes, griffins, chimeras, dragons, hircocervuses, harpies, hydras, unicorns, basilisks regain possession of their city'.[15] The trans-formation here occurs as it does in Carroll's word puzzle: how do we shift from animal stories to story animals? Again, a space is needed, as in Maurilia's postcards, to make the two series contiguous: this space takes the form of books, written surfaces. The square can be read with the following metaphorical connotations: humanity cannot totally dominate its environment because every remedy it implements becomes a new environmental imbalance; but if, by hypothesis, humanity were able to exterminate all the species that threaten its dominion, there would then be the monsters of the unconscious, the monsters of humanity itself ready to destroy it. The fact is, however, that this talk about monsters is made possible by the passage along the edge between one and the other series. To express it another way: if the animals that occupied the world can be put in books, the animals in books can occupy the world, which is an effect of language. This is much less and much more than an ecological fable. It is the vertigo of the possible metamorphoses that language can enact through its unlimited becoming. Unlimited becoming, of which Deleuze offers an ample explanation, is the specific mode of surface adventure: language that from one series can produce two; that can divide and multiply series so as to enact the transition from past to present, from discontinuity to continuity. Unlimited becoming is unlimited metamorphosis: Alice becoming bigger and shrinking, but also Alice reciting 'Father William' and then another poem in tune with the first but entirely different. Unlimited becoming is then narrative prolif-eration: as in the case of Shahrazàd, who tells the story of the merchant and the demon, and then of the three old men who save the merchant with their stories. All this is barely resolved within the scope of semantic or intentional interpretation. Depth is immutable permanence of being, to which semantic interpretation can be usefully applied, whereas unlimited becoming is the series of events in which being manifests itself by changing simulacra. The ancient negativity of the simulacrum is the only thing to which one can be positively attached.

Recalling the model of transformation contained in the description of Moriana, or rather the study of such a model made by Calvino in the short story 'Dall'opaco' (*Adelphiana*, 1971) we can come to define the effects of the mechanism as this form of pure becoming that logically results in paradox. Deleuze defines paradox as that which initially 'destroys good sense as the only direction, but it is also that which destroys common sense as the assignment of fixed identities'.[16] In the famous paradox of Chrysippus ('If you say something it passes through your mouth; now if you say "chariot", a chariot passes through your mouth'), just as in the squares of Mariana of Maurilia and the other cities based on a double series, two series come into circulation to create an uncontrollable movement in which the attributes of things are irresistibly transformed. Paradox has to do with infinite becoming and the metamorphic possibilities of language – because paradox allows two possible series to occur, with one continuously transforming into the other. Infinite becoming is not only the fact that Theodora's animals can dizzyingly replace each other, and each empty box comes to be filled mechanically with a newly arisen species. It is also the fact that animals can become books and books animals; that the obverse can become the reverse and the surface depth; that the mirror is another way of imagining the paradox we already know from *Through the Looking-Glass* – just as the traveller arriving in Valdrada will see two cities: one upright and one reflected upside down. 'The mirror increases a thing's value, at times denies it. Not everything that seems valuable above the mirror maintains its force when mirrored. The twin cities are not equal […] they live for each other, their eyes interlocked; but there is no love between them.'[17] The invisibility of Calvino's cities comes from their perpetual non-identity with themselves, from their splitting into images that maintain in discourse a paradoxical mode of speaking and in so doing reject the defining of discourse's identity with respect to itself, something characteristic of traditional writing. What paradox attacks is the principle of identity. The endless series of simulacra replaces the original form, the archetype behind the identity of all things.

As mentioned previously, the two types of chapters clearly identify their narrators, with the numbered ones conveying Marco Polo's tales and the unnumbered ones reporting Kublai Khan's observations. At the outset of the book the plural *maiestatis* (royal we) brings us to understand that the scribe puts himself in the same category as Khan and listens to what the fabulator Marco Polo tells him. Fabulation and writing seem quite distinct in terms of both the spacing of the text and its stylistics. The chapters in which Khan carries out his reasoning serve to delineate and organize the parts of the book (the cities) and at the same time reveal the activity of the scribe: writing. The unnumbered chapters are stories reported by Marco Polo – fables from elsewhere that someone has told and that the scribe welcomes as quotations in his discourse: fabulation. It seems to me that in terms of literary games this distinction, clarified here by the form of chapters, should always be made. Writing serves to delimit the material space of the game and to administer it: how the chapters are put together, whether they are numbered or unnumbered, how the parts follow one another making use of a progression derived from the presence of certain inscribed signs (names or otherwise) or break apart into autonomous spaces. On the other hand, fabulation is not necessarily linguistic, as is evident for example at the beginning of the book, when Marco Polo 'newly arrived and totally ignorant of the Levantine Languages [...] could only express himself with gestures, leaps, cries of wonder and of horror, animal barkings or hootings, or with objects he took from his knapsacks'.[18] I set aside for now the problem of fabulation. But with Marco Polo the fabulator and Khan the scribe, Calvino brings me to consider that writing and fabulation are equated with what in game theory is called game and play, or the rules and the game, respectively. The game is merely an abstraction, like Khan's boxes understood as a matrix of possible moves, without regard to actual moves. Game is the out-of-context, meta-game or normative form of play. This closely aligns with the model Khan uses to interpret his cities: the empty chessboard, its squares as the spacing of nothingness, that is, discrete units with no meaning of their own but capable of ordering all possible cities and that correspond to the function of writing in the text. Writing is but a matrix of moves. Game is defined by Von Neumann and Morgenstern in *Theory of Games and Economic Behavior* as the totality of the rules that describe it, making Khan's model a descriptive abstraction, the grammar or bureaucratic criterion of the game, administering it from a distance.[19]

The unlimited becoming of writing discussed to this point indeed has a boundary: the boundary of grammar. Grammar is like Borges' Library of Babel, capable of composing an infinite tangle of unlimited episodic recurrences. The grammar on which writing is based is an irreplaceable administrative tool for western societies. But then, can grammar actually recompose the infinite bricolage of language? It can if conceived as an illusion of power, or God-power, like the illusion of God-order-recurrence introduced by Borges. Khan attempts to imagine a model containing all the infinite becoming of the possible and to rearrange it into a coherent vision. Coherent, let us remember, is the opposite of paradoxical; it means one-way. Therefore, it does not matter whether Marco Polo speaks truthfully or deceptively, speaks only of Venice or confuses cities – because in the systemic abstract totality of information, unlimited becoming is nullified by reducing all citable cities, or all possible metamorphoses of cities, to a limited number of almost Platonic 'forms'. These 'forms', spoken of explicitly, include not only current cities but also past or future ones: the annulment of becoming. What Khan pursues in his ramblings is nothing but the grammatical order mentioned above. What is interesting is that here this grammatical order is clearly linked to the exercise of power as a breaking up and marginalizing of the empirical in order to control it in non-empirical form, which is what any grammar does. From a very Borgesian point of view, the God-order is present even in the most subterranean and infinitesimal disorder. The story of the atlas reduced to a chessboard is all here: 'knowledge of the empire was hidden in the pattern drawn by the angular leaps of the knight, by the diagonal passages opened by to the bishop's incursions, by the lumbering and guarded steps of the king and the humble pawn, by the inexorable ups and downs of every game. [...] By disembodying his conquests to reduce them to the essential, Kublai had arrived at the extreme operation: the definitive conquest, of which the empire's multiform treasures were but illusory envelopes.'[20] We have arrived at exactly the opposite end of everything we were saying before; not only because this reduction is annihilation of becoming, but because, whereas before the illusory effects of language were the devices with which to operate, now in these unnumbered boxes are the signs of annihilation reflecting the total illusoriness of the world. This is the business of Lacan's '*manque à etre*' (lack of being).

Calvino's book gathers within it, concentrated in the model of the cities at the very heart of the game, the illusions of a pure epistemology capable, by way of some trick of discourse and semiological novelty, of fixing the metamorphoses of the possible in an exhaustive grammar. Only this then leads back to a nothingness that is Khan's chessboard square, a planed wooden inlay. Summary of the story: the grammatical domination of written spaces, the exercise of absolute power over writing, is an illusion of the surface. Thus far we are in line with the most advanced western epistemology that dotingly explains that the sign is not the thing, the signifier is not the meaning, that it is all a matter of a few discrete elements, which in themselves are not signifiers, that they are nothing. This is also the point reached by the current tendency to think that everything is contained in the text, in the writing, that is, in the rules of the game. The relationship between limitless becoming and its generative model leads to the crux of the issue: but at the crux there are only rules, no fabulation, no game. In essence one is always just telling oneself what the game is like but never playing. Contemporary textualism clearly demonstrates that it does not know how to put fabulation back into the circle, and thus it is doomed to simply remake grammars. One clear example is Roland Barthes' brilliant *S/Z*, the most obsessive description of the rules that determine writing that I know of, with the implicit fallacy that rules and game are the same. I leave out 'creative' examples because those that come to mind only show how the mirages of writing can make passive laughingstocks out of those in the field. Writing is nothing more, culturally, than a bureaucratic tool for administering territories. The *topos* of writing is the theological and/or bureaucratic *topos* of the world-book. The modern primacy of writing does not detach scribes from their work but rather increasingly binds them to their roles, causing them to become ever more submissive and bureaucratic. *Bouvard et Pécuchet* (*Bouvard and Pécuchet*) offers a detailed account of this illusion. In Flaubert's tale, the endless bricolage of the world annihilates or overcomes the possibilities of dominating the world demiurgically through the writing of books about it, and thus the two heroes find themselves for what they were: scribes, submissive scribes. In Calvino, too, there is an account of this illusion, with much the same outcome: the realization of the original 'manque' on which writing and its rules, the order-grammatics-power that administers the world, are founded. But further on, if I read the reasonings of Khan correctly, the discourse goes round in circles to another possibility: 'The square on which your enlightened gaze is fixed', says Marco Polo to the Great Khan, 'was cut from a ring of a trunk that grew in a year of drought: do you see how the fibres are arranged? Here you a barely discernible knot can be made out: a bud tried to sprout'. The quantity of things that could be read in a little piece of smooth empty wood overwhelmed Kublai'.[21] Taking this passage as a conclusion to Calvino's *conte philosophique* (philosophical story), I return to the infinite becoming enacted by the writing in the boxes it administers. But the perspective is somewhat changed from this side. It is not so much the fabulation taken in by the writing that matters but the fabulation that the writing emits. Khan's chessboard square is eventually proposed as a box furrowed with traces that must be followed one by one, until a story can be fashioned out of them through meticulous observation. We have now returned to the problem of Maurilia's postcards or the squares as inducers of fabulation. For this business we need to think perhaps of the illustrations in old adventure books: spaces charged with exotic tensions that, because of the eidetic force of their traces, are producers of commentary and fantasies. Let us return to the third city, Zaira: 'A description of Zaira as it is today should contain all Zaira's past. The city, however, does not tell its past, but contains it like the lines of a hand, written in the corners of the streets, the gratings of windows, the banisters of the steps, the antennae of the lighting rods, the poles of the flags, every segment marked in turn with scratches, indentations, scrolls.'[22] Everything is well expressed: traces have memories in them, but these memories cannot be developed discursively as a sense in and of itself separate from the traces. The quality of the traces is the silence surrounding motivations and meanings. To say anything about Zaira, to explain its memories, we need only to stretch them out – to trace the city's inscribed lines, like the fibres of Khan's wooden chessboard square, the grids of the windows, the handrails of the stairs, all the vicissitudes of an itinerary of signs. The sense, memory and past of the traces cannot be grasped here or there, in a precious turn of phrase, in the fullness of a word, in some symbolic aspect or in a revealing figuration: it cannot be grasped in the traces but in the spacing of the traces. Meaning does not lie in a space of memory to be recovered, as for Proust, but in the spaces of memories spread out like a carpet – in an inscription of something, scratches that the presence of someone or something one day produced. And yet such a presence at the moment of reading is lost forever, having become absence. Zaira's parable is this: surface does not reveal itself but instead retraces itself.

The eidetic is thus a quality specific to the surface because by thickening the details to be traversed it abolishes any possibility of wide-ranging perception. The reading of the boxes then somewhat resembles the reading of a code of instructions that redraws, step by step, the path of a drawing.

In this regard Tamara is described as follows: 'Your gaze scans the streets as if they were written pages: the city says everything you must think, makes you repeat its discourse, and while you think you are visiting Tamara you are only recording the names with which it defines itself and all its parts.'[23] The city is a figuration carried out with words, arising from a correspondence between the written sign and a drawing to which it refers. It is not a matter of referents but that the traces reduced to literal form acquire an ostensive character: they indicate areas, corners, intricacies, labyrinthine deviations on the page. They deposit and distend the continuous metamorphosis of language into spacings that, like Khan's square, are empty assemblages. Here we say 'names', because proper names are elements of discourse without referents and are therefore empty assemblages that are filled mechanically with the surpluses of reading. We must think of reading as a series always exceeding writing. The procedure is thus to inscribe, not describe, the city-squares, leaving empty referential spaces that reading will then fill. This is gleaned from the chapter on Zora: 'This city cannot be expunged from the mind is like an armature, a honeycomb in whose cells each of us can place the things he wants to remember: names of famous men, virtues, vegetable and mineral classifications, dates of battles, constellations, parts of speech.'[24] The box is a matrix of possible readings. But this does not correspond at all to the ancient polysemy. If it did, the surface narrative would lose its literalism and reintroduce itself as a new kind of allegory. It is instead the exact opposite: traces function like those words without a referent (e.g., 'unicorn') that logicians call null: it is the overall pattern that matters, not the meaning underlying the traces. In the city of Eudoxia there is a carpet in which the entire city is reproduced: looking at it closely, one realizes that 'each place in the carpet corresponds to a place in the city and all the things contained in the city are included in the design'.[25] What is the effect of the design? 'Every inhabitant of Eudoxia compares the carpet's immobile order with their own image of the city, an anguish of their own, and each can find, concealed among the arabesques, an answer, the story of their life, the twists of fate.'[26]

It is only by explaining the traces that we come to square the surplus of reading with the void of writing. To explain again means to follow all the correspondences between discourse and drawing, between drawing and induced words, between induced words and that discursive manifestation of memory called fabulation. Fabulation arises from this continuous exchange of factors in a proportion that bridges an initial inequality. Fabulation is thus first and foremost exchange. The city of Euphemia is a city where merchants from seven nations convene at every solstice and equinox. At night by firelight each says a word such as '"wolf", "sister", "hidden treasure", "battle", "scabies", "lovers" – the others each tell, each one, their stories of wolves, sisters, treasures, scabies, lovers, battles'.[27] They exchange words and each word produces in the other a tale. This is a small-scale model of induced fabulation: offering words, phrases, objects or names inscribed in a box, like a catalogue of narrative possibilities. It is a game of exchange because it modifies the narratives we already knew into others that are not our own. But to understand these new narratives induced by the words of others we must free ourselves from our own words. This is what we learn in Hypatia: 'I realized I had to free myself from the images which in the past had announced to me the things I sought: only then would I succeed in understand the language of Hypatia.'[28] To play at reading is to exchange words in this way, but it is also to lose identity with our own tales and to discover that other tales invade us: 'And you know that in the long journey ahead of you, when to keep awake against the camel's swaying or the junk's rocking, you start summoning up your memories one by one, your wolf will have become another wolf, your sister a different sister, your battle other battles, on your return from Euphemia, the city where memory is traded at every solstice and at every equinox.'[29]

All these cities are, it seems to me, reductions to formulas or minimal parables of fabulatory possibilities. They are made to induce narratives, to exchange memories, but they also include the rules of this operation. The tale is outside of writing precisely because it is its effect: the novelistic or the marvellous are modes – moods that are learned from writing by contagion but then develop their disease independently in the body. Fabulation is related to the dream in this, as the dream, while not being language, can suggest itself with language, but its paths do not develop in language but in the body. Dream and fabulation are two identical activities arising from different states of the body. Dream is the greatest disruptor of surfaces because, rising from the depth of the body, it confuses them, condenses them, ruins their spacing. 'Nothing is more fragile than the surface', says Deleuze, which is 'always threatened by a monster even more awesome than the Jabberwock – by a formless, fathomless nonsense'.[30] Thus in Chloe everyone experiences the vibrations of their mutual presence, but no one carries the vibrations of their body beyond an exchange of glances with others. The body's adventures are kept within the limits of the imagined, the imaginary. The perfect game is this mentalization of relationships: 'A voluptuous vibration continually stirs Chloe, the most chaste of cities. If men and women began to live their ephemeral dreams, every phantom would become a person with whom to begin a story of pursuits, pretences, misunderstandings, clashes, oppressions, and the carousel of fantasies would stop.'[31] The true game of bodies is something else: it is their mixing. The true game of writing is the distance of the traces, which are dead as soon as they plough the plane, the celluloid in which the dream stretches out losing its depth as a dream, becoming absence or loss of the dream. Zobeide was built in the image of a dream; many men had the same dream and wanted to reproduce it in a city so that it would come true: 'New people arrived from other lands, having had a dream like theirs, and in the city of Zobeide, they recognized something of the streets of the dream, and they changed the positions of arcades and stairways to resemble more closely' the dream image.[32] The first to arrive in the city, meanwhile, had already forgotten about the dream and 'could not understand what drew these people to Zobeide, to this ugly city, this trap'.[33] The fabulation is either inaugural or it is nothing. Like the dream transcribed in the morning, it is a sign of a cut and a new beginning, deposited in grooves that preserve its exact consistency as the dream no longer exists. The fabulation contains within itself the unlimited becoming and all the metamorphoses to which we subject ourselves – and as such it is unfixable, always inaugural and always immediately lost. Writing calls to it, seeks it with its own moves. To find it, it must escape itself, if it can manage to. Therein lies the problem of writing today.

The draw of *Le città invisibili* lies, in my view, in contrasting and then circulating two possible tendencies in contemporary writing: a) that of textualism – the spacing of the surface as an analysis of discourse and reduction of the narrative to the rules that determine it; b) the tendency to use the textual surface as an inducer, illustration or type of figural writing that activates effects that move from the page and into the body. There is a misconception regarding the first tendency that is worth dwelling on and one that Calvino transcribes well: the model used by Khan to interpret his cities 'contains everything corresponding to the norm. Since the cities that exist diverge in varying degree from the norm, I need only foresee the exceptions to the norm and calculate the most probable combinations.'[34] This passage can be compared with Barthes' idea that 'the unveiling of the codes of literature' is the most provocative act that literature can perform: modern writing then seems to be writing that by unveiling the norm would enact its transgression.[35] The sense of both discourses can be expressed thus: by calculating the combinations of permissible moves starting from the rules (norms, codes) of a game, the optimal strategy (exceptions, transgressions) can be deduced (predicted). The misconception is that as soon as we have a game that is more complex than the matchstick-based Marienbad, it is no longer meaningful to talk about optimal strategy and thus about calculating exceptions or transgressions. Here I rely on what Enzo Melandri says in *La linea e il circolo* [The line and the circle]: 'the strategy of a game is not deducible from its rules'.[36] The match or play is not reducible to the game. Strategy always transcends the rules. In the game the rules are only negatively useful, to fix how far one can go; positively one must resort to more than that, to timing and induction, imagination and flair at bluffing. For strategy is not a calculation, it is only a local induction if done with style and ease. If we maintain the correlation between game and literary product, all theories of contemporary textualism explode, because they are based on an identification between rules and game. Melandri's thoughts on this kind of confusion, which are common in structuralist thought, should not be overlooked.

Strategy transcends rules because it cannot be calculated from them, just as fabulation goes outside the text because it cannot be reduced to the written word or any of its grammar. One can thus say that a strategic use of writing refers only to writing as a matrix of moves – an inducer of other things that go beyond the page. To explain how this induction occurs, consider the form of commentary. Manganelli showed that annotating a book, existent or non-existent, is an act of fabulation. From here we can begin a discussion of how the external development that a text produces is always fabulation, whether in the form of commentary, as mine is, or in the form of paraphrase, or simply in the form of account, mentalization, discursive or dreamlike activity, chatter, gossip or delirium: these are all examples of operations of the text developing outside the text. We know what logical operations consist in: the deriving, from certain formal premises, of all the transformations allowed by the rules that are given along with the formal premises. Wittgenstein in his notebooks arrives at this most blunt formulation: 'The concept of the successive application of an operation is equivalent to the concept "and so on"' (*Tractatus Logico-Philosophicus*).[37] This 'and so on' applied to fiction has some analogy with the formulas that conclude fairy tales: for example, 'and they lived happily ever after', or all those other formulas with temporal operators such as 'always', 'never again', 'for all my life', 'and since' or 'since that day'. Temporal operators are the formal premises for a development beyond the fairy tale that can be mentally traversed in an unlimited way. The rules of development are the narrative event to which the operator refers. On the other hand, fairy tales are a typical case of text developing beyond itself, being in essence strategies of cultural adaptation.

According to the rules of fabulation of the surface tale, the squares of Zora, Eudoxia and Euphemia seem clear enough to me. But in Sanguineti's *Capriccio italiano* there is a game that more closely resembles our own; it is the game of guessing a novel, with someone asking questions and others having to answer. When 'they ask a question whose last word ends in a, or in o, or in u, we would always say no, and that if it ended in e, or in i, we would say yes'.[38] This is the most pertinent example because here the rules of development are letters, that is, non-metaphorical or non-semantic units. This falls under the literalism we mentioned above. In surface narrative all transformations can be made between units, but not metaphorical transformations, only literal transformations. The need for literalism is related to the ultimate need to liberate the narrative from the global metaphor in which everything risks being confused. A game is such only if it keeps its units intact, says Elizabeth Sewell. The confusion-totality-continuum of all global metaphors is the depth of body and dream. Sewell writes: 'The dream tends toward oneness but the mind is separate from this process and can, in waking, set the dream into words, thereby establishing a measure of control over it and communicating it to other minds.'[39] It is in the body and the dream that the game deposits its traces; that fabulation enacts its ultimate effects. But to do so it must distance itself from itself – for the story to become a dream, as in Alice, it must liberate itself from the dream and become pure surface.

Notes

1 Gilles Deleuze, *The Logic of Sense*, trans. Mark Lester, with Charles Stivale (New York: Columbia University Press, 1990), 42.
2 Deleuze, *The Logic*, 10.
3 Deleuze, *The Logic*, 72.
4 Deleuze, *The Logic*, 9.
5 Deleuze, *The Logic*, 9.
6 Deleuze, *The Logic*, 10.
7 Italo Calvino, *Invisible Cities*, trans. William Weaver (San Diego: Harcourt, 1974), 9.
8 Calvino, *Invisible*, 20.
9 Calvino, *Invisible*, 20.
10 Calvino, *Invisible*, 20.
11 Elizabeth Sewell, *The Field of Nonsense* (London: Chatto and Windus, 1952), 98.
12 Calvino, *Invisible*, 30.
13 Calvino, *Invisible*, 105.
14 Deleuze, *The Logic*, 11.
15 Calvino, *Invisible*, 160.
16 Deleuze, *The Logic*, 3.
17 Calvino, *Invisible*, 54.
18 Calvino, *Invisible*, 21.
19 John von Neumann and Oskar Morgenstern, *Theory of Games and Economic Behavior* (New York: Science Editions, 1964).
20 Calvino, *Invisible*, 123.
21 Calvino, *Invisible*, 131.
22 Calvino, *Invisible*, 10–11.
23 Calvino, *Invisible*, 14.
24 Calvino, *Invisible*, 15.
25 Calvino, *Invisible*, 96.
26 Calvino, *Invisible*, 96–7.
27 Calvino, *Invisible*, 36.
28 Calvino, *Invisible*, 48.
29 Calvino, *Invisible*, 36–7.
30 Calvino, *Invisible*, 82.
31 Calvino, *Invisible*, 52.
32 Calvino, *Invisible*, 45.
33 Calvino, *Invisible*, 46.
34 Calvino, *Invisible*, 69.

35   Roland Barthes, 'Drame, poème, roman', in *Théorie d'ensemble* (Paris: Seuil, 1968), 39.
36   Enzo Melandri, *La linea e il circolo* (Bologna: Il Mulino, 1968), 946.
37   Ludwig Wittgenstein, *Tractatus Logico-Philosophicus*, trans. F. P. Ramsey, *The Ludwig Wittgenstein Project*. https://www.wittgensteinproject.org.
38   Edoardo Sanguineti, *Capriccio italiano* (Milan: Feltrinelli, 1963), 45.
39   Sewell, *The Field*, 53.

6
'The virtues of the gorilla' ('Le virtù del gorilla', 1974)

In a pamphlet entitled *Visita del Gorilla Quadrumàno (teatro di stalla)* [Tour of the quadrumanous gorilla (barn theatre)], a group of students from the University of Bologna, organized by Giuliano Scabia, describe their project begun in the month of June in the Apennine Mountains near Reggio Emilia, in tiny villages such as Ramiseto, Busana, Ligonchio and Villaminozzo: 'We discovered that in these areas, until about 30 years ago, there were enacted plays, called by old farmers who told us about them, *rime* (rhymes) and *farse* (farces); these plays were enacted during carnival time in barns, where farmers would pass winter evenings together.[1] Two things particularly struck us as theatre students: the way in which, with the pretence of theatre, these farmers (who for some of us are grandfathers and great grandfathers) passed the time together; and how they produced "culture" autonomously, by way of their own, if very poor, means.' The rediscovery of a few pieces of barn theatre by the student Remo Melloni was the source of the students' project: 'Among the texts we chose one called *Il Gorilla Quadrumàno*, or "a tall and ferocious simian," a figure capable of truly extraordinary feats: at times a monkey, at others a human, and at others a magician.' In short, the play is the story of a Portuguese king who, to embellish his garden with various marvels, sends his servants Salam and Codghin in search of the gorilla. They lock it in a cage and teach it to speak and reason like a human. But at the end the gorilla is revealed as the most human of all the characters, punishing the vices of the courtiers, serving (as in various similar fables) as a magical helper to the hero and bringing the comedy to a happy end.

In its rough outline, I would say that the account has many parallels with another re-enactment of the myth of the giant ape – that of the 1933 film *King Kong* – except that American culture could not allow for a pact of friendship with the beast, and thus the film ends tragically. Instead, in *Il Gorilla Quadrumàno*, peasant culture conceives of the beast as a mediator between human desire and the exigencies of nature, as well as between society and its distant origins. This widespread folkloristic motif has as many interpretations as there are situations in which it appears. For example, in addition to Vico, Kafka too took up this motif, paradoxically re-evoking it in the story of a gorilla educated in human society and transformed into an able performer. But the motif's underlying importance comes from the fact that every time it is evoked, a judgement is put into play by present society of past society, of the varying possibilities of an accord between present society and its distant origins. It is evoked time and again when there arises the need to revisit the problem of social relations, for example in Rousseau, who transforms the beast into a child by way of a mythological process in which the place left by the ancient giant or beast is filled by a child, a modern metaphor for all creative vitality. The beast sparks this grappling with present society, with which we can come to terms only by way of an identification with an earlier form of language.

One may wonder what sense there is in exhuming and disseminating this figure, which is emblematic to a degree of the rediscovered play, and of its symbolic role within rural culture. First it must be said that the type of recitation employed by the students is very simple, minimally nuanced by a comic tic invented for each of the characters. In substance it is not a true and proper theatrical recitation but more akin to the public demonstration of the possible uses of an instrument: the instrument is a basic text such as *Il Gorilla Quadrumàno*, and the demonstration is that this instrument can be used by everyone, with no need to be a star of the stage or an anti-star of the avant-garde.

From this arises the first virtue of the Gorilla, and of this type of theatrical practice: performative expectations are kept to a minimum, and thus they are fully met. In other words, people laugh, joyfully throw back their heads and engage in playful a back-and-forth with the actors – with a general lightening of the mood, a melting of the societal reserve that comes about with festivities. Sociability is most detectable in celebration, and thus in comedy, notably in celebrations such as the carnivals that mark the change from work to non-work, and, deeper still, changes in season and in the economy. A focus on sociability is thus implicit in this theatrical project, along with spectacle as an excuse to throw a party.

And yet the activities of the Gorilla troupe, and the personal activities of Giuliano Scabia, consist not only of putting on small productions.

They also and above all consist of enacting an entire series of preliminary operations aimed at reconnecting the threads of society. The model is that of old itinerant peddlers who travel from house to house with an announcement, but one based on sparking a rapport based on gab, which is perhaps the part most difficult to grasp for a sceptical intellectual. There is a practice of gabbing that in small social settings functions to unite the group, along with a precise way of sparking cohesion by exchanging ceremonial phrases and thus lowering social reserves. In urban society one knows that this method is often viewed with a certain distrust, but I would say that every time there arises the need to re-establish the sense of a social group, or to indicate identification with a group, the practice of ceremonial gabbing reappears – for example, in various forms of underground American culture as a system of introduction and recognition. The fact that this technique of gabbing is as important as the spectacle itself – to Scabia, to the Gorilla troupe and to the overall results of the enterprise – is evident in the premise underlying this type of theatrical practice. Put succinctly, this premise is that the first political move should be to build societal frameworks, places of collective identification. Such a proposition is not new, but perhaps the non-pedagogical dimension in which it is being relaunched is new. It seems to me that we have at last begun to understand this: that societal strands cannot be reconnected if within the relationships with others there intervenes someone in the guise of an instructor, of a pedagogue, or of a clarifier of public ideas; at most such a situation may regroup people around ideas that they already have in common, but it does not increase communication in societies such as ours whose identificatory groups are fragmented into the solitary lives of their individual members.

In this way the problem of the nature of sociability and of social communication is re-proposed in its full extent, being that sociability is only partially verbal, built of words that inform people of the carryings on of the world. Sociability is nurtured above all by specific gestural systems, of behavioural metaphors, of an understanding of the timing of reciprocal actions and responses and of a collective economy of sensitivity that no professor can teach us. First this means that social dramatizations are the large-scale models to consider: weddings, baptisms, carnivals, parades and public gatherings. And second, it means that our loss of the meaning of these events, of these large productions of collective gesturality, is the loss of our sense of society and the entrance into our lives of solitude. It is not so much the loss of words to reach others but of the gestures, of the forms of bodily movement and barest means of behaviour needed to identify with others. If I have understood something of the activity of the Gorilla troupe, I would say that its hypothesis tends in this direction and not towards a reactivation of popular phantasms evoked by old texts of barn theatre (keeping in mind the necessity of distinguishing phantasms from social metaphors). The metaphor of the Gorilla or large beast seems to me extremely apt at sparking this sort of collective gesturality because the spectacle searches out the foundational modes of communication in a social group; and those who are enacting it are students who seem to have understood that such things are not learned in classrooms, mulling over the words in books, or in the sophisticated little theatres of the *élite*, pretending to have gone mad.

This is at the heart of this unusual *studio* (project, study, investigation), if *studio* is the right word. Vico's monsters and Rousseau's innocents speak a *stralingua* (a primeval glossolalia or animalistic hyper-language), a language that precedes all other languages, an originary source that seemingly filters up through to the present. Linguists would say that this is an ideological mistake and that it has nothing to do with the inner workings of true languages. All the same, is the idea of a *stralingua* not perhaps a metaphor of basic social communication, a utopic metaphor of a communicative virtue that passes across the various codes that divide groups? There is a reason, I repeat, that the motif of the mediating talking beast reappears whenever problems of sociality arise. The choice of *Il Gorilla Quadrumàno* was not by chance. In it the Gorilla is clearly a 'rube', pointedly referred to in the text as a 'wild animal man', who is also the wild man of the old carnivals. His language of choice, the language of the person who wrote and recited this comedy in barns, is the 'denatured' language of Ruzante: a way of speaking that is somewhat apparent in the dialogues of Salam and Codghin, but one that arises from the cracks in the text through rhymes and a form of Italian used as a foreign language, by someone suffering from a maladjustment to Italian. The *stralingua* of the beasts, like the 'denatured' language of Ruzante, is not a language in and of itself but the symptom of a maladjustment and the dream of a form of communication capable of expressing human desires through this linguistic maladjustment. And herein lies the political crux of this metaphor and of this enterprise, as far as I have understood it. If political language is, and should be, the vehicle of the needs and desires of the various social classes, it soon becomes clear that these necessities and desires must pass through a standardized jargon, through languages that do not belong to the people constrained to use them, such as bureaucratic, literary, or contractual versions of Italian, or the language that the Gorilla must learn when he is put in the cage. But if necessities and desires constitute the cultural discourse par excellence, then we must admit that there exist many regional varieties of political discourse, of the expression of necessities and desires – as many as there are differing dialects, argots, idioms and originary languages of various cultures. If one takes up the profession of being a student, what else is there to study today? The large systems of thought are not of much use in this regard.

The maladaptation to Italian is a maladaptation to a bureaucratic, administrative, raving society in which Molierian doctors have become prison wardens and children are taught from infancy to emulate these same ravings, which then become a symbol of a state of society desperately wanted by all. And so, welcome be these visits of the Gorilla who leaps over verbal persuasion, giving us the idea that there exist gestures – specific ways with which a local culture expresses its own needs. These visits reveal matters that do not pertain to an abstract discourse on the state of the world but to matters that are invisible to those who always think about abstract discourses on the state of the world: how we greet one another, how we laugh, how we celebrate holidays, how we indicate consent and dissent, how we show both respect for speech and joy in its expression, within various groups. In short, these visits bring us back to a discourse on the limitless variety of political languages, and even more so, to the vast metaphors or deep meanings that cultures arouse and through which cultures express their desires. This wayfinding, which is the true virtue of the Gorilla, is something worth reflecting upon, among the many bizarre ravings with which each day we feign intelligence.

Note

1   A selection of photographs and other documents relating to the 1974 travelling performances of *Il Gorilla quadrumàno* can be viewed here: *Nuovo Teatro Made in Italy*, https://nuovoteatromadeinitaly.sciami.com/giuliano-scabia-gorilla-quadrumano-1974/. Film footage of the play with English subtitles can be viewed here: *Mediateca Gorilla Quadrumano*, https://www.youtube.com/watch?v=8Bt4-Rif8sQ.

7
'The archaeological bazaar' ('Il bazaar archeologico', 1975)

I.

For a purview of the syndrome that is modern existence it is worth returning to the point of departure. From Rimbaud to the Dadaists to the Surrealists, the onus of having to be modern is wedded to a passion for fragments, objects, relics of a past lacking context, ruins of a history by now lost to history: new silences that arise where once not long ago there was a language capable of speaking of original experience and of the justifications behind these objects. The passion for *objets enfouis* (buried objects) and the passion for *enfouissement* (burial) seem to be metaphors of the unconscious and of repression, and perhaps they are. Underlying this are what Walter Benjamin called the 'remains of a dream world', with lingering oneiric elements upon awakening; the awakening of the modern era is a rather rough one.

In his Paris notes, Benjamin writes: 'Balzac was the first to speak of the ruin of the bourgeoisie. But it was surrealism which first allowed its gaze to roam freely over it. The development of the forces of production had turned the wish-symbols of the previous century into rubble, even before the monuments which represented them crumbled.'[1] The modern acceleration of history, or the development on the rails of history that is called progress, counts among its most illustrious victims the illusion of being able to prolong the dream up to the very moment of full wakefulness, perhaps even inspiring abstract poems; this illusion ruinously collapsing together with the idea of literature leaves in its place the persistent notion that the dream is only a lost object; that everything lost is part of the nature of the dream and thus is what must be sought out.

Take, for example, Rimbaud's *enchantementes* with modern man: 'What I liked were: absurd paintings, pictures over doorways, stage sets, carnival backdrops, billboards, bright-coloured prints; old-fashioned literature, church Latin, erotic books full of misspellings, the kind of novels our grandmothers read, fairy tales, little children's books, old operas, silly old songs, the naïve rhythms of country rimes.'[2] A folkloristic litany that passes from books of alchemy to collections of *conneries* (nonsense), but one divorced from the spaces which produced it. This is nearly the same litany presented by Eluard in *Poésie involontaire et poésie intentionnelle* and is also at the heart of Breton's research project: objects marked by a historical dislocation that renders them bewildered and bewildering and it is within this dislocation that the very loss of an origin imbues the cast-off, once forgotten objects with a sense of fascination. This is the bazar in place of the museum, in the sense that the collection of objects at a bazar is organized according to a varying taxonomy not subject to a logic of classification that feigns an impersonal authority.

For evidence of Breton's and the Surrealists' interest in such dislocated objects, see for example *Nadja*: 'searching for objects that can be found nowhere else: old-fashioned, broken, useless, almost incomprehensible, even perverse – at least in the sense I give to the word and which I prefer – such as, for example, that type of irregular, white, shellacked half-cylinder covered with reliefs and depressions that are meaningless to me, streaked with horizontal and vertical reds and greens, preciously nestled in a case under a legend in Italian, which I brought home and which after careful examination I have finally identified as some kind of statistical device, operating three dimensionally and recording the population of a city in such and such a year, though all this makes it no more comprehensible to me.'[3]

In short, these are forgotten objects that emerge in the guise of junk or debris in a sinking context, of which there no longer exists a history to tell – because history, every story, must rely on the epical 'once upon a time', or otherwise presume an identification with the past. But with these objects no identification with the past is possible: the reasons behind their production are not the same for which we seek them out and disinter them from oblivion. If the worth of an object's use changes, so too change the codes as well as the excess codification associated with how the object is placed within a cultural context. And this context can be rearticulated only incompletely, because what cannot be rearticulated are the reasons for the object's original production and its specific uses, which linger like a lost dream whose essential points are varyingly remembered and forgotten.

II.

Having arrived at this point, narration – which is always a salvaging of a past to which we lay claim through the epic, through a genealogy that makes of this past our origin – clears the way for the collection, the gathering, of vanished systems, testimony of which is only a testimony of a loss.

Apart from the Surrealists, T. S. Eliot perhaps best interpreted the new situation, using the only key which with poetry could still cobble together a representation of the world: 'A heap of broken images'. *The Waste Land* was the most forceful example of this sort of project, because in it the dereliction of monuments surpassed by advances in production puts into focus and defines the estranged perception that characterizes modernity. These monuments are actual lost monuments that have become inexplicable in modern cities ('the walls of Magnus Martyr') or works of literature still transmitted orally that appear as sonorous fragments lacking contextual references that would otherwise render them meaningful. Thus, in the amalgam of all these memories, lines of tragic verse are mixed with popular jingles, fragments of daily chatter with erudite commentary. This once again is the bazar – this entirely modern practice of collecting forgotten and useless objects, which has nothing to do with the practice of *cabinets de curiosités*, because it does not tend to organize and classify but rather tends, as Benjamin indicates, towards a 'stubborn and subversive protest against the typical and the classifiable'.

The modern passion for collecting is a *quête* (quest) for traces of the past that voice in their present silence this entirely new human condition that is being without origins. In the bazar of the collector everything appears as an anomalous flux, an archaeological *bric-à-brac* of cast-off things, fragmentary images of an estrangement that can be expressed only with the echolalia of senseless discourse, as in Eliot: 'These fragments I have shored against my ruins / Why then Ile fit you. Hieronymo's mad againe.'

III.

Walter Benjamin, in his essay on Eduard Fuchs, lays claim to the privileged position of the collector with respect to history. Fuchs is a pioneer because in his studies at the margins he undermines an idea of historical continuity, proposing a science of the past no longer based on representation and evaluation but on the inventory of minimal signs, of pieces of peripheral information, which when put into juxtaposition cause a re-evaluation of the present's conception of the past. That is, the collector affirms the specificity, the uniqueness of every past, and throws into doubt historicism's eternal, uninterrupted and unified image of the past.

Benjamin discovers that the study of fragments, from fragmentary archives of the past, guided by the object and not by an a priori context structured around an idea of totality, increasingly becomes a reagent of estrangement from the present – because it introduces into the present a view of objects as traces or relics, objects such as *Das Andenken* (souvenirs). The gaze that Benjamin discovers in Baudelaire is of this type: 'If it can be said that for Baudelaire modern life is a reservoir of dialectical images, then it implies that Baudelaire stood in the same relation to modern life as the seventeenth century did to antiquity.'[4] In other words, the modern gaze is an archaeological gaze, which gathers being not as an originary unity remoulded in worldly terms but as a fragmentarity of ruins, a continuum of having been.

By way of comparison, consider that in *Ursprung des Deutschen Trauerspiels* (*The Origin of German Tragic Drama*) Benjamin defines seventeenth-century allegory as one in which the world appears to the observer as full of petrified ruins. In modern (and baroque) allegory, 'history does not assume the form of the process of an eternal life so much as that of irresistible decay'. By way of other comparison: Eliot, in *Gerontion*, begins in this way his discourse on speaking in fragments, a reconsideration of seventeenth-century metaphysical poetry that leads to *The Waste Land*: 'My house is a decayed house … '.

IV.

That which Benjamin discovers by roundabout means, through Baudelaire and the surrealists, through baroque drama and Kafka, swiftly leads to an overarching perspective in which modernism defines itself at a distance, a sort of archaeological gaze turned back upon itself. The relict, the souvenir that Benjamin brings forth, carries out the function of rendering impossible the identification of a past event, beginning with that homogenous and totalizing continuum that is called history.

As he states in *Gesammelte Schriften* (*On the Concept of History*): 'Historicism justifiably culminates in universal history. [...] Its method is additive: it offers a mass of facts, in order to fill up homogenous and empty time.'[5] Subverting this view is non-homogenous time, discontinuous and overflowing with debris and cast-off objects and forgotten emergences, the hypothesis of an alternative history. This is the flood over which history has had to spread its silence in order to be able to propose itself as a linear and continuous development of a transcendent entity: men, white men, consciousness, reason, civilization. The ideal alternative history for Benjamin is a history capable of re-invoking each of its objects and moments, each of its castings off in a *'citation à l'ordre du jour'*. In this regard, Hannah Arendt is one the most articulate commentators: 'Collectors are those who gather objects without regard to their "importance", or tradition puts the past in order, not just chronologically but first of all systematically in that it separates the positive from the negative, the orthodox from the heretical, and which is obligatory and relevant from the mass of irrelevant or merely interesting opinions and data. The collector's passion, on the other hand, is not only unsystematic but borders on the chaotic, not so much because it is a passion as because it is not primarily kindled by the quality of the object – something that is classifiable – but is inflamed by its "genuineness", its uniqueness, something that defies any systematic classification. Therefore, while tradition discriminates the collector levels all differences.'[6]

And it is this sort of incisive history that climbs back up and beyond canonical selections and puts back in play *objets enfouis*, incomplete and fragmentary objects, studying them as one would famous monuments. To the fragmentary and discontinuous, to the excluded and forgotten, is entrusted the task of calling into question the illusion of a linear and continuous development of human history, and thus the exclusions carried out in the name of this concept of development: to direct our gaze back upon events and cultures and groups and practices whose existence we will not quantify, limiting ourselves to the selection that history has made for us.

V.

Throughout his work, Benjamin consistently studied modernism as a form of lived history and as an inventory of motivations. Reading this inventory now isn't so much worth the trouble as understanding what it conjectured well and what it didn't. It is also worth taking up the inventory again and expanding it in a way that its voice becomes one of the many with which a full space is built, the space of an era that will have died as soon as we have been able to define its essential motivations – an era that we will be able to see at last as anonymous, without exceptional creators, without authorized voices, without the primacy of the cunning of the best, if we wish to take seriously the hypothesis of an alternative history.

As a sample of discourse, or testimony, a declaration such as what we find in the first chapter of *L'Anti-Œdipe* (*The Anti-Oedipus*) by Deleuze and Guattari serves to define the situation in which we find ourselves speaking: 'We live today in the age of partial objects, bricks that have been shattered to bits, and leftovers. We no longer believe in the myth of the existence of fragments that, like pieces of an antique statue, are merely waiting for the last one to be turned up, so that they may all be glued back together to create a unity that is precisely the same as the original unity. We no longer believe in a primordial totality that once existed, or in a final totality that awaits us at some future date. We no longer believe in the dull grey outlines of a dreary, colourless dialectic of evolution, aimed at forming a harmonious whole out of heterogeneous bits by rounding off their rough edges.'[7]

That which the authors here put into play are, quite clearly, the conclusions of Maurice Blanchot on the word fragment, the word of the exteriority of the Other, irreducible to the identity of the Self and of the Id. Such a fragment is an entity not derivative of a preceding totality but a splitting off from an originary totality that has the effect of an interruption: this interruption, Blanchot says, is not an impeding of becoming but, on the contrary, is that which triggers becoming 'in the rupture to which it belongs'. Becoming is a progress of cuts, of interruptions and of differences. The privilege of the fragment is that of pure difference, irreducible to a negative form of identity. That is, the fragment cannot be considered as what it is not (part of a totality), and thus it is neither negative nor positive with respect to an originary totality, but rather it is neutral and external.

Thought and language based on the fragment are a mode of conceiving of the relationships of worldly entities not as harmony, agreement or conciliation but as divergence and disjunction: 'an arrangement that does not compose but juxtaposes, that is, leaves each of the terms that come into relation outside one another, respecting and preserving this exteriority and this distance as the principle – always already undercut – of all signification'.[8]

More than an additional proposal of a systematic philosophy, fragmentary thought is a denouncement of the inefficiency of systematic thought at amalgamating the storehouse of accumulated materials, of the impossibility of unificatory methods that assign a place for every object and an object for every place, and of the collapse of the identificatory principle of the orderly totality that is History.

For Mikhail Bakhtin, this is the decline of the power of monologic voices intent on rephrasing all explanations as if from an individual transcendent speaking I, man, white man, spirit, thought, consciousness. Bakhtin explains better than any other philosopher the principles of ideological monologism, conceived of as an affirmation of the unity of existence transformed by an idealism stemming from the unity of consciousness: 'The unity of consciousness, replacing the unity of existence, is inevitably transformed into the unity of a *single* consciousness; when this occurs it makes absolutely no difference what metaphysical form the unity takes: "consciousness in general" ('*Bewusstsein uberhaupt*'), "the absolute", "the absolute spirit", "the normative consciousness", and so forth. Alongside this unified and inevitably *single* consciousness can be found a multitude of empirical human consciousnesses. From the point of view of "consciousness in general" this plurality of consciousnesses is accidental and, so to speak, superfluous. Everything in them that is essential and true is incorporated into the unified context of "consciousness in general" and deprived of its individuality.'[9]

And thus, according to Bakhtin, it happens that in monologic thought empirical voices acquire individuality only if they err, because when these voices speak correctly they always derive or emanate from consciousness in general. Partial voices become recognizable only when they deviate in error, when they stray from the pre-established line of *dénouement* or become lost in zones of bewilderment or aberration, and thus are no longer reducible to the 'correct' form of thought.

After all, the sole image of thought that philosophy can invoke in order to defend itself from idiocy is the totalitarian 'everyone knows': the rule is that a philosophical concept only holds up if it can respond to this requirement of universality. What then is this universality, this 'everyone knows', or this 'everyone thinks' with which the unity of existence reaffirms itself in various combinations, pulling itself together again, questioning the possible existence of a truly inclusive way of thinking, a way that takes into account even those who refuse to think, negate knowing and refute intelligence and the agreement of good sense that intelligence presupposes? Once varied foreign voices that do not participate with consciousness, voices of madness and idiocy, acquire citizenship rights on par with the rights of wise voices, voices of good sense, there no longer exists the possibility of a unitary utopia, nor of any utopia.

VI.

It is exactly this rupture of the unity of thought that modernity causes, obscurely, adventurously, to arise from the heap of cast-off things. From here there comes the tendency to directly reproduce marginal voices, to transcribe and publish them: diaries of deviants or autobiographies of outcasts, protocols of the insane, collections of dreams. The recovery of documents of this sort is in keeping with the collection of cast-off objects, having the same motivations.

Hannah Arendt informs us that Walter Benjamin's library contained many rare children's books and books by alienated writers. In the realm of writing, these pieces stand out as marginal voices able to recount something of the bewildered and bewildering condition of finding oneself out of context, outside of the univocal historical context that systematic thought loves to imagine. Everything lost in the daily selection of History seems to possess the essential quality that modernism has always sought out: that of putting into circulation words omitted by history and thought, words whose very nature is that of having been left out and cast off, fragments that have lost their contexts. Such words serve to define and give voice to a fundamental silence: that of those who are not authorized to speak, or those lacking a 'self' with which to speak.

History's unmitigated *quête* is a search for identity for various social groups: in this sense History is always epical, the recitation of the genealogies of origins by a bard, whose function is that of conferring worldly identity and thus power. Now the words of those who have not been able to participate in this assigning of identity have become more persuasive, being the only words that are not epical.

Almost all of Benjamin's visionary inquiries grapple with the possibility of modern humanity still conceiving of History in some form, even if without the exclusionary logic that every story implies. The first step is thus of distinguishing what History has excluded from what History has glorified – the objects that have remained in obscure archives from those that have entered museums – in short, archaeological objects from historical ones.

VII.

Archaeological objects are those objects whose internal motivations cannot be recovered: the motivations that produced them in the context of a specific past; historical objects, on the other hand, are those objects whose motivations have been recovered, and which come to function as metaphors of a contemporary past. The subtle distinctions between these two ways of treating objects can at times blur, but the two types of poetics underlying them are not so easily confused.

What History lacks is the sense of the death of objects, aiming at reviving or recuperating what is proclaimed, by suppression of a context or extinction of a tradition that is lost, exhausted and extinct, and thus extraneous. What, on the contrary, is missing from archaeology is the total comprehension of events, that is, of the motivations of the world as it is, aiming not at recovering or reviving but at finding the lost object, which is precisely the testimony of a loss, of an inaccessible discontinuity, or, in other words, of the interruption of a continuity as the mark of becoming.

The differences distinguishing these two approaches are thus located not so much in relation to the object studied but in relation to the criteria of observation, even if each may have its privileged objects, as is true of all forms of observation. History has always been the story of leaders and of monuments, whereas archaeology is rather a story, like Ruzante's, that 'yesterday came from the field'. This is to say that the privilege of the historical object lies in the fact that it can be placed at the centre of a web of developments, or seen as an index of a directionality, while the privilege of the archaeological object lies in the fact that it is at the edge of possible developments, with its own continuity trickling out, exhausted: as the saying goes, it didn't make history.

Historical criteria are always, in spite of themselves or not, teleological, in as much as they must direct their efforts at revealing a directionality of objects, which is what gives the objects meaning. But to reveal one must interpret, and to interpret one must compare familiar motivations with unclear intentions, that is, give voice to the intentions of others in the language of my motivations, reprojecting them as the intentions of others. This is exactly the way to produce the literary effect of identification, on which historical poetics has based a large portion of its resources. One can thus understand how the historical novel or a work of historiography are separated by only a very thin literary convention, not so much by way of the formal fiction that props them together as by way of the poetics and rhetorical annexing that they hold in common.

Archaeology instead introduces the principle of the difference of the other with respect to the self, of the difference between elsewhere and here, and thus of the impossibility of identification with these distant points. Archaeological poetics for this reason cannot do without the literary effect called *straniamento* (defamiliarization or disorientation), as an indication of something with which I am not able identify because it refuses to serve as my direct mirror, pointing back to an actual past that I cannot relive, and thus carrying me to a unfamiliar land where the possibility arises of coming to terms with the existence of the other whom I am not; of the other whom I do not know.

This defines archaeological poetics as a rediscovery of an alternative to History, or as a vision of the objects that History has cast off. In this mode, History no longer appears as destiny, nor as a grammar of human actions, but rather as a series of emergences kept in check either by their reduction to forms of identity according to a *telos* or a monumental plan that leads all the way to us, or by their removal or casting off when they can no longer be adapted to fit these forms of identity.

VIII.

History, both in the form of historiography and of literary adaptation, epical or novelistic, tends always to create the sense of large assemblages of facts through the artifice of *agnizione* (recognition): that point, central scene or declaration of a truth in which various discontinuities are dispelled through revealing their direction – in as much as all the discontinuities, the molar mass of facts known and unknown, carry good or evil, consciously or unconsciously, towards that point of *agnizione*. This is the moral of the story, the *dénouement*, which pre-modern narration could not do without. Now the point of *agnizione* is by nature anagogical, 'lifting up', subliming or stirring the ugly mass of the results of materialism's pure events, to then transform them into signs, symbols or additions to the consciousness, of a destiny comprehensible by means of a doctrine or rational proclamation: something that recounts to us the world in which all events 'must' transpire, in which all that becomes 'must' have an explanation. In this sense, History and Literature are in agreement, neither being able in any way to justify itself without this analogical transfiguration of facts and objects into signs of another vaster and more inclusive truth, this being the subject named Man: the subject of all predicates and of all metaphors, the subject-owner of consciousness, he who knowingly makes all choices.

Archaeology instead has a declining or sorting vocation: it does not provide to the molar mass of events any point of *agnizione*; it is always focused on localized and molecular concentrations, and it is not able to make the leap from quantity to quality, to choose for itself an abstract axiom to account for a focused totality of events. It mimics or enacts a regression, and thus lacks a view of the overall.

This is because regression, as a descent through all time-filled matter, means that at the molecular level focal points or points of *agnizione* disproportionately multiply, requiring the point of view to be perpetually updated. In terms of optic metaphors, if perspective vision is the metaphor best suited to historicism, then eidetic memory is the one best suited to archaeology.

IX.

Archaeology is based on the forgotten. As Benjamin teaches us, the forgotten is never simply singular; of the individual or of the individual object. Everything lost by that fictional figure of justice, which is the witness or the testimony of its birth, bears in itself the trace of an area that does not belong because it falls outside the familiar paths that lead from the depths of time to us: something that thus takes part in the nature of the dream because it is not fully able to be contextualized within our physical reality. Its presence is a remnant of prehistory that pushes in on History to gain entrance, to find a situational context. This situational context may be located through its historicization, by its transformation into a sign of some historical truth. But what it cannot find is the language of the motivations that produced it, the language needed to express its original experience.

And this is a problem of poetics, because the possibility of affixing forever a lost object within a historical assemblage is to a degree an illusion of reawakening. The text or language that affixes it is a fragile tissue that assures a weak mediation between dream, prehistory, the unknown and physical reality as to how the world is ordered. It is what happens to dreams when they are transcribed upon waking: nothing gives us the certainty that what is thwarted is analogous to what is affixed through the dim light of memory and the arrogance of the pen – not even the specious theory of the Freudian slip. To affix the dream is a *quête*, a mode of chasing it, just as one says 'chasing a dream', an expression to be read literally.

The lost object, the fragment that is unable to carry us back to the originary unity of a design, introduces into the present the effect of a subterranean, invisible apocalypse that has just passed or that is still occurring: as in certain horror stories in which an unusual presence upsets the normal continuity of everyday life, in this rupture there arises a fundamental silence that is called terror because it is inexpressible, unresolvable and lacking discernible motives. Archaeology is always an archaeology of silence (according to an idea revealed at the beginning of Michel Foucault's *Madness and Civilization*), of an emergence that, being mute, forces those who must classify and explain into a raving delirium – as the living rave over the dead who are unable to respond.

X.

All this is well and fine. But if the dream is a metaphor of estrange-ment, or of a piece of what is lost, the tissue of the text that affixes it is nothing but a convention based on laws of western linguistics, familiar to everyone and for this reason accessible, a rule of the historical present in which we live.

For example, the memoirs of assassin Pierre-François Lacenaire, published in 1836 and read (as far as I understand) as a novel, were taken up by Breton as an example of dark humour. In another example, the memoirs of Schreber, published in 1903 in a volume that betrays its strangeness by announcing under its title *Memories of My Nervous Illness* the phrase 'president of the senate of Dresden', were taken by Freud as a classic example of paranoia, later becoming one of the most cited texts in psychiatry. The memoirs of the parricide Pierre Rivière, admitted as evidence in 1835 on the suggestion of a judge, were taken up by psychiatrists or phrenologists of the time to define the mental state of their author, then conversely by Michel Foucault as an archaeological object capable of disconcerting psychiatric thought. The 1921 study of the alienated Swiss painter and poet Adolf Wölfli (by doctor Walter Morgenthaler) was later taken up by Dubuffet and included in the issues of *L'art brut* (Outsider Art), as an extraordinary example of the artistic capabilities of the alienated. Louis Wolfson, a schizophrenic from New York, who, not bearing to speak, read or hear English, invented a system of instantaneously deconstructing English words that transmute into fragments of foreign languages. He recounted the principles and use of this linguistic system not in English but in a French that he picked phrase by phrase from dictionaries and grammar books. His memoir, *Le Schizo et les langues* [Schizophrenia and languages], was published in 1970 by Gallimard publishers, with a preface by Gilles Deleuze. It seems upon reading to be an archaeo-logical object, written in an inexistent language, instantly recogniz-able as something strange and unclassifiable. But Deleuze's preface unpacks its inner workings to show us the deeper bodily logic that is schizophrenic thought.

There is a similar trajectory to that of the completed dreams of these texts: that of their origin-based marginality; they become documents of a marginality that is explosive because it is anti-historical (composed of what history has excluded) and then fade away among discoveries whose historical importance is undeniable. As traces of forgotten areas, such documents become memories and the recovery of a different truth that history is unable to recognize because history has removed it. But this different truth lies in the truth of its removal, that is, in the truth of History. The truth of these documents derives from History.

And this is the paradox of archaeology. We must always refer to some sort of grammar, otherwise all distinctions would fall between monumental examples and atypical emergences. If History is a vast grammar of human behaviour that our civilization has never stopped proposing, with the understanding that this grammar is nothing but a mechanism of removal, we must begin from here in order to speak of what History has removed.

We cannot speak of the dream if we do not begin from wakefulness; we cannot speak of the other if we do not begin from the self; we cannot speak of insanity if we do not begin from normality. And so too archaeology is a discourse on the other and the different: archaeology must begin from History, from that arbitrary selection to which we must anchor our study of objects that have been excluded, buried or forgotten in the very course of selection.

XI.

When archaeology is framed as 'critical history', as for example in the work of Enzo Melandri, it becomes necessary to conceive of it as a genealogical retreat that then climbs back to a position ahead of historical removal: 'before the bifurcation of the conscious and unconscious of the phenomenon in question'. At stake here is a retreat, adds Melandri, but not 'to the unconscious as such, but rather to that which rendered it unconscious'.

This means that – taking archaeology as a recovery of the past, as a return to a substance given the name of culture, the unconscious, the human, or the imagination – what results is nothing but a shoddy reform of the values of History. The presumed archaeology is instead the impossibility of the recovery of the object to an ideology or a style, and thus is not a greater fullness of the offered reality but one of its alternative positions in contrast to choices already carried out – its 'different' quality in contrast to the traces that History and its supporting grammars predicate as the destiny of man.

The alternative perspective is based on the principle of bringing forth examples that strip historical grammars, both linguistic and social, of their absolute value; because if it is true that we need grammars in order to comprehend the real, it is also true that we need to know how to recognize what is different in order to catch sight of alternatives, which are not grammars.

But inversely we know that there is a substitutive game of alternatives with new grammars, which bring us back again to the discourse of the point of departure. In this regard, the objections of Jacques Derrida to Foucault, to his *Storia della follia* (*History of Madness*), to this silence that archaeology must interrogate, should be kept in mind: 'is not an archaeology, even of silence, a logic, that is an organized language, a project, an order, a sentence, a syntax, a work? Would not the archaeology of silence be the most efficacious and subtle restoration, the *repetition*, in the most irreducibly ambiguous meaning of the word, of the act perpetrated against madness – and be so at the very moment when this act is denounced?'[10]

I take this response, understood as a warning, to mean: it is not the recording of a primitive or innocent word that archaeology enacts. When archaeology desires this, it is already on the other side. We cannot make use of these objects, we cannot make them speak or transform them into mouthpieces of something that we would like to recognize as 'life', as 'presence', with which to make books or literature. Their silence is like that of insanity: to follow insanity means following or choosing its silence, and above all maintaining this silence with respect to the 'notion' of insanity. We cannot make this silence speak, we cannot make the insane speak. It is rather the insane who take the words out of our mouths, the words in search of representations with which to prove themselves true.

The insane, as with all things extraneous and unknown, can only serve as our mirror through the rationalizing of the idea of insanity and of extraneity, to the utter advantage of those who use this idea as a defence, and to the utter disadvantage of those who are defined by this notion. Regarding this rather important point, with which contemporary anti-psychiatry must also grapple, Derrida has said something not to be forgotten: 'the misfortune of the mad, the interminable misfortune of their silence, is that their best spokesmen are those who betray them best; which is to say that when one attempts to convey their silence *itself*, one has already passed over to the side of the enemy, to side of order, even if one fights against order from within it, putting its origin into question'.[11]

XII.

For the surrealists the study of archaeological objects was a type of descent into the underworld, into the subterranean city where all the streets re-converge. In Breton's *Nadja* this scheme becomes precarious: the path veers off at a sharp angle and brings the imprudent seeker of the unknown, the lover of archaeological objects gathered from the *marché aux puces* (flea market), back to the world of normal life, with a use of oneiric elements upon awakening characteristic of the lost–found figure of Nadja. The game of identification doesn't hold up in the end: the search for identity in the other fails because the other is in fact the Other, that is, the extraneous and unknown, and rational thought is of no help. The search fails with the discovery that the essential form of extraneity, that of insanity, is a physical extraneity and thus inaccessible. Nadja among the insane is the moral of the story.

The idea that this book is a novel is completely contrary to what Breton had in mind. *Nadja* is a precarious book, the trace of an extraneity found and then at once lost: a book that does not obey the constructs of a project, that repudiates being a book, that attempts to be a pure emergence. It is a book-occurrence, not only because it speaks of an estranging occurrence, such as the encounter with Nadja, but also because it shows that the account of this encounter is a coincidence: an emergence and not a scheme. Nevertheless, if this occurrence is equivalent to the discovery of an archaeological object of incalculable value (Nadja appears to Breton like that half-cylinder found at the *marché aux puces* or, in other words, like an inexplicable presence with which we cannot identify), and if the report is documentary and not literary, the report becomes a record or anamnesis of a past illness (and therefore does not follow the hegemonic project of the novel of presenting examples with which all can identify but, on the contrary, reveals the loss of identity of the observer when facing the unfamiliar object): in the end, is this not a book that we consume with all the fascination of a novel?

The scheme of escaping from the scheme of the book is Breton's reversal; this reversal is also a form of recovery, which allows him to back away from the precipice of retreat and to look at things from a distance, as Lino Gabellone has noted. From this shift, however, come into focus several things: if Nadja is a quasi-allegorical figure of marginality versus normal life, versus the project itself of normality, is she not also the test subject necessary to understand the location of this boundary, as well as to contemplate the precipice with fascination? And thus, is it not exactly this marginality, this insanity, this victim of the removal of psychiatric order, which in the end serves the centrality of Parisian literature, normality, the project of writing and the men in control?

   Scarto (deviation, waste) and margin serve to define the hegemonic position of those who are not at the margin, as well as to find objects of fascination, objects of aesthetic consumption and narcissistic fictions. The archaeological object tends to satisfy the narcissism and aesthetic manias of normal men; it also marks a virgin territory for future projects of rationality, projects of acquisition and appropriation of white, adult, normal men. And it is the denouncement of this sort of appropriation, together with the claim of the object as a trace of a past that no one can identify as their own, that fundamentally defines the proposal of what I continue to call archaeological thought. But when Claude Lévi-Strauss puts ethnology on trial, in *Tristes Tropiques*, he denounces this system of projections with which civilized and normal man reduces all unfamiliar cultures to representations of his rationality, of his motives and prejudices. And when Robbe-Grillet takes issue with anthropomorphic metaphors in literature, he continues along the same line of discourse; he speaks out against the appropriative, undifferentiated gaze – against forms of language that assign all of what is real and true to Man.

XIII.

It is clear that archaeological or unidentifiable objects, ranging from *Nadja* to Louis Wolfson's memoir or Pierre Rivière's autobiography, function as indications of a boundary, of boundaries impassable to 'normal' discourse, to the 'it must be like this, so it must happen like this' with which historical *telos* speaks to us every moment of our lives. Archaeology can tell us something of such boundaries, deconstructing them, revealing their ritual or conventional bases, their repetitive coactions, their normative rhetorics. But it is unable to go much further without wanting to explain what extraneity is in itself, without becoming another rationalization of the unknown and its boundaries.

   These boundaries also serve as the operative basis for the modern novel, beginning in the eighteenth century; it is thus likely that, once inserted into a book, they become fetishized, attracting aesthetic consumption, the appropriation and familiarization of all forms of extraneity. But it is also true that such appropriations have a clearly defined limit, a point at which narcissism no longer finds its own reflection or gratification.

And this is the point at which the impassable boundaries of 'normal' discourse appear only as boundaries of the law and the great unknown beyond these boundaries as the mysterious *arbitrariness of the law*: the vast ritual practices without a basis, the obviousness of customs and of verbal repertoires or of the simple habits of the body, the horizon of presuppositions that marks the limits of what we are.

'The laws', as Kafka writes, 'after all are so old, centuries have worked on their interpretation, even their interpretation has in a sense become codified, and while there is surely room still for interpretation, it will be quite limited.'[12] The parable 'Vor dem Gesetz' ('Before the Law') in *Der Prozess* (*The Trial*) also depicts the law as arbitrary and obligatory – indifferent to the projections of the subject – which is more or less the discourse carried out by archaeological thought, in opposition to the reduction to an easily comprehensible rationality of the arbitrariness of laws, of the origin of laws, of their trajectories and applications, as carried out by historicism.

As a boundary trope, archaeology is a metaphor that Kafka too brings to play in 'The Great Wall of China': it is a mode of working on thresholds, of retracing the construction of barriers, the establishment of laws, the memories of removals and suppressions. Archaeology is the path of historical removals, and its object is always something like the southern groups that the great wall of China cut off, of whom Kafka writes: 'The atrocities which their nature prompts them to commit make us heave a sigh on our peaceful porches. [...] But we know nothing else about these northern lands. We have never seen them, and if we remain in our village, we never will see them, even if they charge straight at us and hunt us on their wild horses.'[13]

XIV.

Archaeology thus appears as a thin Heraclitan philosophy, or as nothing, a reversal of History, a history turned inside-out, an anti-history. It is also a dream, a vision of the empty order that lies under the full order of the habitable physical world (the empty order of boundaries and laws), a metaphor of a loss, of a removal from the origins that looms over every present. And nothing tells us that because History has shown itself to be a failed therapy, that archaeology then can be supposed to be a successful one. History is the search for an identity by a social group, but what is archaeology? A confirmation or a discovery that no identity is acceptable, that no interiority or origin belongs to us (if anything, we belong to the undifferentiated terrain of every origin, like things and plants).

But with fictional figures what is important lies in the adventure across which they carry us, the dance with which they persuade us, the movements with which they conduct us: not the figures themselves, which are always the same. The expository adventure of archaeological discourse thus appears as the spoor of a different path, different from utopia, which is the spatial figure of historical *agnizione*: archaeological discourse is no longer a directed *quête* that carries us to a visitable truth, to the centre of a utopic city in which all provinces are represented in miniature, but rather an wandering *quête*, spatialization and *flânerie*, an uninterrupted encounter with the molecular places of a heterotopic city where residues of extraneity float to infinity, objects and traces of what has been lost, which no museum is equipped to conserve.

From Baudelaire to Rimbaud, Breton, Duchamp and pop art, in terms of poetics, the heterotopic city has been incessantly visited in this way. And this means the end of occasional poetics, of the privileged case, of the meaningful scene, of the special view, because there is no place or object that is not an occasion: each is similar and discontinuous, as important as, but also different than, all the others. It is well known that various pop artists have applied this sort of reordering to unimportant objects, deforming them slightly in appearance and placing them in other contexts; these too are archaeological objects, being traces of an ordinary path found and then at once lost.

James Rosenquist said of his own paintings: 'If I use anonymous images [...] they've been anonymous images of recent history. In 1960 and 1961 I painted the front of a 1950 Ford. I felt it was an anonymous image. [...] I use images from old magazines – when I say old, I mean 1945 to 1955 – a time we haven't started to ferret out as history yet.'[14] And Claes Oldenburg: 'I am for the art of underwear and the art of taxicabs. I am for the art of ice-cream cones dropped on concrete. I am for the majestic art of dog turds, rising like cathedrals. [...] I am for the art of things lost or thrown away.'[15] And George Brecht: 'My impression is that these objects get together in the same what that dust moves in the streets. If we said that one object had a greater value than another and that it therefore got into the piece, well, I don't think that would be appropriate. I don't see it as a matter of choice.'[16]

But still before this, Duchamp's installation of a urinal in a museum overturned the category of the privileged artistic object; this overturning, as in the case of the pop artists, is not so much in the object as in the way of looking that the object beckons and suggests: 'the eyes', as Roland

Barthes writes in response to the novels of Alaine Robbe-Grillet, 'of a man walking in his city with no other horizon but the spectacle before him, no other power than that of his own eyes'.[17] These are the eyes of the *flâneur*, a figure central to archaeological thought, with *flânerie* identified by Benjamin as the falling back into and descent through the crowded time of the modern city.

XV.

Flânerie, aimless wandering, is of great importance in defining the adventure of archaeological exposition, because it proposes this adventure more as a spatial process than as a chronological itinerary. To the historicist, History tends to be identified with a tradition, in the sense of an uninterrupted succession of events that can be situated along a chronological continuum. History has the sense of being analogous to the individual experience of memory, because it is the process of searching for an identity. But this transposition of an individual function to a superindividual field can no longer be justified: there is no reason to make of history a temporal field rather than a spatial one, when the search for individual identity is substituted with the recognition of pure exteriority in relation to ourselves and our origins. It is exactly in those spaces that are marginalized or simply ignored by memory-tradition that there resides that difference without which history is tautology. This difference is found in the corners of streets, in the ignored closets of temporal memory, and is thus a spatial notion.

Archaeological thinking helps us to understand or feel this: that History is always the physical world, with its monuments and its roads, the roads that lead to the monuments, the monuments that give order to the roads, the cities that rise up around the monuments, the roads that connect the cities with important monuments and cut other cities out. The entire geographic matrix, the flat surface of offshoots, the paths that lead one to the other while driving, walking, moving in any way, are paths of history: emigrations, invasions, the path taken by the young man going to the city, etc. Actual city and utopic city, the two constantly blur one with the other, not only in dreams but also in that image of History contained in the elaborate projects to control cities. The city is the visible form of History, where 'space becomes perspective as time becomes history'.

It thus becomes clear why archaeology, if ever a science, is a science of the margins. It is the science of what has been left out of cities, or buried in cities, behind the grand facades or along the dim edges of the avenues.

XVI.

The modern city begins with the large transformations of the nineteenth century – of Paris with Haussmann, London with its various administrative reforms, Firenze, Napoli, Vienna and Barcelona. Everywhere are restructurings called 'amplifications', but which initiate cycles leading to something else, cities enormously multiplied that no longer have fixed routes; monuments yes, but ones that are no longer able to impose order due to the vast growth of peripheral zones. The heterotopic city is one that has lost its centres and monuments, its points of irradiation within the countless offshooting streets. That the adventure of archaeological thought in literature takes place in explorations of cities, from Balzac, Baudelaire and Rimbaud to Breton, Eliot and Benjamin, is not by chance. The heterotopic city is the self-same image of the archaeological bazar in which the identificatory nodes of social groups, squares and monuments multiply infinitely but without true spatial perspectives that entail temporal destinations, or a destiny.

This is the growth of the margin, the increasingly evident presence of an unfamiliar marginality within known paths, which are perceptible as soon as you leave home. The *parades* Rimbaud saw in the heterotopic city and visited in *Illuminations* resemble our own because the reflux is the same: the reflux emerges where and when greater order reigns, where the seriality of signs of power is more noticeable, in the heavily developed areas of the Grand Administration. The reflux of heterogeneous emergences is proportional to the homogeneity imposed by the Grand Administration, because what is cast off is always larger than everything surpassed by the processes of production. And this is theatre, the great modern spectacle, the spectacle of marginalization, but also the novelistic fascination with the other, the different, the extraneous.

Rimbaud records the spectacles of reflux in London in his poem 'Parade': 'Not to be compared with your Fakirs and other theatrical buffooneries. In improvised costumes of nightmarish taste they perform romances, tragedies of bandits and demigods [...] Chinese, Hottentots, *bohémiens*, fools, hyenas, Molochs, old dementias, sinister demons, mingling popular jokes with bestial poses and caresses. They perform a new theatre and sing songs for "good girls". Master jugglers, they transform people and place and use magnetic stagecraft.'[18]

These are the spectacles of the street, the spectacles of extraneity in the 'official acropolis' of 'modern barbarity', as Rimbaud puts it, where millions of people, 'who do not even need to know each other, manage their education, business, and old age is so identical'.[19] It is in the city where everything is at the surface, arrayed in space and heterogeneous, where what is under us, subterranean, is no longer recognizable: 'I thought I could judge the depth of the city! It's the wonder of it that I was unable to seize: what are the relative levels of the other districts above or below the acropolis? For today's tourist, orientation is impossible.'[20]

The places in which identity can be found, in which our paths become clear, in which historical identity can be sought, have fragmented, multiplying infinitely in the spatialization of the modern city, to the point that between citizen and foreigner there is no longer any difference: 'I am an ephemeral and by no means overly discontented citizen of a metropolis thought to be modern', a fitting epitaph to put on his tomb.[21]

Rimbaud speaks of nineteenth-century London. But New York, today, is little different. We are in the centre of the empire, and where there is an empire there is reflux. And thus this 'new theatre' performed by a heterogeneous crowd, the wild parades that Rimbaud recounts: are these not the same spectacles, the same parades encountered everywhere while travelling about, in the archaeological bazars of metropolises, in stations, ports, slums, subways, Grand Central, Port Authority, Times Square, with the floods of multifarious strangers, in the centres of power, the flows of goods, cars, gadgets, diverse multitudes, policemen, blacks, Slovakians, Sicilians, Polish, Irish, Jews?

The backdrops are common, the details too: the storefront windows. Alice in a display on Oxford Street, the old dolls, the kitschy objects, pub signs, lamps from other times, the astonishing nautical instruments on sale at an antiques shop on Portobello Road. Fashion does not suffice to recount this, to recite the magnetic comedy; it is not enough to explain the cold and peculiar passion for the *littérature de colportage*, the *Banbury Chapbooks*, the *Bibliothèque bleue* from Troye, the popular editions of Salani and Treves, the phrasebooks, the confessions of the condemned, of sailors, of anarchists and stowaways, tarot cards, illustrated children's books, pub songbooks, the New Orleans toy museum.

Everything that no longer has a use, which has not made history, is part of the spectacle that satisfies the narcissism of normal people, which offers up this ecstasy of marginality.

Rimbaud helps with comparisons: there are other parades of refluxes, but they are always similar: an opaque inauguration of new realities, a new theatre devoted to exteriority, the clothes of past generations that circulate in London and New York; and those who wear these clothes, the young women with eyes painted like *La Folle de Chaillot* (*The Madwoman of Chaillot*), the young men wearing opera hats, one with an old tram ticket tucked behind the ribbon, the Central Park skater in tails, his confrere Tarzan, the melancholic mime performing alone among the crowd, the seventeenth-century soldier suits like those of the Beatles, uniforms of all sorts, the magnetic comedy, the master jugglers, hippies, fools, crazies, perform with bestial poses and caresses, at times with nightmarish taste.

Note

This piece has its origins in a magazine project that I worked on together with Italo Calvino, Carlo Ginzburg, Enzo Melandri and Guido Neri between 1970 and 1972. The project was based on a series of themes that revolved around the traces, residues and fragments of invisible orders accessible by a path that has nothing to do with evidential criteria, nor with the systematic understanding of an object of study. This is the terrain of archaeology, or of history folded back on itself, where many disciplines (from linguistics to philosophy, history and story writing) seemed to us to have a common ground, from which there arose a beckoning towards that background of infinite Heraclitan traces that is the modern city.

'Il bazar archaeologico' ('The archaeological bazar'), based on a collection of preparatory notes for the journal, should be read alongside Italo Calvino's 'La sguardo dell'archeologo' [The archaeologist's gaze], written for the same purpose and included in *Una pietra sopra* (Turin, 1980). A few years later, Carlo Ginzburg exhaustively treated this theme of traces, publishing a much more elaborated essay entitled 'Spie: Radici di un paradigma idiziario' (in *Crisi della ragione*, edited by Aldo Gargani, Turin, 1979).

Other related books on the topic of importance to me include Guido Neri's study of Claude Simon's *Histoire*, published in an appendix to the Italian edition of the novel (*Storia*, Turin, 1971); the extraordinary work of philosophy by Enzo Melandri, *La linea e il circolo* (Bologna, 1978); Carlo Ginzburg's *Il formaggio e i vermi* (Turin, 1976); and Lino Gabellone's *L'oggetto surrealista* (Turin, 1977) and his postface to the Italian edition of André Breton's *Nadja* (Turin, 1972).

The direct and indirect citations from the work of Walter Benjamin come from the following volumes, all published in Italy by Einaudi: *Angelus Novus* (regarding the conception of history and the references to Baudelaire), *L'opera d'arte nell'epoca della sua riproducibilità tecnica* (regarding Eduard Fuchs and collecting), *Il dramma barocco tedesco* (seventeenth-century allegory), *Avanguardia e rivoluzione* (surrealism) and *Immagini di città*. The citations from the work of Hanna Arendt are from the introduction to a collection of Benjamin's writings translated into English, *Illuminations* (New York, 1969).

Many cues regarding the critique of history, in addition to Benjamin's *Tesi sulla filosofia della storia* (in *Angelus Novus*), come from Friedrich Nietzsche's *Sull'utilità e il danno della storia per la vita* (Milan, 1973). Conceptions of archaeology derive from Kant (*Schriften zur Metaphysik*, in *Werke*, vol. III) explored under the guidance of Enzo Melandri in 'L'archeologia, Foucault, don Chisciotte' in *Lingua e stile* (1968).

With regard to the call to reflect on objects out of context, the shock of the other and extraneity, I must also mention Victor Segalen's *Notes sull'exotisme*, in *Stèles-Peintures, Equipée*, with a preface by J. P. Jouve (Paris, 1970). The concept of the rupture of the unity of thought comes from the third chapter of *Differenza e ripetizione* by Gilles Deleuze (Bologna, 1970).

Regarding the various disorderly readings of the modern city, I cite: Lewis Mumford, *The City in History* (New York, 1961); Jane Jacobs, *The Life and Death of Great American Cities* (New York, 1965); François Choay, *La città, utopie e realtà* (Turin, 1973); Kevin Lynch, *L'immagine della città* (Padua, 1964); William Holford, *The Built Environment*, Tavistock Pamphlet no. 11 (London, 1964); J. B. Charrier, *Citadins e ruraux* (Paris, 1970); *Human Identity in the Urban Environment*, edited by G. Bell and J. Tyrwhitt (New York, 1972).

On the transformation of historical time in spatiality, see G. C. Argan and M. Fagiolo, *Premessa all'arte italiana*, in *Stora d'Italia*, vol. I (Einaudi, 1972). Other cues or suggestions come from Pierre Kaufmann, *L'experience émotionelle de l'espace* (Paris, 1969). On the relationship between space and dreams, the chasing of dreams, see the *Nouvelle Revue de psychanalyse* (5, Printemps, Paris, 1972), an issue dedicated to 'L'espace du rêve'. The reference to horror stories comes from Lovecraft's work, based on an observation been made by Lino Gabellone in a letter.

The references to pop art are from *Pop Art Redefined* by John Russell and Suzi Gablik (London, 1969). The citations from Roland Barthes are from an essay on *Les gommes* by Robbe-Grillet, in *Saggi critici* (Turin, 1972). Observations on the transposition of individual memory to history, and on what temporal memory ignores, come from conversations with Guido Neri.

A few months after the journal project had been abandoned, Calvino published *Le città invisibili* (*Invisible Cities*), in which many of the archaeological ideas that we discussed are elaborated through a more or less semiotic lens. My notes, which I put aside for a few years and then revisited, being published in a journal in 1975, end with descriptions written while walking the streets of London in 1971 and New York in 1972.

Most likely everything that I had to say in this piece, as well as in later related work, are contained in this passage by Benjamin on surrealism:

> He can boast an extraordinary discovery. He was the first to perceive the revolutionary energies that appear in the 'outmoded', in the first iron constructions, the first factory buildings, the earliest photos, the objects that have begun to be extinct, grand pianos, the dresses of five years ago, fashionable restaurants when the vogue has begun to ebb from them. The relation of these things to revolution – no one can have a more exact concept of it than these authors. No one before these visionaries and augurs perceived how destitution – not only social but architectonic, the poverty of interiors, enslaved and enslaving objects – can be suddenly transformed into revolutionary nihilism. Leaving aside Aragon's *Passage de l'Opera*, Breton and Nadja are the lovers who convert everything that we have experienced on mournful railway journeys (railways are beginning to age), on Godforsaken Sunday afternoons in the proletarian quarters of the great cities, in the first glance through the rain-blurred window of a new apartment, into revolutionary experience, if not action. They bring the immense forces of 'atmosphere' concealed in these things to the point of explosion. What form do you suppose a life would take that was determined at a decisive moment precisely by the street song last on everyone's lips?
>
> (*Avanguardia e Rivoluzione*, Turin, 1973, 15–16)[22]

Notes

1   Walter Benjamin, 'Paris, capital of the 19th century', *Perspecta* 12 (1969): 163–72.
2   Arthur Rimbaud, *Complete Works*, trans. Paul Schmidt (New York: Harper Colophon, 1976), 204.

3   André Breton, *Nadja*, trans. Richard Howard (New York: Grove Press, 1960), 52.
4   Walter Benjamin, *The Writer of Modern Life: Essays on Charles Baudelaire*, ed. Michael W. Jennings (Cambridge, MA: Harvard University Press, 2006), 134.
5   Benjamin, 'On the concept of history', trans. Andy Blunden, https://www.marxists.org/reference/archive/benjamin/1940/history.htm.
6   Hannah Arendt, introduction to Walter Benjamin, *Illuminations: Essays and Reflections*, ed. Hannah Arendt, trans. Harry Zohn (New York: Schocken Books, 2007), 44.
7   Gilles Deleuze and Felix Guattari, *Anti-Oedipus: Capitalism and Schizophrenia*, trans. Robert Hurley, Mark Seem and Helen R. Lane (Minneapolis: University of Minnesota Press, 1983), 42.
8   Maurice Blanchot, in Gerald L. Bruns, *The Refusal of Philosophy* (Baltimore: Johns Hopkins University Press, 2002).
9   Mikail Baktin, *Problems of Dostoevsky's Poetics*, ed. and trans. Caryl Emerson (Minneapolis: University of Minnesota Press, 1984), 80–1.
10 Jacques Derrida, 'Cogito and the history of madness', in his *Writing and Difference*, trans. Alan Bass (Chicago: University of Chicago Press, 1979), 35.
11 Derrida, 'Cogito', 36.
12 Franz Kafka, 'Unknown laws', trans. Michael Hofmann, *London Review of Books* 37, no. 14 (16 July 2015): 23, https://www.lrb.co.uk/v37/n14/franz-kafka/short-cuts.
13 Franz Kafka, 'The Great Wall of China', trans. Ian Johnston, *Franz Kafka Online*, http://www.kafka-online.info/the-great-wall-of-china.html.
14 James Rosenquist, 'What is Pop Art?', interview by Gene R. Swenson, *ARThews* (February 1964), http://www.artnews.com/2017/04/03/from-the-archives-james-rosenquist-defines-pop-art-in-1964/.
15 Claes Oldenburg, '*I Am For …* (Statement, 1961)', *The Walker*, https://walkerart.org/magazine/claes-oldenburg-i-am-for-an-art-1961.
16 George Brecht, 'An interview with George Brecht', interview by Henry Martin, *Art International* 9 (20 November 1967): 22.
17 Roland Barthes, 'Objective literature', *Critical Essays*, trans. Richard Howard (Evanston: Northwestern University Press, 1972), 24.
18 Arthur Rimbaud, *Complete Works*, ed. and trans. Wallace Fowlie (Chicago: Chicago University Press), 238–40.
19 Rimbaud, *Complete Works*, 239–40.
20 Arthur Rimbaud, 'Cities (I)', trans. John Ashbery, *The New Yorker* (30 January 2011), https://www.newyorker.com/magazine/2011/02/07/cities-i.
21 Rimbaud, *Complete Works*, 238.
22 Walter Benjamin, *One Way Street and Other Writings*, trans. Edmund Jephcott and Kingsley Shorter (London: NLB, 1979), 229.

8
'The comic body in space' ('Il corpo comico nello spazio', 1976)

I.

Merleau-Ponty describes two types of bodily movement, one abstract and one concrete, one connected to sight and the other to touch: the first appears as an act of pointing out (*Zeigen*), the second as an act of grasping hold (*Greifen*). These two ways of moving, which are usually complementary, are connected to behaviours that are defined as virtual and those as real. For example, my body has a different way of moving if I indicate to someone the location of a pen, or inversely if I move a hand to grasp the pen. In the first case, my body is the expressive means of a spatial thought and of the recognition of a set of objective laws of a space, and in the second case, it is an instrument of occupying a space, familiar or not, but in any case one that is not interpreted.

The treatment of eros in the films of the Marx Brothers very clearly reflects their strange utopia. This is the utopia of a primitive condition in which there is place for neither ideas nor feelings, and one that is bent solely on touching, disrupting, wrecking and invading space. Simply consider the scene from *Horse Feathers* in which Thelma Todd, sitting on a sofa, is assaulted from all sides by the three brothers. For them eros is never translated into words or other symbolic substitutes but appears suddenly in the movements of crudely touching, hugging, chasing or jumping into the laps of the women who come within their reach. The crude act of grasping, as manifested in the eros of the Marx Brothers, especially Harpo Marx, is an eradication of cognitive behaviour when faced with the erotic object: it is an instantaneous localization of the stimulus, without the steering of a virtual behaviour that more precisely identifies the stimulus. Such an act falls into what can be called a concrete movement. The whole body takes part in a concrete movement, without identifying what part of the body is drawn by the stimulus: it is an infantile and pathological behaviour, locked in the dimensions of the instant and the concrete, without the ability to abstract stimuli or to decipher them through the objective laws of a space. It thus tends to locate them instantaneously through touch.

II.

Merleau-Ponty writes: 'The normal subject's body is not merely ready to be mobilized by real situations that draw it toward themselves, it can also turn away from the world, apply its activity to the stimuli that are inscribed upon its sensory surfaces, lend itself to experiments and, more generally, be situated in the virtual.'[1] The impossibility of situating oneself in the virtual is the impossibility of rendering movement abstract, with the consequent necessity of laboriously deciphering the objects to point out and the movements to do so: this can be the equivalent of aphasia in relation to the use of the body in space. This laborious deciphering of the objects to point out, which become confused when massed together – material presence indistinct from abstract categories – is called atopia. Grasping hold or touching for the body is entirely different from pointing out. Goldstein's experiments on the antinomy between *Zeigen* and *Greifen*, between grasping hold and pointing out, form the basis of this entire discourse.

What is also perceptible here is a model of deciphering not only comic behaviours but a range of general expressive behaviours (in literature and theatre). It is as if differing ideological premises were to lead from time to time to the founding of an expressive utopia on one or another of these behaviours. For example, the entire theatre of ideas, or theatre that uses an actor to discursively engage with a problem or theory, from Molière to Brecht, is based on the utopia of a purely virtual behaviour. The actor recites to indicate something at a distance. It is clear in Brecht's theatre that the verb *Zeigen* defines the process of estrange-ment at the centre of his conceptual project. In contrast, nomadic theatre, from *commedia dell'arte* to music hall, American burlesque or vaudeville, and Artaud's theatre, is entirely based on real, not virtual, behaviours. Actors recite by grasping hold of and touching other actors and objects on stage, throwing themselves directly at stimuli instead of pausing to recognize them (kicking, smacking, chasing, thieving). In the type of theatre that Artaud loved to define as 'anarchic', the privileged verb is '*saisir*' (*Greifen*): not only grasping hold of bodies on stage but grasping hold of spectators, working on their nerves and charming them like snakes. For Brecht, instead, spectators must remain lucid and detached.

The metaphors of mental lucidity and of visibility (virtual or distant contact) are replaced in anarchic theatre by the opposite of visibility and mental lucidity: the pinnacle of true theatre for Artaud is '*aveuglement*', blindness, and catastrophic delirium in which all bodies become entangled, the point at which we lose track of every virtual behaviour and abstract movement, when the process of locating stimuli becomes increasingly frenetic, overwhelming, relentless. In silent comedy films this type of situation usually erupts in a brouhaha or mêlée, which is the climax of the comedic action.

It should be noted that this theatre based on physical contact (hitting, kicking, stealing), and in general on non-abstract behaviours, has always been considered a 'low' form of art – inferior and working class – according to the ideological hierarchies of modern culture. One of Artaud's merits is to have opened up a non-biased consideration of this mode of using the spatial body. Artaud's reference to the Marx Brothers is evidence that, if on one hand he considered Elizabethan and Jacobean theatre to be a quintessential example of the theatre of cruelty, on the other he also considered nomadic comic theatre (which then gave rise to silent comic cinema) to be an example of a use of space unlike the sort found in bourgeois theatre.

III.

One of the clearest models of the brouhaha in silent film is Laurel and Hardy's *The Battle of the Century*. In the film Laurel needs to injure himself (in order to collect insurance money) so Hardy places a banana peel on a sidewalk for Laurel to step on. Instead a delivery man carrying pies slips on it, then gets angry with Hardy and throws a pie in his face. Hardy throws a pie back but hits a passer-by, who responds in kind, and soon a huge crowd joins the battle. The square in the end is packed with people covered in cream seeking revenge with forced gestures, in a spectacle that involves everyone, but which excludes the human dimension – the thinking human capable of virtual thought. The finale of the brouhaha is the triumph of impulsive action. Another similarly elaborate brouhaha, in which the actions of touching and bodily aggression shatter the most basic societal conventions, occurs in *You're Darn Tootin'*, once again with Laurel and Hardy. Here a massive scuffle is sparked by a gust of madness that causes first Laurel and Hardy then all passers-by to hit and kick each other and rip off each other's pants, leading in the end to a free-for-all of men in their underwear assaulting each other with spasmodic joy.

All the Marx Brothers films are crescendos towards brouhahas. Regardless of the qualitative level of a film, when the moment of this type of 'celebrated anarchy' is reached, the uproariousness and disruptive action become a source of crazed excitement, not only for the characters but also the spectators. The brouhahas of the Marx Brothers, however, do not follow a mechanical crescendo (as in Laurel and Hardy's *The Battle of the Century* and *You're Darn Tootin'*) in which the same gesture infects an entire crowd. As opposed to the hallucinatory character of the crescendos of Laurel and Hardy, with the Marx Brothers there is a comic orientation towards an unhinged extroversion, for which their films do not tend towards a concentrated, unified, obsessive and forced gesture but rather towards an explosion of all possible gestures within a distinct space. In their films, the brouhaha is in some ways purer, less contaminated by the constructed dynamic of the gag: it takes the form of a collection of real or concrete behaviours, in which there are no longer distinct gags but instead a single overwhelming mêlée. The dynamic of the gag, in contrast, is usually based on a shifting between two types of examined behaviour (virtual and concrete), or on their misfortunate inversion. It is not by chance that the canonical running gag is very rare in the films of the Marx Brothers. If the brouhaha is fundamentally based on concrete movements that culminate in the act of touching, the gag is based on a shifting of, or playing with, the twofold movement of the spatial body. Thus, the gag and the brouhaha stand at the two poles of the comic body's gamut and define all its possibilities, up to the limit of abstraction.

Here are a few examples. In *Picking Peaches*, Harry Langdon has to shoot a revolver, but instead of pulling the trigger he makes the sound 'bang bang' with his mouth, resorting to a virtual behaviour instead of the called-for concrete one. The gag in *Long Pants*, when Langdon tries to attract the attention of what turns out to be a manikin, is a perfect example of virtual behaviour (signalling) in inappropriate circumstances. In *Haunted House*, Keaton finds himself in the midst of ghosts running about and begins to try to direct them with the gestures of a traffic policeman, substituting a concrete movement (the identification of the stimulus and escape) with an abstract movement completely out of place (the directing of traffic). All of these examples show the tendency of Langdon and Keaton to substitute concrete movements with abstract ones.

On the other hand, there is a type of opposite inversion. In the simple case of an actor who falls into a manhole, the character behaves as if he were in a familiar place without the need of spatial interpretation, of an appropriate virtual behaviour. This is what Bergson called the comic element of automatic repetitiveness. An elaborate example of this occurs in *From Soup to Nuts*, in which Laurel and Hardy serve lunch. At the beginning is a scene in which Hardy scolds Laurel for his rash behaviour (which is not adequately interpretative) and as a result decides to take it upon himself to carry an enormous cake to the table: his bearing of the cake is triumphal and expresses the certainty of the character's behaviour, that is, a familiarity of the character with the space that he is crossing. In the meantime, however, the family's dog has taken a banana and dropped the peel in Hardy's path. Hardy of course slips on it and lands headfirst in the cake. The space that the character assumed to be familiar is transformed, carrying the gag to its finale.

Other examples show the possibility of a mix of the two behaviours. For example, Hardy is hit by Laurel, then begins to process it mentally. The haphazard movement of locating the stimulus is substituted by the process of identifying the stimulus, a sign of an attempted virtual behaviour that then turns into the opposite: Hardy suddenly and roughly responds by hitting Laurel back. When Chaplin is about to kick an adversary and is caught in the act, he turns his behaviour into abstract movements (dancing, pirouetting) that bring into play an inverse process. This symbolic behaviour, such as dancing, is another form of virtual behaviour, because it does not directly point at the stimulus, while instead kicking someone corresponds in the most economical way with the idea of a concrete behaviour, because it points directly at the stimulus.

IV.

All of this is tied to the problem of the spatiality of the body in diverse circumstances. If I am in my own room, I move differently than when I am crossing a street full of traffic. All the comic effects of the clumsy character (pratfalls, running into things, breaking things by mistake, being hit by flying objects, etc.) derive from the failure to recognize a space that requires interpretative behaviours, that is, abstract ones. The two types of movement depend on a use of the body as an instrument for occupying space, becoming one with surrounding space (non-interpreted space), or inversely as separation and interpretation at a distance from space, 'distracted by the world', as Merleau-Ponty says.

An antimony is always present, between occupying-touching and showing or deviating in expressive movement, by virtual means. There are moments in which Buster Keaton turns into an acrobat (for example in *The General* or *Steamboat Bill Jr.*) and takes over a space with his body, transforming it into a precise mechanism whose movements become one with his own. The Keatonian utopia is here at its apex: to make of one's own distinct body a model for virtually occupying space, defining its laws and internal inner workings through entirely mental means, that is, from a distance. All the machines that Keaton invents for carrying out movements from a distance (for example in *The Navigator*) are a confirmation of this. To virtually occupy space in this way is equivalent to the idea of mechanically administering a space.

Nothing could contrast more with the Marx Brothers, who do not tend to administer a space so much as invade it in a coarse and physical way, to leap all over the place, to spread disorder such that everything is transformed into an indistinct mêlée. But here a problem arises: it is not with my own body, limited and separate, that I am able to concretely invade all spaces. I am capable of invading all spaces only by using my body as an inexhaustible source of flows – flows of objects and flows of words – the introduction of material and symbolic things into the world. Only by considering my body as a source and channel of flows – flows of food and flows of excrement – can I come to think of a space that is entirely full, a space in which all encounters and all mixings are possible, but above all one in which society functions as a single body, such as the body of the enormous giant that embodies the Carnival. The carnivalesque conceives of a space in which there is no separation between individuals, between the inside and the outside of individuals, or between interiority and exteriority, due to an extraordinary abundance of food, words, excrement and flows of every sort that move inside and outside of bodies, out of mouths or asses and inside asses (enemas) or mouths (ingurgitations). This is a utopia that can be explained only by excluding isolated individualism and thinking of an entirely collective form of comedy.

The even-handed divvying up of the brothers' exploits between Harpo and Groucho, with Chico acting as their go-between, reflects the two differing ways of occupying space by way of two types of flow that arise from the body: the flow of words (symbolic) and flow of objects (material). Indeed, Harpo reacts to every possible situation by pulling objects out of his pockets, just as Groucho invades every social situation with a loquacity that much less than discourse is rather the raw material of discourse. To undertake this occupation, certain characteristics are necessary. The expressive and articulate body of the mime would never be up to the task: what is needed is a grotesque body that goes everywhere, which is erratic and disjointed in all its movements and above all does not follow the harmonious paths of the mime.

V.

Of all the brothers, Harpo best expresses the sense of a space that is to be only occupied and filled up, not to be administered, measured or negotiated by way of virtual behaviours – a space in which the precise distinction between bodies and objects is eliminated, because what counts is the invasion of pure corporeal materiality.

To Harpo the quality of the objects doesn't matter, only their abundance. An abundance of objects is ecstasy for him. In *Horse Feathers* he leaps under a cascade of coins falling out of a payphone as if it were a delightful shower. In *A Night in Casablanca* he wins big at roulette and dives into a sea of tokens. The equivalent to this ecstatic accumulation of objects is their elimination – random, intentional or unintentional, and always with the greatest indifference. One example is his famous act of letting silverware pour out of his sleeves. He also calmly pulls out from his clothes mattresses, dogs, sleds, guns, mousetraps, alarm clocks and even limbs that, even if fake, muddle a bit the distinction between his body and the array of objects he carries about. This confusion between Harpo's body and his objects is heightened by a recurring move: when someone asks him who he is, he shows them the objects on his person, as if these objects formed a sort of autobiography. Or better: it is as if these outpourings of objects could remedy any need for symbolic communication or virtual behaviour.

Harpo is someone who picks up everything. His stealing reflex is an extension of his tendency to pick up and touch everything within reach and is also an inversion of his contrasting tendency to expel objects. In this way surrounding space circulates within and outside of him, together with the objects that come and go, blurring the lines dividing interior and exterior. Harpo's body is no different than the things that he collects. He carries about on his person a miscellaneous stash of flea market junk. But in eroding the distinction between himself and what he carries in his pockets, Harpo refuses both metaphorical dealings with objects as well as humanizing the spaces in which he moves. He participates in the inert materiality of objects (a typical example of which is his way of sleeping, of letting a limb impassively drop as if it were lifeless), living thus in a universe without any possible virtual dealings and without dreams, a universe of pure corporeal existence without mental extensions. He reacts as if he were jumping to the demands of an exclusively physical law, displays deeply corporeal automatisms (eating, grasping, running) and lowers human movements to those of animals, with whom he acts as a kindred being. He can also be squished under carpets, between mattresses or inside suitcases, all of which are simply inert objects. Harpo is a concentration of the utopia of an entirely full space, full of people and material objects all blurred together: a utopia that is also a sort of solemn alienation from everything that is important, dramatic, unique or based on qualitative or abstract evaluations. For him one thing is worth any other, a can of sardines is the same as a diamond necklace, in the sense that he doesn't know the difference. Because of the collapse of these evaluative categories, his joy of abundance can never be exhausted: material is always only material, and all objects are to be collected because they can all be food for his body and flows to occupy and invade the surrounding space; this is the utopia of a completely material space, before the intervention of any evaluation or abstract definition.

VI.

Comic film actors make use of wide range of objects as instruments of aggression and thematic indicators, but in spaces administered through virtual means by a mime, as in the work of Keaton, Langdon and Chaplin, the objects tend to lose the sense of their raw materiality and transform into something else, for example, Keaton's ingenious machines or Chaplin's or Laurel and Hardy's animated objects. The converting of an object into a different one is evidence of possible metamorphosis, but the metamorphic principle of reality, once called the 'revolt of objects', contains evidence of its own reversibility. This is because the 'revolt of objects' entails the integration of these objects into human behaviours. The result is that if comic actors integrate an object within a performative space, they do so because it transforms the space into a metaphor of pure human presence. The metaphoric space, together with the virtual ensemble of the actor, thus becomes a space that is animated and animistic, in which everything is both symbol and practical meaning for those who inhabit it. Even in the case of 'enemy objects', the humanization of the performative space is always at the foundation of every means of external administration.

It is the proliferation of objects that eliminates this point of view, as happens in moments of crisis or during brouhahas in which there is indeed a 'revolt of objects'. The amassing and proliferation of objects introduces the sense of the extraneity of objects and of their purely material presence. If silent comic film is for the most part a space in which the object takes on a 'human' dimension through metaphor, in the case of Harpo and his objects, things take on a presence in which they shine with pure materiality. Only with Harpo is there the systematic proliferation of objects with which to invade the performative space and dissolve its metaphoricity. This is in large part the comic utopia of the Marx Brothers: the utopia of a series of scattershot collective movements that dissolve all dividing lines, both between the various actors (Harpo and Chico who become Groucho in *Duck Soup*) and between the actors and things – between objects and persons. The utopia of invasive comedy is always connected to the idea of a collective body that incessantly advances, crushing in upon you. The fact that the Marx Brothers always chose crowded places for their acts, places where the assembled spectators are dragged into the action in a messy brouhaha, and where various 'important objects' (works of art for example) are debased and stomped on (such as the painting in *Animal Crackers* that Harpo uses as a blanket), reduced to any sort of common use in more or less the same manner in which the bodies of spectators are treated (they too are attacked and stepped on), is a good indication of the Brothers' orientation and of their utopic space that must not be administered but simply occupied.

A scene comes to mind from *A Night at the Opera* in which Groucho's small ocean liner cabin is invaded by a dizzying array of people. Groucho enters, and in opening his steamer trunk finds Chico, Allan Jones and Harpo stowed away inside and all asleep. Then two cleaning ladies arrive to make the bed, followed by a manicurist who begins to clean Groucho's nails, a ship's engineer and his assistant, a young girl looking for her aunt, and then four waiters with trays of food. When at last Margaret Dumont arrives and opens the door, everyone comes violently tumbling out. In this scene the idea of the grand brouhaha is at its peak.

In carefully watching this scene, a few rules of this type of comedy come to light, showing its underlying collective character. First is the need to inflate bodies and objects: individuals and pieces of furniture, people and things that no one knows where to put, such as Harpo who behaves like an inanimate object and continues to sleep. Within the tight cabin everyone continues to do their duties, the manicurist attends to Groucho's nails, the engineer fixes the pipes, the passenger makes a call, Harpo who is asleep rolls all over the place, the cleaning ladies make the beds, etc. The crowd here becomes a single body melding into the space of the cabin, an all-out body in which each person loses his or her own singularity, continuing nonetheless to perform a specific bodily action: space as the intersection of concrete movements and flows. This is the rule of flux: space here is occupied by flows of bodies, as in other cases by flows of objects; but there is no difference. Bodies and objects in this space are not clearly separated, being both presence and material. They become corporeal space, the idea of a space entirely full and without voids in which the void is nothing but a momentary effect of movements, of gestures, which then suddenly disappears amid other movements and gestures.

P.S. When I was at Cornell University, almost every evening I went to see Marx Brothers films. Over the course of a year, I drafted a book of about 500 pages that I called *Harpo's Bazaar* (because Harpo, being mute, was my favourite). Then when I realized that I would never manage to finish it, I threw the manuscript into the trash. A few pages survived, the part called 'The comic body in space'.

Note

1   Maurice Merleau-Ponty, *Phenomenology of Perception*, trans. Donald A. Landes (London: Routledge, 2013), 111.

Figure 8.1   Gianni Celati, 1976, by Carlo Gajani, during Carnival in the Pilastro quarter of Bologna. Dressed in top hat and tails, Celati is comically reciting, 'Io sono dottore e professore, / primario e secondario/ nell'ospedale triclinio quadriclinico e policlinico, / io curo i crampi, i calli ed i duroni, / unghie incarnate, scarpe rotte e geloni, / col sovrano rimedio del clistere, / non c'è mal che resista al mio sapere' (I am doctor and professor,/ primary and secondary/ in the triclinic quadriclinic and polyclinic hospital,/ I cure cramps, corns and calluses,/ ingrown toenails, broken shoes and swollen toes,/ with the supreme remedy of the enema,/ there is no ailment that can resist my expertise). Reprinted by permission of Gillian Haley.

9
'Counter-information on power: on Foucault's *Discipline and Punish*' ('Contro-informazione sul potere: a proposito di *Sorvegliare e punire di Foucault*', 1977)

There is a passage in *Discipline and Punish* in which Foucault declares that it is time to cease describing the effects of power in only negative terms. Liberal, illuminist discourse, when dealing with power, can only see what it calls injustice, brutality, inhumanity and tends to speak of reforms that will bring about a more humane Law. Modern cultural discourse is preoccupied with exclusion, censure and repression, focusing on secondary, negative aspects of a mechanism. But it is exactly the negativity of pre-bourgeois power, the excess of power's spectacle, the futile supplication of the subject's body, that modern power must avoid, despite often failing to do so.

Submissive bodies instead of martyrized ones: not mutilated bodies but ones studied, analysed and reassembled as positive mechanisms. Precise movements to be executed, a comprehensive training on bureaucratic minutia that seem incomprehensible, rituals of formal precision that in time become routine, functionaries that make note of the smallest gestural imperfections. It is above all a gaze, but not that of the functionary: the functionary is commutable, without the need for visible individualization (such as a uniform) as for example with town criers spreading the king's word. It is the gaze of a mechanism, which does not operate in exterior space like the grand spectacles of monarchical power, but instead operates within the internal space of our bodies. Foucault uses the image of Bentham's Panopticon to describe this gaze that from a central tower monitors and analyses the movements of prisoners. This brings a didactic nursery rhyme to mind, which was common in the nineteenth century, of the child who sucks its thumb only to have it snipped off by a great tall tailor. Premodern folklore lacked this educational technique: its fables explained how to overcome dangers in the woods; modern nursery rhymes prescribe behaviours necessary to avoid punitive sanctions. Herein lies a new educational discipline, according to which the isolated subject interiorizes and reproduces a mode of surveillance, an impersonal gaze that hones its gestures.

For example, in the context of the military, the brutality of a paranoid colonel is a farce as conspicuous as it is secondary; that is, what counts are the calculated movements the soldier is trained to perform, the efficiency of a body that performs gestures alone that are precisely established by a diagram. It is not the external brutality of the force that assaults the body as a totality but the infinitesimal correcting action on the detached parts: the arm that must move in this way, the shoulders that must remain in this position, etc. This is not what organizes and divides the ranks, what creates the miracles of choral harmony that the heads of state so enjoy (characteristic of coordinated exercises) and what finally orients various individualities according to analytical patterns, each in its own place. In short, it is a discipline that transforms what at first was a mass into subjects, a heterogeneous clot in which myriad contaminations and insurgencies were possible. The subject arises from the engineered segmentation of the horde. It is born as an interiority, a harmonious personality, a unitary consciousness and positive mechanism that produces the sense of the Law.

How to explain the parallelism between the rise and development of the sciences and the mechanical creation that is the modern subject? Various historical, social and psychological sciences study humanity, observing and monitoring its basic rituals, outlining the form of its ideal body (social or individual), disassembled and remade according to a positive model, one that promises a good return on investment. Analyses, identifications of useful gestures, profits on bodily investments, capitalization and good yields go together. They create a type of normal subject to serve as a cultural standard. A sociological survey differs from a police interrogation in legal terms but not in the type of analytical gaze at work. The school exam that so often returns in our dreams is not an esoteric (psychoanalytical) system of symbols but the reality of our process of individualization by way of selective mechanisms and the analytical gaze of modern power.

While there are several predecessors to this work of Foucault's (Bataille especially, namely his theories on the transition from monarchical sovereignty to the modern state), no one before Kafka so accurately described this general process by which the subjects of a police state are set off on an endless journey of examinations, designed to integrate into themselves the principle of tribunal surveillance as world conscience.

Kafka is an example of counter-information on power, carried off into the thickets by experts and espoused as an example of esoteric symbolism or cultural curiosity. Must we wait for the work of Foucault to also become a cultural curiosity and end up grouped with other books on piquant historical problems exhumed by archivists and imbued with populist ideology (what is selling at the moment)? And yet his is a book neither for experts nor humanists curious about what is happening in the world. It is a book to be used for everyday life, to be consulted and questioned at work and at the centre of institutions. And to use it means putting yourself on a level wherein the functionary's analytical gaze, the expert's examination, the police interrogation, cease to be part of an annoying routine and become instead emergency situations. How will the experts who so emphasize Foucault's nihilism come to terms with such situations? Will they do so as is usually the case with cultured discussions, analyses, judgements and defamatory sanctions? It is best to say right away: books of this sort, if they are used, are guerrilla war machines, as are all forms of counter-information.

To end: it is not possible to use this book without realizing that the grand histories of nations – History – is precisely the implementation of the analytical gaze of disciplinary regimes. Here we see in the end that archaeology, as the counterpart of history, cannot result in a specialized discipline but only in a practice: otherwise it remains antiquarian history, which is precisely the clever recycling of piquant themes to satisfy cultural vices. Why is it that the great histories of modern nations have never praised, along with other technological achievements, this extraordinary technological development that is disciplinary surveillance, the bureaucratic police-like tracking that keeps tabs on the most insignificant details of all social relationships? It is precisely because, says Foucault, this was the grandest technological achievement, but also the least confessable. On the other hand, Foucault has already shown us that, if the confession is a false proof that serves the police state, history does not develop by way of admissions and confessions but through repressions, rationalizations, deviations and silences. Archaeology is not the ideological illusion of an alternative history but a practice of counter-information that breaks a silence and a code of silence.

10
'On the era of this book' and 'Alice and the occurrence ...' from *Displaced Alice: Collective materials (on Alice) for a survival manual*

'On the era of this book'

I.

The setting of this book is Bologna between 1976 and 1977.[1] I was teaching at the University of Bologna and in November 1976 started a literature course swayed by the moods of the moment. I began by reading in class Victorian works of so-called nonsense, in other words, drivel or foolishness, such as comic passages from Edward Lear's *Book of Nonsense* and Lewis Carroll's two fanciful books on Alice: *Alice in Wonderland* and *Alice Through the Looking Glass*.

The lessons were relatively well attended. Many came to pass the time, as if watching a variety show, while others came to judge what I was saying according to the dogmas of their political indoctrinations. I have in mind a bearded student with a timid, serious air about him and a military haversack around his neck who was a member of a far-left group that fed on phrases from the Third International. One day he announced his dismay that I was holding lessons on such unserious things instead of grappling with the problems of society. I believe that he left traces in the book, with his grave calls for order, only then to disappear amid the thronging voices discussing uncertain matters.

It took some time before I could make sense of the reactions and debates that arose among the students, with shifts in position according to various political slogans. The point is that this student and others at a certain point began to seriously discuss the adventures of Alice, but it seemed to me that they were always talking about their own situations as students away from home, away from their families. The phrase 'displaced Alice' was born from their displacement.

This displacement grew from their dealings with penny-pinching landlords, the poor meals at the cafeteria and the lack of places to gather other than on the street. I don't think that Bologna was any less welcoming than other cities to life as a student, but the enormous increase of the student population caused crowding, often with the feeling of a slum, with visitors streaming in from all over drawn to the intense life on the streets. It was a city with an exaggerated abundance of encounters, a setting for a coming-of-age novel, such as Enrico Palandri's *Boccalone*.

In *Boccalone*, Palandri describes a city of walkers, 'high walkers', as he calls them. Bologna was a city of wandering students who often attended class to simply sit down more than for any other reason. Given the overcrowding of the rented rooms, many faced the problem of where to go during the day, above all during the winter months. It is not by chance that the student protests started punctually in the spring when it was more agreeable to be out in the streets. Even the occupation of the university always had the feeling of a seasonal ritual. When university buildings were occupied, the wanderers finally felt as if they had a place where to relax. Some slept there on makeshift mattresses; during the day they would play cards or invent things to do – apart from meetings, which called to mind the Leninist occupation of the Winter Palace in 1917, when the Bolsheviks defeated the Mensheviks.

II.

One day in March 1977 the police stormed the university district in Bologna, firing teargas canisters. I happened to be there by chance and took cover behind a column. A teargas canister landed a few feet from me, and I saw someone suddenly leap out from behind another column and send it back towards the police with an elegant lob. He was smartly dressed and wearing suede gloves (the teargas canisters were hot, and gloves were needed to throw them back). We exchanged a few words, and I understood that he was there for no other reason; he had come just for that occasional sport that gave some entertainment. But the next day, after students had erected barricades in the same area of the university, I don't think that any more skirmishes broke out. Everywhere there was an air of leisure, of defying authority, without ideological decrees, accompanied by the sound of someone cheerfully playing the piano behind a barricade.

Apart from the fictions of revolutionary gravitas, what gave meaning to the student uprisings was the overwhelming desire to be rid of constraints, to unlock the cage of social domestication. This was accompanied by the suspension of certain conventions determining socially acceptable sexual behaviour, with easier love and the idea of a liberation from sexual taboos that soon led to patheticism or a neurotic promiscuousness. Another common aspect to the student uprisings was the need to rationalize events in retrospect, hiding the gratuitous or purely corporeal excesses and everything else that did not fit into the ideological canon. This need was felt above all by the leaders to give shape to the struggle against power, here too in keeping with the Leninist uprising of October 1917.

What changed in March was this: that first the police, then the official channels of information, collaborated in a sweeping rationalization of events that had taken place in Bologna. The events in summary are these: the murder of a student, shot by the police, the ransacking of a radio station by a police squad, and the arrival of a contingent of tanks dispatched at dawn to the city gates as if to declare a state of siege. The wrecking of the radio station – Radio Alice – was a paranoid act, and also illegal. The killing of the student was senseless, if we exclude the possibility that that the police seem irresistibly drawn to acts of this sort, something that cannot be ruled out. It was also a stupidly bullying decision of Minister Cossiga to send tanks as if we were in Budapest in 1956. These were not acts aimed to maintain public order, but rather ones meant to instigate more heated conflicts, and to make scattered student protests appear to be a state of emergency.

The press and TV news, however, were just as interested as the police in inventing a state of emergency. The Bologna affair was covered by the press in photographs that portrayed it as a major spectacle, from folkloric images of menacing far-left militants to others of Bologna seeming a miniature Budapest. It was one of the more soothing rationalizations, in which the 'youth' became carriers of an ideally revolutionary future, yet one unfettered by the harsh sermons of the official left party. Afterwards, many authoritative figures felt it necessary to express their opinions on the 'new utopia' of the March movement, which had been endowed with cultural prestige, with some of the movement's representatives courted by TV. For a moment the students who had marched in the protests found themselves at the centre of public attention, while the beleaguered revolutionary fiction became the stuff of entertainment in a sideshow of current affairs.

In September 1977, on the initiative of Mayor Renato Zangheri, the City of Bologna held a conference on dissent in order to bring the new opposition movements into peaceful dialogue. It was a diplomatic attempt to defuse some of the furious hostility of the Communist Party towards the groups at the centre of the March events. And yet it was at this conference with international reach drawing people from near and far, that it became evident that a memorable season of intellectual fervour in Bologna was over. The city took on the air of a spectacle devoted to the press, the conference came across as a miniature carnival produced for television, and things took a turn for the worse, with the announcement of armed groups who soon would be taking matters into their own hands, including showing off for the mass media.

III.

In March 1977, the university was occupied, and lessons suspended; I was sorry to interrupt my course. To keep teaching during the occupation I had to negotiate with the authorities and sign a document in which I assumed responsibility for any resulting damage. I collected several books on the customs, morals, reforms, family life, literature and sexual habits of the Victorian age then handed them out to those willing to copy out passages on cards to circulate among the other students. The cards made their rounds, and at a certain point almost everyone wanted to write, each going off in their own direction. That system of writing based on things read or talked about in class gave the comforting illusion of knowing what was being discussed; the fulcrum of it all was the figure of Alice.

The name Alice had been in circulation thanks to American counter-culture and had become a codeword referring to that loose coming-together without hierarchies that was called a 'movement'. In Lewis Carroll's book, thanks to a magic mushroom, Alice grows in size and shrinks to the point that she loses her sense of identity; for this reason, she was associated with a destabilizing experience, such as taking LSD. And yet behind her childish appearance there emerges the sense of a new individual, for the most part destabilized, caught up in continual change, but freed from precepts such as 'you should' and more aware of the importance of how 'you feel'.

This focus on feeling was foreign to traditional politics. It arose through various sources of existential inspiration, but also through new films and songs. Bob Dylan's songs were particularly popular and often played on Radio Alice; they announced a radical change in contemporary ways of feeling from which there arose yet more means of dissent, other means of confronting social domestication, no longer directed at the mirage of a revolutionary future. The figure at the centre of these new visions was no longer the hero of the working classes, the hero of a battle with the forces of the upper classes, but the ordinary individual lost in the uprooting of all the classes and in exile from depressing petty bourgeoisie neighbourhoods, one seeming nearly identical to the next.

All this was part of the spirit of the times, felt in the air and heard in the street, in which one trusted without knowing exactly what it was. This spirit was evident, too, during class discussions in which everything seemed to come up: love, psychoanalysis, politics, rock music, German cinema, new ways of writing and thinking. For about a year Bologna was an open-air laboratory in which ideas and opinions circulated at high speed, with hurried messages and echoes of the overheard that were almost immediately overtaken by yet new ideas. Then it all ended: afterward there began an era of a new dogmatic economy, with an even more enfeebling domestication of the human animal.

IV.

This book was first published nearly 30 years ago. Its unconventional form arose from the way in which it was composed – the collecting of notes, filing cards, little crumpled pieces of paper, recordings and speeches that continued discussions that had been going on for a year. For this reason, the writing has the appearance of hurried note taking, with uneven sentences, frequent repetitions and everything seeming fragmentary and scattered. I the undersigned editor was responsible for assembling the pieces, which I initially took up in order to keep some fragmentary record of what was being said, and then with the idea of putting together a book at the request of a friend who had just started a small press – the psychoanalyst Elvio Fachinelli, who was interested in the book for the same reasons for which it would today be tossed in the garbage by the experts in our famous publishing houses.

Fachinelli was interested because this assemblage of entangled, messy discourses had no safety net, with a clownish air strongest in the parts in which serious matters were broached. Born in an atmosphere of euphoria for everything external, for random chance happenings and meetings, the book does not hide its somewhat deceptive character: like a person who after donning the mask of wisdom immediately tires of it, tossing the pretence into the weeds amid laughter and jokes. But what makes the book still legible, I think, is the return of a spark of a special *allegria* (light-heartedness, mirth) that arose for no reason but for coming together with others. I refer to the pages in which Alice's adventures are explained in terms of automatisms, mechanical movements, intense swerves, avoiding the usual psychological interpretations and 'poetic' gratifications of interiority.

The line of thought is this: psychological explanations always speak of the individual closed within the *sancta sanctorum* of the self. Instead, physical and mental automatisms cause external movements that we share with others; for example, we understand the ways in which Alice moves because they correspond to automatisms that could be our own, and which are never closed within the private interiority of someone. And it is exactly this exteriority when combined with light-heartedness that causes an expansive movement that makes evident a commonality with others. It is important that this exteriority material-izes as a bodily impulse, surging with desire, without the hindrance of psychology, without vigilant states of consciousness, which always have an inhibitory effect on the automatisms of the body and the mind.

The light-heartedness that sought to wind its way through this book must always reject the idea of knowledge as a state of conscious-ness, the stagnant knowledge of qualified professionals. It must instead embrace an unhindered, jesting approach, with highs and lows according to the moment, because positivity is always a question of moments – the atmosphere, the intonation of the moment, whether exhilarating or distressing, in which a mental opening becomes evident. The adhesion to the moment transcends all types of knowledge, every kind of interiority, because it redirects our attention to occurrences outside of ourselves; and as it becalms competitive anxieties, it helps us to envision a possible community, without 'messages'.

G.C., November 2006

ALICE AND THE OCCURRENCE. THE HEAD THAT LEAVES BEHIND THE BODY BRINGS JOY. WAIT, FIGURE, FALLING/ BEFALLING. THE FALL INTO THE INSIGNIFICANT AND THE LOSS OF RIGHT SIZE ARE NOT AS TERRIBLE AS THEY SAY. ALWAYS THE RETURN TO BOOKS FOR GOOD CHILDREN.

Collective writing, December 1976
Alice's hole is never where you think it is. A stable hole, that already knows where it is. It is only spectacle, a theatrical or touristic fiction. Means of control propose stable holes to us, holes that exist only for

taking us far away, on exotic trips. But the question lies in wait in the occurrence that brushes by; you are unaware that it is on the verge of happening, then it happens, and before you, within your being in the world, there opens a possibility. The occurrence is an opening of comprehension. It is useless to theorize the occurrence, and useless too to hold it up as a model once you have lived it. For these reasons Alice's hole is not a model, it is only a movement of falling.

Alice falling into the hole dreaming: a departure by means of an alternative path with the head remaining here with the body. An escape from traps. Alice remains in the meadow. The physical fact of drifting into a dream state, in bed or on the toilet or while reading. That which causes you to move from one place with your head is something felt, always strongly physical, but also an opening in comprehension. You are reading and at a certain point realize that your head is going somewhere else, unexpectedly, that you are escaping in order to feel your body. Where are you? In your head or in your body? Alice has major problems of identity.

The physical sensation of the body that summons the head back to itself. There is a jolt, as when we wake up suddenly or emerge from the effects of a drug. A swerve of intensity between stupor and awakening. As if the body were to summon the head back to itself, inspecting its knowledge to put it back in order, to discover an identity: Who I am? What time is it? Where am I? Alice no longer knows who she is. Where has she left her body and where is her head going? She tries calling herself back, appealing to her schoolroom knowledge: 'In what latitude and longitude might I be?' And with words learned at school she attempts to call herself back while lost in the movement of falling.

> The head is a monster that devours everything and reanimates everything; it grows or shrinks depending on what it eats.

Useless to attempt to protect oneself with knowledge against occurrences. Alice is the opposite of the old way of remaining on the defensive instead of running after occurrences: the old way of negating what there is, with a sense of guilt for what there is not (the revolution). It is a fact that everywhere there are heads taking off on their own; and that there is no way to keep them in the place where they belong; and that too many no longer believe in the story that impulses must be kept in order by the precepts of reason. The fall of Alice can also seem an 'ego-trip' but without the ego. A trip without interiority: restored as a pure positive movement, without fault.

> Protecting yourself from occurrences with knowledge is the old way of remaining always on the defensive.

Thoughts on how to write, December 1976
One must attempt to write and speak elliptically, leaping and syncopating; communicating not by way of readymade phrases but figures of

movement in such a way that things escape, slip away. Using speed and rhythm against the sense and knowledge of the proper academic. Falling into Alice's hole with a spontaneous movement, then following the rhythm, chasing after the rushing flow and all the shifts of discourse that trail off underground. In such a way one may come to understand that befalling is a falling into occurrence, is a falling/befalling. Alice is born of a movement of this sort, with everything contained within this initial movement: the fall into the hole, the subterranean trip. The first manuscript was indeed called *Alice's Adventures Underground*. Only later came the gift-wrapping of the product, the title closer to the ambitions of children's literature, and the opening poem 'All in the golden afternoon' that explains what the escape means.

Falling/befalling

Lesson on mechanisms, December 1976

Alice is full of a waiting for occurrence. The occurrence is desire: desire is the waiting for occurrence. In Alice there is the waiting for a story with pictures and conversations: 'what is the use of a book […] without pictures or conversations?' And suddenly a figure appears in response to the waiting, a figure that carries her inside of the story that she had wanted: the White Rabbit with its waistcoat and white kid gloves complaining because it shall be late. This is a swerve with respect to a literature for children that is misleadingly childlike. This swerve happens quickly, by way of an automatism of the response, like a swerve of potential in open unbound intensities. And it is the speed of Alice's response, or of her desire to follow the rabbit, that leads to the question: what does this mean? Useless to theorize the occurrence, to doggedly ask what it means, what sense does it have: 'when she thought it over afterwards, it occurred to her that she ought to have wondered at this, but at the time it all seemed quite natural'.

Desire is the waiting for occurrence.

The figure is the trace that follows us whenever we fall into an occurrence. Falling into an occurrence is like getting lost in a hole whose path is unknown. Social upheavals produce occurrences, swerves of intensity, and in so doing respond to the waiting for occurrences. And yet Alice's movement is an expected/unexpected event, the inconceivable occurrence, that takes the honest and modest Lewis Carroll unawares, putting him on the trail of a White Rabbit that the Victorian age had not yet met.

Falling into an occurrence is like getting lost in a hole whose path is unknown.

The first mechanical junction in Alice's adventures is an automatism, like a railway junction. It produces an intensity and a swerve of intensity, a new way of wandering with one's head. The parts of the mechanical junction are: 1) the waiting for occurrence, 2) the appearance of the figure to follow, 3) the movement of falling/befalling. Or: the waiting for a figural story (dreams are pure figural thought), the appearance of the White Rabbit, the falling into the hole as a falling into occurrence.

Later Alice wants to pass through the little door that leads to the garden, hoping to shrink as if she were a collapsible telescope. Once more the desire for an occurrence; then a response to the waiting: a small bottle appears with the words 'DRINK ME'; and there follows another falling/befalling: Alice shrinks as she had wanted. There is no occurrence without the desire for something to happen, without the joy of following the trail of a figure, and without an opening into a system of as-yet unexpected possibilities. In this sense the figure of falling works as a figure or metaphor of comprehension, that is, of under-standing, delving into. Here there arises a task larger than us, beyond us: to become helpless, small, insignificant, stupid/strange/alien, or to lose the advantage of 'the right size' (of Alice).

The ensuing adventures of Alice revolve around the instability caused by having lost the right size, with fluctuations towards the two extremes: becoming too small or too large. Too small: a powerless body not tall enough to reach the height of the little table on which there rests the key to her desires. Too large: a grotesque body, ill-suited to manoeuvring through the house into which she has chanced (chapter IV), or mistaken for a serpent by the haughty Pigeon trying to protect her nest.

The fall into the low and insignificant is the fall into the instability of desire, into the perpetual instability of 'how you feel'. Adult discourse follows the equation: desires = childish whims = random temptations = things lacking importance and therefore insignificant. Desires are fragmented longings not reassembled according to a dominant path that leads to the paranoia of everything. They are scattered automatisms, chaotic, pushed and veering off, always too weak or too strong in relation to an end. For this there is always a precarious finalization of desires. That which matters in desires is the swerve of intensity that they produce in relation to an initial reality. Towards what? Where? 'Which Way?' asks Alice after eating the very small cake. Yet it doesn't matter whether she becomes small or large. It is the automatism that in generating a swerve brings us joy, Alice's real scoop.

In these processes the ideal of a harmonious body is lost along the way, turning into a symbol of power. It is as if there were a basic conflict between the swerving of desires and the symbolism of power and of harmonious beauty. Those who have visited the palace of Queen Victoria on the Island of Wight will better understand this conflict, seeing the type of art and furnishings preferred by the queen. It is a world in which

> The fall into desires is the fall into the low and insignificant.

> Desires are scattered automatisms, chaotic, pushed and veering off, always too weak or too strong in relation to an end.

the instability of desires does not exist. Everything is dominated by 'as one should', including art. Everything of the age is dominated by the symbology of all that is stable, strong, balanced, without uncertainties of 'how we feel'. The age of steel: trains, steamships, grand bridges, the Crystal Palace, machines of every sort, famous Victorian engineering, and above all the great industries that came to dominate the careening of class struggles.

Images of power are common in newspapers and other publications of the time covering the new industrial cities experiencing exponential growth: Manchester, symbol of a new era, Leeds, Birmingham, Sheffield. One catches the sense that the power of these changes is capable of creating a new city of God, inspired by the austere Victorian figures of 'as one should', such as the men behind the Crystal Palace (1851), exponents of the power of human labour such as Samuel Smiles, believers in reforms such as John Bright, or advocates of the formative power of public schools such as Thomas Hughes. Society is viewed as an enormous mechanism that unstumblingly moves down the road of infinite progress. Alice is off to the side of all this, a body without power.

Desires render the body powerless: too big or too little, discordant, lacking the ascendent harmony of the symbol of power reclaimed by the middle classes. In Alice's becoming too big there is a fragmenting of the body in discrete parts: overly long neck, feet that move on their own. With her long neck Alice is mistaken for a serpent. In becoming small an animalization takes place (children are animals) – a symmetric inverse of becoming big and adult, in which there is at work a humanization of the body towards a harmonious model, the harmonious perfection of the human being. The model of the harmonious body is based on Greek statuary, traces of which remerge in the myriad copies collected by Queen Victoria, in the ideals of the middle classes, in eighteenth-century education, in pre-Nazi eugenics, in so-called orthopaedics ('the art of correcting and preventing deformities in children's bodies'), and in the industry of making mechanical devices for straightening both the bodies and heads of children. *Alice* is not born as a book for good children.

Carroll's illustrations in the first manuscript of *Alice* resemble Lear's little figures, most of all Alice when she is too small, reduced to head and feet, and also when she is too big, having grown into a kind of tree trunk with a head at the top. But these caricatural tendencies, like an escape from the ideal of the harmonious body, and from the 'as one should', are even more evident in the secondary figures, for example those illustrating the songs of Father William: unbalanced and discordant, like those of Lear's characters, hyperbolic anglicisms, deformed bodies.

Desires render the body powerless, discordant, lacking the ascendent harmony of the symbol of power.

Instead, Tenniel's illustrations, which more commonly come to mind, set Alice's gestures in harmonic theatrical poses: Alice with slight gestures of surprise, curiosity, fear; the entire theatrical farce of human feelings rendered familiar and recognizable. Tenniel's illustrations stand in contrast to the discordant and unbalanced movements of the desires that animate Alice.

Note

1 'Sull'epoca di questo libro' e 'Alice e l'avvenimento ...' ('On the era of this book' and 'Alice and the occurrence ...'), *Alice disambientata: Materiali collettivi (su Alice) per un manuale di sopravvivenza* (Florence: Le Lettere, [1978] 2007), 5–11, 66–72.

11
'Soft objects' ('Oggetti soffici', 1979)

At a certain time in my life, I read and reread in a state of relative aston-ishment these statements by Claes Oldenburg, copied below for your information:

> I am for an art that is political-erotical-mystical, that does something other than sit on its ass in a museum …

> I am for the art that a kid licks, after peeling away the wrapper …

> I am for art that flaps like a flag, or helps blow noses, like a hand-kerchief …

> am for art that is smoked, like a cigarette, that smells, like a pair of shoes …

> I am for art that flaps like a flag, or helps blow noses, like a hand-kerchief …

> I am for art that is put on and taken off, like pants, which develops holes, like socks, which is eaten, like a piece of pie, or abandoned which great contempt, like a piece of shit …

> I am for an art that tells you the time of day, or where such and such a street is …

> I am for the art of underwear and the art of taxicabs. I am for the art of ice-cream cones dropped on concrete. I am for the majestic art of dog-turds, rising like cathedrals …

> I am for the art of bar-babble, tooth-picking, beer-drinking, egg-salting, insulting. I am for the art of falling off a barstool …

I am for the blinking arts, lighting up the night. I am for art falling, splashing, wiggling, jumping, going on and off …

I am for the white art of refrigerators and their muscular openings and closings …

I am for the art of rust and mold. I am for the art of hearts, funeral hearts or sweetheart full of nougat …

I am for the art of things lost or thrown away, coming home from school. I am for the art of cock-and-ball trees and flying cows and the noise of rectangles and squares. I am for the art of crayons and weak gray pencil-lead, and grainy wash and sticky oil paint, and the art of windshield wipers and the art of the finger on a cold window, on dusty steel or in the bubbles on the sides of a bathtub …

I am for an art that is combed down, that is hung from each ear, that is laid on the lips under the eyes, that is shaved from the legs, that is brushed on the teeth, that is fixed on the thighs, that is slipped on the foot …[1]

In my contemplative mania I contemplated these statements, finding in them many utopic promises that had nothing to do with utopic Art – because the statements are only a list of ordinary objects, gestures, occurrences and uses, transformed into a list of forms of art. This involves such a high level of attention for all the ordinary objects and gestures and uses with which we come into daily contact that it leads one to believe that the utopic promise might only be that of absolute ordinariness.

This is great minor petty bourgeois art. Hardly the great major poetic Art of all humanity, which was all just a farce to give the rich something to talk about. These are the ordinary arts of those who are no longer within or outside fervid utopias, fervid politics, and who know not what to do with Art specialized in saying extraordinary things. It is the art of the age of fluctuating currencies, of fluctuating philosophies, of politics that are as transferable as currencies according to an exchange rate no longer guaranteed by any golden reserve. Art after Fort Knox; but this has already been happening for some time.

I would that you take note of the type of adhesion that these minor arts imply. Not the enthusiasm of those who say 'Great! Wonderful! Super!' and not the enthusiasm of those who proclaim, backed up by some field of study, 'It's interesting because …'. These are phony enthusiasms because they are judging, approving, sanctioning; they are the enthusiasms of those interested in something because it is a part of their role.

I mean another enthusiasm, not judging, not approving, not sanctioning, simply accumulative, everything in the exteriority of the most ordinary gestures, repeated without qualms, without critical judgements.

The art of the petty bourgeois is not that demystifying and critical stuff that noble modern Art should always be; because, to believe in demystification and in criticism, one must be inside a fervid utopia, a fervid political world, and spin about like a top thinking that your interests in life are right and sensible.

Cold utopias are the ones necessary for survival because they involve you in effects, depending on choice and chance. Fervid politics engage the head, never leaving your head empty, forcing you to always repeat the exact same message, according to the programme: struggle, commitment, democracy, participation, chauvinism, marginalization, movement, workers, socialism.

Laidback enthusiasms with little to proclaim. Think of the soft dissonances of cool jazz; the barely perceptible sharp notes; methods of engaging with effects, but barely hinted at, escaping on half-notes. The rhythm section is no longer separate but part of the collaborative search for strange coincidences; the feeling is of finding pleasing things by chance.

This is to say that the objects, gestures or occurrences that grab and engage me have nothing special or unique about them: they are out there in the world and serve what they serve; they are not metaphors of anything, mean nothing particularly interesting, dear or rare; we are unable to make symbols out of them; they simply have the virtue of existing somewhere and having some sort of effect on us.

The evaluative criteria of your enthusiasms are thus reduced to the reaction 'I like/I don't like', without needing to add illuminating explanations, to convince anyone that your interests in life are correct and well founded. 'I like/I don't like' is an evaluative form that doesn't allow replies, avoids the process of aligning oneself with tastes, of searching for the right reasons, of consulting with experts so that they can tell you what 'proper taste' is.

One of the philosophic matters circulating in recent years is that modern humanity has become impoverished in experience; this experience of the world has become so paltry that any attempt to communicate it as constituting some meaningful knowledge of the world can only be seen as an act of naïveté. This is true not only because in the quantifiable world experience has nothing special about it, even in special situations, but also because it is not a form of officially sanctioned knowledge. In the quantifiable world Ulysses becomes an average Joe, maybe a bit paranoid.

Most of the information about the world that common modern mortals accumulate during their existence comes in mediated forms by way of newspapers, books and various versions of the mass media. Fragments of daily routines, carefully blended with overheard talk and a certain number of futile warnings, constitute their experience, which cannot be communicated as a form of knowledge, but only palaver. We cannot recount our own lives if not in the stale and trivializing mode of chatting; those who take their lives as something truly exemplary, to offer up to others as a form of education, have missed the punchline. Modern humanity knows that experience teaches nothing; for this reason, we are all on par, regardless of what a given person might have done.

Knowledge, from the beginnings of the modern world, is an entirely different thing: science, which distances itself from the uncertainties, biases and randomness of talk. To communicate knowledge, I must pay heed to a model from which are expelled all the futilities, illusions, deficiencies of 'I like/I don't like', most of all those deceptive things – the sensations of the subject. I cannot invent a sociology of urban behaviours wandering around a city; at most I can produce some talk about my sensations, the traces that bind me to certain things in the everyday. To communicate knowledge, I must collect a certain number of objective facts that surpass the possibilities of direct experience and find a way of assembling them while abstracting my subjective sensations and traces. This is the way of science, the only authoritative basis that we are still willing to understand.

There are many things to say about this split between knowledge and talk. The matter that interests me the most, however, is that in this world of vast numbers and equivalent subjects there is no room for a connoisseur of lived experience, only an authority on the knowledge of data: the scientist, the expert.

Indeed, our sense of reality is dominated by experts; there can be no evaluative criteria, social selection, supposition of truth, without the intervention of experts. But the fact is that the reaction 'I like/I don't like', with which I loosely orient myself in plying the myriad inputs of the external world, is exactly what is missing from the expert. It is a question of taste, as they say.

I don't remember any longer who said this: taste, in its variability, is the main role of the subject, that which renders it always different, never identical to another. As Roland Barthes said, the subject is neither describable nor bounded, because it is based on an infinite accumulation of 'I like/I don't like'.

For long there existed an amusing outgrowth of philosophy, termed aesthetic, tasked with introducing even in these regards some guiding principles with which to explain to common mortals what should be pleasing to them and on the other hand what was not deserving of their attention. In retrospect, however, it becomes evident that these guiding principles vary depending on historical context. We thus pass from evaluative aesthetic criteria to historical ones; 'proper taste' (neoclassic canon) is replaced by the criterion of appropriateness to the historical moment, according to an 'innovative/non-innovative' paradigm.

But innovative with regard to what? The 'historical moment' is a pure abstraction, a mode of affixing an incalculable molecular transition: an infinite passage of effects and heterogeneous things, astonishing occurrences, and everyday situations, from which we extract a selection of exemplary events, much as do the newspapers every morning, so that we have something to talk about. It is only in relationship to the assumed exemplarity of certain events that one can speak of historic progression; the evaluative criteria of the expert become a game of separating exemplary events from unexemplary ones.

Something progressed would be something placed on a line of development that then 'remains' there as a monument for centuries. There is no possibility for historical selection without this idea of the exemplary monument that 'remains', unbending and unbreakable, in the midst of infinite anonymous occurrences.

Moreover: to be exemplary means to teach, to serve as an exemplum; and an experience that teaches becomes knowledge. And here is the keen idea with which they trick you, especially in left-wing regimes.

The modern routine, piddling and trivial as it is, the incompleteness of the signs that bind us to the real, the randomness of every expression and passion, the variability of every subject, in short, all that which communicates, to modern humanity, that 'experience does not teach', by means of the trick of historical appraisal, becomes once again knowledge, instruction, outstanding example. In this way someone can once again believe it possible to fob off their own life ('life!') as something meaningful and edifying. Once again someone pulls in Art as the solution to the banality of the minor arts, hardly exemplary, hardly edifying, that we all daily practise in our anonymous routines.

Over this there weighs the obsession with steel, of what is tough and durable, of non-perishable experience, of what 'remains' and does not fade away. Think of the great iron constructions of the late nineteenth century, symbols of a non-perishability created by men, or rather experts, not by God; neoclassic non-perishability is a product of nature, whose monuments also include Homer and Raphael; nineteenth-century non-perishability is always based on engineering, creations of experts in a reality dominated by experts.

What happens if instead, as in the case of Oldenburg, randomness and perishability are exalted, things that can be consumed and that are soft rather than hard? If privileged objects are no longer those destined, by high decree, to end up in the museums of historic memory, but those that individuals in their daily experiences consume in random corporeal encounters?

Why haven't aesthetics and adjudicatory criticism ever extended their superintendence over food? Have they instead always flaunted an anti-gastronomic rancour?

It is because the superintendence (whether neoclassic or engineering) of food must eliminate the moment of consumption, that is, of taste as a flavour that touches the tongue for a moment before the food is swallowed, being consumed together with the food; the superintendence must consider hard objects – not consumable ones – eternal in their historical standing.

Food, colourful ice cream that I like to lick because of its colours, all this is mere consumption. The criterion 'I like/I don't like' can be applied to what is consumable, what I want or don't want to consume, but not things in the distance I can only contemplate. The subject of experience does nothing else, for the entirety of the day, but consume tastes, consume loves, the taste of eating or making or touching something, of wandering and getting lost, of going to the cinema, drinking, always smoking, etc. To the odious philosophizers who still differentiate an 'authentic' experience from an 'inauthentic' one, it must be said that experience is not something that you have or give, like knowledge; it is the consumption of an object found or a gesture made, and nothing remains, as on your tongue after having eaten a desert. For this reason, we are all equal subjects with respect to experience, because experience truly does not teach but consumes us and does not remain as a patrimony to administer.

For example: the critic of consumer society, who often *turns* to Art or some other fervid utopia such as salvation, or some other ideology of the eternal, of non-perishability, of anti-consumerism, of the experiences that we carry around. But are not critics always this: the opposite of the taste of consuming things?

I like all things that are dated, that carry the clear sign of the moment and the place in which they came into the world, all things that are too evident and obvious, with nothing to hide their randomness, that are not made to last centuries but to be immediately used; I like pies because they never last very long; I like old trench coats (the ones worn by Humphrey Bogart) because they are a photograph of the past.

And so of course I like Öyvind Fahlström's painted simulations of Krazy Kat cartoons, Warhol's silkscreens of Elvis Presley, George Segal's plaster statues playing pinball, but most of all (most of all) Claes Oldenburg's pies, porkchops, hotdogs, hamburgers and ice cream cones, made of plaster or canvas but full of the talk of food, bringing to mind the sensations and signs, the spectacle of eating that food. I find one authorized artistic superintendent (Giulio Carlo Argan) that has it in mind to ruin the flavour of this food for me in an absurd fashion. I quote:

> Oldenburg identifies *consumer society* with the most common type of consumption, food: it is implicit that *mass culture* too is a sort of food. For Jasper Johns the most identifiable sign of American collective identity is the US flag with its stars and stripes, and for Oldenburg it is industrialized and standardized American food: the hamburgers, hotdogs and ice cream cones that are daily produced in enormous quantities, like fuel feeding engines, the digestive tracts of millions of Americans. The *models* are not even the actual foods, but their colourful images in advertisements: it is clear that in *consumer society* first comes the image in an advertisement and then the thing. What is the meaning of this process? It can be ruled out that with his gaudily painted plaster and papier-mâché foods Oldenburg's intention is to celebrate the *humble values* of existence: the banquette to which we are invited is clearly a *banquette of nausea*. It can also be ruled out that those enormous and repellent foods can be viewed as symbolic of society: if anything, they are reversed personifications, depersonifications, as if to say that in consumer society, being autophagous, people are a sort of consumable good, such as food.[2]

I would like to point out how the superintendent is unable in any way to take the things for what they are, for their flavour. That is, he feels compelled to understand the things for signs of other things, as parts of a code. And so, when he sees something, he does not allow himself to be carried away by its effect; his power lies in hurriedly consulting the code and then explaining it to us. In the quoted passage note all the italicized words: these are the key terms of the code he has consulted and with which he explains the matter to us, as an expert, without ever allowing his head to air out.

Consultation of the code will lead neither to contact nor participation with the taste of the thing, because if this were the case, one would have to recognize something positive in participation, the consumption of taste (taste is something that is consumed). But the positivity of consumption is exactly what negates the permanence of the 'hard' artistic object that is not consumable: if it were consumable, it would not be Art-Monument-Example-Explanation, and it would not be allowed a place in the Eternal Museum.

The only solution is to find at all costs the negativity of the object: the object must negate the taste of its consumption, it must be by definition 'critical' towards that which it represents, it must be demystifying, *ollallà*, negator, negative, not expressing a taste but a distaste.

And so, to summarize: Oldenburg's foods represent mass culture, which represents the falsification of taste in advertising that leads one not to the taste but to the distaste of the thing, which is a negative judgement of the thing. As was the intention to demonstrate, signed: the Superintendent.

Oldenburg's canvas hamburgers, and to an even greater extent his colourful ice cream cones, bring to my mind the relationship that I have with real foods. These foods are ostentatious signs of abundance and of artificial colours, as found for example in New York; they are also a transient observation of exteriority, an enchantment of the fake encountered in storefront displays and commercials. In this regard, only a strange censorial process allows me to distinguish between true and false, and to transform taste into distaste; the censorial process consists of overlooking the connection to exteriority that these objects imply.

If you have tried to savour a truly artistic and super-colourful ice cream sundae, you will understand that the enchantment of the object originates in the zone of illusion that radiates out from its colours, form, flavour. The zone of illusion is one of transitional objects, or the zone of experience (according to Winnicott) 'between the thumb and the teddy bear, between the oral erotism and true object-relationship'. In short, the zone of taste, of painted lips, of colourful ice cream, that is no longer good inasmuch as it is coloured, but because it functions as a transition between the eroticism of my lips and the exteriority through which I reach it; an empty zone in which I situate and consume the taste.

Beginning with several studies by Marcel Mauss, attention was given to certain empty receptacles without meaning, but fillable with almost any meaning, as for example the empty words 'thing', 'stuff', or in French 'truc', 'machin', etc. The zone of taste, of the transitional object, is an empty receptacle, stuff that connects you to the external world.

In mulling over these matters, I think it becomes clear why the experts tend to disregard the intermediary connections with external reality that objects such as Oldenburg's inscribe. I believe that this is because the nominal eroticism of consuming ice cream is something traditionally neither admissible nor celebratory – because petty bourgeois eroticism consists entirely of extraordinary regressions, regressions to magical infantile zones at the very margins of our bodies, to spaces that appeal directly to the senses. All these regressions imply the petty bourgeois who lack collective rooting and involvement in fervid utopias, deprived of abstractions: 'sensual and contorted'. It is relatively clear that the magical zones of petty bourgeois *mana* are concerned almost entirely with the body and with connections with the external world – that is, with routines both anonymous and little edifying that constitute the enacting of their sensuality.

A transitional object (for example Linus's blanket that he drags around everywhere) has this feature: to fill the gap between the body and the external world, to create an illusory void that is then filled in with 'I like/I don't like' by way of activities such as touching, sucking, watching, etc. Empty space that is endlessly filled by things that carry me away, that cause me to rave or hallucinate, familiar things seen a thousand times that all the same enchant me, like something randomly encountered, stuff that grabs your attention, a place without an aura, Minnie and Moskowitz's mystic hotdogs and cows that fly in the air.

Porous objects that absorb my eroticism but don't represent or reflect it; soft objects that I penetrate savouring their exteriority with borrowed lips and eyes.

And the same holds for Oldenburg's *Soft Typewriters*, soft technological objects with a soft design, signalling the end of hard nineteenth-century steel typewriters.

Observation: Winnicott's discovery of transitional objects can be compared to the discovery of the curvature of space, of material that adapts to the space it penetrates, of space that adapts to material by folding around it as it expands. As in Einstein, but here the space is subjective.

It is not so much a question of choosing between major Arts and minor arts, when the soft transitional objects (whether Linus's blanket, a doll, or little manipulable gadget) are manifestly minor, entangled with movements of the body as it adapts to the spaces of ordinary exteriority; all of Oldenburg's statements cited at the beginning are a list of these minor arts; you can reread them.

Objects penetrated by exteriority that bridge the gap between the inner and outer; bodies that are open because they are soft, manipulable or adaptable to being penetrated: like a finger in foam that enters entirely without tearing anything.

Well, eroticism is the connection and only connection that I have with this Einsteinian-routine-Winnicottian space, in which I adapt my body through objects and related minor arts.

All petty bourgeois cosmology can be boiled down to the sensuality of the body, not of observation or contemplation. And it can be deduced that the art of the body is made of soft objects.

Ways of recognizing soft objects if you happen upon them while out and about: they are not dense like monuments, they always seem incomplete in some way, they look a bit like Peter Blake's pub doors or Robert Rauschenberg's printed rags, they are always capable of containing other things inside of themselves, tram tickets, nativity scene statuettes, car company logos.

Soft objects are for the most part *assemblages* of familiar objects, gathered together without any formal or aesthetic homogenizing criteria, but according to the adaptive relationship of my body with the external world – with the places I have crossed, with the swerves with which I wander, the bars I have frequented, the tags that have remained attached to my suitcase.

Soft objects are for the most part made of remains, the remains of devastated cultures, the remains of expired situations, the remains of discourses that I have never managed to finish, the remains of a love that left its traces behind, the remains of people that I have known.

The soft object can be compared to a sponge: it absorbs expressivity but does not reemit it. For this reason it is always cool, like 1950s jazz. Its effects of absorption are soft, like a Lou Reed song that absorbs your bad mood and redirects it, scatters it, but does not bring it back with judgmental undertones.

The soft object absorbs and dissolves your sorting codes (old/modern, reactionary/progressive, well-made/ill-made, unclear/comprehensible) instead of spitting them out again fixed in abstract categories, in selections that are not based on taste but on judgement (note: taste is that of savouring, sucking, touching, looking at, entering things; the aesthetic taste of contemplating from a distance is a taste of looking and nothing else; when I say 'aesthetic' I mean a manner of looking constituted as a form of judgement).

The soft object tends to focus on effects not judgements, on the reaction 'I like/I don't like'. This is not to say that this reaction lacks sorting codes; it is that here the original code, based on the habits of my body, fades in meaning, remaining a residual effect, a response that is automatic yet full of contradictory interferences. The soft object is entirely contradictory.

It is the hard objects, monumental and lacking porosity, put somewhere to be contemplated, to train your manner of looking, that force your sorting and selecting codes to confirm the categories and suppositions of truth.

The most renowned theorist of hard objects (also the least daft, the most skilled, the most attentive to the minor arts) is perhaps Bertolt Brecht. His problem is that the theatrical object is not something edible but rather a mirror that instead reemits to us our codes of reality. His actors must not express but show character, or in other words, they must not play on the enchantment of the effect, but on the reduction of the effect – not on the emptiness of the zone of illusion, but on the web of sorting and selecting codes. What we must activate when faced by these theatrical objects is not so much sensuality but observation; everything becomes a lesson, a message, an example.

That all of this would shift, from the narrow confines of the experts, from the networks directed by superintendents, to a general practice, to a matter of habit; that at a certain point many people were to begin trading and collecting objects of this sort; that *assemblages* of familiar objects, collections of postcards, poems about ordinary minor arts, drapes made of old fabric, myriad recycled scraps, old jackets, new carnivals, lost passions, pre-war actors, punk outfits, colourful glasses, were to amass in a continuous collage, spaces that are never-circumscribed, spectacles that tempt you to join in, with a widespread sense of a new socialized taste: all this can be traced to the spread of what is known as mass culture.

The superintendents always felt compelled to find fault with mass culture, perhaps because they were neoclassic. However, all this by now has become the production of reality in a general sense (not the work of 'artists', 'writers', etc.). Cultural goods have proliferated in a chain reaction that the critics of artistic goods were unable to predict.

On the other hand these critics have always been a bit behind with respect to goods: this is inevitable, given their problem of contemplating from a distance, instead of using and consuming the objects that they encounter in the world. The critic cannot be but a mobile cadaver since they cling to an absurd privilege: the privilege of not being a member of the masses.

Goods are concrete remnants of a necessarily abstract relationship with the world; they are the connection between my shell and externality, like food, sex and affectivity. But because by now there is no way of distinguishing things from one another, it is also useless to argue that food, sex and affectivity are a trap, in the world of goods. They are what they are; the trap is believing that you can tell the true from the false.

Notes

1   Claes Oldenburg, 'I Am For ...', in *Environments, Situations, Spaces* (New York: Martha Jackson Gallery, 1961); reprinted in an expanded version in Claes Oldenburg and Emmett Williams, *Store Days: Documents from The Store (1961) and Ray Gun Theatre (1962)* (New York: Something Else Press, 1967), 39–42.
2   Giulio Carlo Argan, *L'Arte moderna 1770–1970* (Milan: Sansoni, [1970] 2002), 280–1.

12
'Adventure at the end of the twentieth century' ('L'avventura verso la fine del XX secolo', 1982)

From a conversation with Luca Torrealta and Mario Zanzani in October, 1982. Zanzani and Torrealta asked Celati about had most inspired him to write, the relationships between adventure, experience and history in writing, and if Celati's various travels, such as those in the United States, were related to his interest in adventure.

Adventure books are what first drove me to write. At university I immersed myself in eighteenth-century English novels. I also had an intense passion for Stendhal's *The Charterhouse of Parma*, a novel of Italian adventures written in French. To find something adventurous in Italian literature takes going back to the wonders of Carlo Collodi's *Pinocchio*, or to the first part of Ippolito Nievo's *Confessioni d'un italiano* (*Confessions of an Italian*), or back even further to Ariosto's *Orlando Furioso* and other chivalric poems of its era, one without comparison in European literature.

In various mythological traditions there exists the figure of the trickster, a sort of demigod capable of nearly unimaginable jokes and scams. And yet tricksters are always incomprehensible, with their actions never corresponding to clearly defined desires, a bit like children, who, lacking precise ideas regarding socially acceptable objects, play with whatever they find at hand. This is adventure. Adventure can also arise from states of desperation, when everything desirable collapses around us, bringing us to the edge of something unrelated to our usual needs, wants or dreams. Such desperation provides us with the means to escape the status quo and is dependent on the ability or possibility of putting ourselves in hopeless situations. As Walter Benjamin wrote in his essay on Goethe's *Elective Affinities*, 'Only for the sake of the hopeless ones have we been given hope.'[1]

Adventure stories blur historical and geographical facts, rendering them fluid and indeterminate. Robert Louis Stevenson's Scotland, for instance, in books such as *Master of Ballantrae, Kidnapped* and *Catriona*, is a land made timeless by how it is evoked, situated in an indeterminate *illo tempore* at the margins of History. Another example: Conrad. His books always seem to be situated in unrecognizable eras and concerned with abstract journeys, because we are always at the end of the world, a world that will never be fully explored. And Kurtz in *Heart of Darkness*, so immersed in historical coordinates, surrounded severed heads on poles, is a vision of prehistory.

In Conrad's travel journals there are references to a precise period of European colonialism, but the book based on them promptly heads off in a different direction. At the beginning is a discussion of the maps of Africa with all the names covering the 'heart of darkness', but then comes an account of the ultimate inscrutability of Africa and the places marked on the maps. Geography assigns placenames to maps, causing us to think that we should know places because we know their names, with the presumption that everything is knowable, everything already indexed in our historical consciousnesses, desires and habits. But adventure can only be born out of a vision that has obliterated History and its facts and figures.

Adventure is also the story of a cycle of experience, such as Buck's story in *The Call of the Wild*. Jack London sees this cycle as something connecting us to human prehistory. I have always liked this book and long wanted to translate it. At times I felt it had much in common with Kafka, in that there is always something reminiscent of human prehistory, or an isolated community in difficult settings, of various adventure stories in which explorers end up in timeless places.

When I was young, I felt the desire to travel to America like a call of adventure. The United States had on me the effect of an apprenticeship. I carefully observed my American friends, studying their ways of dealing with money, possessions, work, family and friendships. They seemed more structured than me. When I arrived for the first time in America, it was the beginning of the 1970s and I went to live in a large wooden house whose door was always open. A key to lock it didn't exist. That sense of certitude that no one would come to rob us while we were away (during vacations no one at all stayed there) went a bit to my head. It seemed the dream of an edenic space, for me entirely new. The place where I lived, Ithaca, New York, is an area of five finger-shaped lakes, with thick woods at the foot of the hill on which stands the Cornell University campus. In the evenings I would often walk down towards the lakes and eat at a farmhouse, together with others like me, discovering food very different from what I was accustomed. It was country food, from old frontier communities, that here continued to be the only form of eating.

It was food made mainly from the garden, old recipes, the triumph of boiled beans, homemade bread, every so often beef stew, but only for special occasions. That food went together with other aspects of country life, far from the city: such as the messy farmyards, the worn-out clothes, the old and simple furniture, the 1950s cars and pickups, the rough utility poles with dangling wires that seemed even older. I observed these traces of the past that lingered in areas of the countryside, in upstate New York, Connecticut and Massachusetts, and also in the south, in the Mississippi Delta. At a certain point I concluded that the US was a country more stuck in time, infinitely more conservative than Europe, more tied to a patriarchal past.

Those who ate in that farmhouse paid a few dollars, without knowing what they would eat, and were obligated to wash the dishes and clean the floor. The head of the family looked people over as they arrived and didn't let everyone in. Those whom he didn't like were sent packing without a word. He couldn't stand so-called hippies or what he considered their ilk. Here I witnessed old ways of life. Everything had the taste of things passed down, and everyone carried themselves with a certain reserve. After three months of eating there I had exchanged all but two or three words with the head of the family. The phrases he spoke required neither response nor explanation, but rather implied the certainty of his very words, according to the dictum, 'I am what I say', a patriarchal dictum of those who feel absolutely in the right.

Yes, it was a period of great change, but for me difficult to make sense of. Between that farmhouse and the university campus on the hill there were just a few miles, but the path offered spectacles that would have incredibly bothered the farm patriarch. Things heated up in the spring, with at least half the student body joining together, going around barefoot, shirtless, or in bras. Along the road that led from the hill down to the wooden house where I lived, many bars and restaurants displayed signs that forbid entrance to anyone not wearing shirts or shoes. Those signs summed up the contrast between the old patriarchalism and the new modes of behaviour arising in the acropolises of knowledge, such as the Cornell campus where I had arrived. Here I witnessed the staging of an edenic state open to everyone. Students put on display an extreme independence of the individual that took various very theatrical forms. I saw a type of exposition of the self, of one's own personality, then becoming the style of new forms of spectacle. I remember my first rock concerts: the riotous exhibitions of eroticism, a sign of the liberation of the individual. At these concerts many people went around half-naked or made love in tents.

Was the countercultural sexual revolution the end of patriarchalism? No. I think that American patriarchalism has never died. From Martin Luther King's assassination to those of Jack Kennedy and Bob Kennedy, it has never stopped being a densely ultraconservative and paranoid force – the same that attacked unions in the 1930s and has hung or burned African Americans up to recent times. It was a misunderstanding to believe that the countercultural movements would liberate us from all this.

Things were very different in 1979 when I went back to the US and visited some old friends with whom I had lived in close fellowship. One in particular, whom I saw in New York, seemed unrecognizable. What had happened to the austere anti-bourgeois Lacanian thinker? Careerist books were displayed around his apartment, opened to show the title and author's name (his own). In only a few years a colossal change had occurred in American life. The new epoch had arrived of the categorical imperative 'Smile!' It was as if the old forms of behaviour had collapsed, the reserved ways of life and muted display of feelings common in the countryside. The Vietnam War had been the deciding factor, with soldiers who could burn down an entire village in minutes, Nixon caught on tape saying to Henry Kissinger 'We'll bomb the bastards off the earth' (referring to the Vietnamese), and other soldiers, after outings to the Napalmed countryside, left not knowing what to do, apart from taking drugs, playing baseball, or looking at porno magazines. And meanwhile the dollar weakened against the value of gold, leading to a long-term decline in the US economy. At the same time, however, the fascination with wealth and excess grew, European-style, surrounded by images of new cars, fancy houses, smiles, and African Americans beaten by the police. In poor black neighbourhoods from Harlem to South Chicago, houses were burned, and piles of garbage grew higher and higher as officials looked on. In 1979 I visited Mark Twain's hometown, near St Louis where *The Adventures of Tom Sawyer and Huckleberry Finn* was set; it was there that it seemed to me that America with all its stories was done for. I would read new novels and toss them aside almost at once. Every place was by now the same as the next and in this sense without recourse.

From 1970 to 1971 I would sometimes travel on Fridays with a friend from Ithaca to New Jersey to stay at his parents' house; on Saturday mornings all the weekend ceremonies were staged in front of me. There for the first time I noticed a sense of unreality in American social life, as if everything were artificial. In those suburban habits and gestures there lacked an underlying context, with the resulting sense that everything around me hung on framework for a life without a past. The houses seemed built of clichés and wealth behind which were visible the signs of an uprooting. Not the uprooting of those forced to abandon their homelands due to invasion by a more powerful group, but the uprooting of the newly wealthy or of social classes that move to new neighbourhoods because they want to appear as if they were newly wealthy. This is now becoming a widespread model, based on the conviction of the autonomy of the individual with respect to the environment: the conviction that, thanks to money, one can live anywhere, without underlying contexts, without traditions. There is a film by Peter Bogdanovich, *The Last Picture Show*, that recounts the end of two older ways of country life. End of the adventure. Now perhaps there remains only the adventure of micro-histories, such as those to which Carlo Ginzburg has dedicated himself: something miniscule, overlooked by Grand Monumental History.

It is in Ginzburg's 1976 book *Il formaggio e i vermi* (*The Cheese and the Worms*) that the idea of micro-histories emerges most clearly. In recent books and films there is evident the related discovery of the murky limbo in which most people have led their lives. Not the grand schemes to rid the world of Evil, but a dimension of life in which there are only ordinary details. Yes, from this everyday limbo comes the idea that language and experience are two things ever more distant from one another, mutually untranslatable. Experience is absorbed by the clichés with which we talk about it, abolished or drained by topical chatter. This is the fog of words within which we live. Amidst the triumph of the topical, there are some today demonstrating the necessity of starting over, beginning from something that has been emptied in us.

In recent narratives there seem to be characters who are no longer psychological types or symbolic figures, but 'no one'. And yet we attentively follow them because they are also 'everyone', the figure of the ordinary human in the walk of life. The adventures of ordinary humans are all micro-histories that play out in dimensions to which no one pays much attention because they are not sensational. It is the commonplace of life that comes to us. And it is this that we find in the work of new directors, writers and artists who do not chase after the triumphal chariot of topicality.

But the critical point is this: we no longer believe in definite and categorizable feelings, such as those in popular novels. Contemporary narration has abandoned interiority as the last homeland of humanity.

It seems to me that this mode of perception is particularly evident in the work of Werner Herzog. In his films there is the sense of a radical human uncertainty, of an uncontrollable Evil. The series of films, *Kaspar Houser*, *Aguirre*, *Stroszek* and *Nosferatu*, end with a vision of an unstoppable spread of Evil, after the display of Klaus Kinsky as a vampire who seems dazed by the blood of the girl. Hence evil, vampirism, appear as creaturely constants, from the origin of time, from the foundations of humanity. At the end there emerges the idea of an Evil as something that binds us all from the depths of time. *Nosferatu*, like *Kaspar Hauser* and other films by Herzog, pull the flag of progressive optimism down from its flagpole. And this is where we find ourselves, in a world dominated by topicality, in which people are no longer able to believe that we have only small islands of knowledge to which to cling. It is as if we were by now all at the mercy of our own representations, of our illusory progressivism, than the actual dangers hanging over us: catastrophes, wars, political depravations.

Note

1 Quoted in Hannah Arendt, introduction to *Illuminations: Essays and Reflections*, by Walter Benjamin, ed. Hannah Arendt, trans. Harry Zohn (New York: Schocken Books, 1969), 17.

Figure 12.1 Gianni Celati, 1979. Reprinted by permission of Gillian Haley.

13
'Fictions to believe in: an example' ('Finzioni a cui credere, un esempio', 1984)

Luigi Ghirri lives in a white house in Formigine, a small town not far from Modena.[1] Travelling across the countryside on the way to his home, everywhere, in all directions, cultivated fields are visible, stretching to flat horizons together with roads jammed with frantic traffic, old farmhouses, factories, little geometric houses and an endless array of billboards wherever you look in space.[2] The area where he lives, outside of town, seems a miniature simulation of those American middle-class suburbs composed of little single-family houses outfitted with yards. Unlike American suburbs, however, here everything has been paved, with asphalt spread all over the place, apart from the cultivated fields that can be seen in the distance.

In front of Ghirri's house an enormous space is bordered by rows of single-family houses. This enormous space is entirely empty and covered with asphalt. It cannot be viewed as a piazza, because it is too vast, and no one ever goes there; only at night is it used as a parking lot by trucks. On the far side of this expanse of asphalt is a solitary bar, it too almost always empty, called I think Bar Las Vegas.

There exist thousands of places like this that are spreading over the surface of the earth. Their emergence is almost always marked by that strange fixity that empty space assumes, space for which for some inexplicable reason no one can find a use. And it is on these hunting grounds that architects embark on grand adventures, with their gazes always directed at a future whose outlines remain anyone's guess.

What Ghirri has done and continues to do is the opposite. He has effected a radical clearing out of the usual intensions or reasons for looking, showing us at last a way of looking that does not go snooping out spoils to be seized, that does not go hunting out extraordinary adventures, but one that instead discovers that everything can be interesting because it is part of existence.

There are little geometric houses that would never have attracted most photographers, in that they would normally represent a world without interest, a state of perceptual boredom. Ghirri has understood their pictorial potential, depicting them in their simplest and most essential assumptions. In these little geometric houses Ghirri has discovered a regularity of lines, symmetries and colours which people have used in an attempt to decorate the everyday void as best they can. He as discovered that, if observed front-on, they can stimulate the mind and imagination as much as a famous monument, for the technique used to deal with space in these little houses involves perspectives similar to those of the fifteenth century, symmetries of a neoclassical type, with colours at times reminiscent of Piero della Francesca. In short, he has discovered that those boring houses are a form of life, an example of culture within emptiness.

An undertaking of this sort is a story, one that is anything but dark and gloomy, of places that are emerging over the surface of the world in which we feel lost. In any story what is most important is the threshold of intensity that is chosen to recount things. If the intention is 'wanting to see (or to describe) the exceptional', the threshold of intensity must be high, and it is usually necessary to resort to sensational topics: photography in such cases often resorts to visual assaults, unusual facts, artistic views, seductive and decontextualized horrors. In his most recent images, Ghirri has managed to lower the threshold of intensity of his account to the point at which he is able to eliminate every reference to the unusual and the topical. Yet this allows him to give much more emphasis to the slightest shiftings in colour, the barest nuances, to the outlines of things, and most of all to his extraordinary way of conceiving and imagining the external world.

Some young people at a beachside bar, so dark all around that it seems as if they are on a stage to perform an episode of their existence.[3] Being night, the photo is lit solely by an American-style sign above the tables outside the bar, slightly out of focus as are the faces of the young people. Herein is a minimal resonance that Ghirri is able to cut from out of the dark. But this resonance is already a way of thinking and imagining the external world: it is like the discovery that we are strangely capable of understanding what goes on outside us because our thoughts are already external, already part of the world and of existence. Here there is no longer an interior being that imagines the world as a thing completely different from itself; through this photograph, we like the young people have always been and will always be part of the picture.

In another recent photograph, there are some bath houses on a beach, between which the sea is visible.[4] The sun is at our backs, probably three-quarters of its way across the sky. There is only one distinct shadow, beyond which is all faded colours. There is such a silence in this photograph, such a lowering of the threshold of 'wanting to see the exceptional', that we are at last allowed to appreciate appearances for what they are worth. Because at this point appearances, which underpin representations of the external world, are much more important to us than any overarching interpretation of the external world. Appearances concern not only the acute vision of the artist but are all that we have to orient ourselves in space.

We believe it is possible to stitch back together appearances scattered across empty spaces, through an account that organizes experience, and thus gives relief. There is no story in the world that is worth telling, if it does not give relief (even tragedy gives relief, while showy exposés of reality do not).

We believe that everything that people do from morning to night is an effort to come up with a credible account of the outside world, one that will make it bearable at least to some extent. We also think that this is a fiction, but a fiction in which it is necessary to believe. There are whole worlds of narrative at every point of space, appearances that alter at every blink of the eyes, infinite disorientations that require above all a way of thinking and imagining that is not paralysed by contempt for everything around us.

Notes

1 This essay appeared in a collection of Luigi Ghirri's photographs and writings by both Ghirri and others: Luigi Ghirri, *Paesaggio Italiano/Italian Landscape* (Hamburg: Electa/Gingko, 1989).
2 The term Celati coins here, 'case geometrili' ('geometric houses') refers to houses designed by *geometri* (surveyors who also design small buildings), but also plays with the fact that many *geometra*-designed houses tend to be boxy with simple geometric features.
3 The photo referred to is 'Porto Recanati, 1984', which can be viewed here: Luigi Ghirri. 'Porto Recanati, 1984'. Instagram, 23 April 2023. https://www.instagram.com/p/Co2tS-WrkiU/.
4 The photograph referred to is 'Riccione, 1984', which can be viewed here: Luigi Ghirri. 'Riccione, 1984'. *Artribune*, 23 April 2023. https://www.artribune.com/wp-content/uploads/2018/05/Luigi-Ghirri-Riccione-1984.-Courtesy-Collezione-Fotografia-MAXXI-Architettura.jpg.

Figure 13.1 Gianni Celati, 1984, by Luigi Ghirri. © Eredi Luigi Ghirri.

14

'A system of stories about the external world' ('Un sistema di racconti sul mondo esterno', 1986)

In the following piece I describe some aspects of the stories that we tell in conversation with which it might be possible to imagine an ordinary representation of the external world. Many of my points stem from the writings of Harvey Sacks, William Labov and Livia Polanyi; I owe much to the suggestions of Guy Aston, with whom I discussed many of these ideas. Nothing would have been possible without the work of Ervin Goffman.

I.

To start I will discuss obviousness and how we need obviousness to make ordinary landscapes. A common trait of conversations is the extreme poverty of descriptions compared with far more numerous comments. There are repertories of comments that are used with the specific intent of obstructing descriptions: for example, 'That's obvious', 'It's clear', 'That's normal'. These phrases above all comment on the ongoing verbal activity and denote that it serves no purpose to talk about something that we all know.

Another group of comments of this sort: 'Of course', 'I get it', 'Everyone knows that', '*Per forza*', '*Cela va sans dire*', '*Natürlich*'. There is the suggestion in such expressions that there exists in the external world a normal course of events, and that, by abiding by it, it is possible to know how to behave. All this assumed clarity naturally entails a trade-off, which consists of a blindness to certain details of places and panoramas in which we have been, and to the variety of appearances encountered. Our blindness stems from the fact that it is impossible to see anything considered of no importance and thus taken for granted. Moreover, if these ritual comments continually tell us that out in the world things are going on without anything particularly worthy of our attention, drawing attention to the details of a place or event starts to sound obvious, like saying 'all people have ears'.

It is this notion of assumed clarity that in most conversations, until you come to a story, makes it impossible to imagine anything of the external world except this: that it consists of a usual panorama.

For example: 'What did you do in Bolzano?' 'Nothing, the usual stuff, I saw some people'. Or: 'How did it go yesterday evening, what did you do?' 'Nothing, we went to eat at Vito's'; 'Oh, the guys went boating and we hung out on the beach'. Without a doubt during a day on the beach many things must have occurred, but here there is no reference made to them to say what happened, but rather expressions to indicate that the day consisted of usual events and that there is nothing else worth mentioning.

Similar comments are possible; however only in certain circumstances. With an outsider or a foreigner, we are always obligated to describe something, while with members of our own group we can take for granted that they know what we are talking about and that descriptions are unnecessary. Only with a member of my group or someone from my area can I say, 'Of course', referring to a scene or behaviour that to me is normal.

The repertories of such comments based on a notion of supposed clarity are part of the set of instruments we use to draw lines of separation between insiders, who belong to our group or environment, and outsiders. These repertories are in short, a way of testing someone: if someone is not an outsider, they must be able to recognize things that are obvious to all members of the group.

Taking for granted the existence of a course of ordered events about which we know more or less everything, we, together with others, construct a usual panorama: and this panorama is so obvious as to lack any need of observation or description.

Taking something for granted means doing away with describing it. We take something for granted according to certain presuppositions, with these presuppositions being the opposite of descriptions.

The term 'presuppositions' can in reality mean many things. Here I use it in the sense of 'background expectations': all that which we assume is made in a certain way or that will operate in a certain way, without seeming to be a problem, which in any event for us represents obviousness.

For example, if tonight I have plans to see a film, it means that my background expectations take for granted certain necessary conditions:

that the cinema is open, that I will be able to get there, that I won't have a heart attack beforehand, that nothing will keep me at work, and that today, too, evening will fall as it does every day.

This set of necessary conditions generates a description of what for us is obvious, if we decide to go to the cinema. Obviousness can be defined in this way: a way of making the conditions necessary for conducting yourself along a course of ordered events, which is taken for granted.

To be less general, various levels of presumption can be distinguished, becoming apparent every time we say or do something. For example: (a) basic presuppositions: if I am to do a job for my whole life, I have to assume that no natural, military or economic events will happen that will make my work impossible; (b) presuppositions of reciprocity: in love, friendship and business I assume that I know other people's underlying expectations, so that we can get along, until proven otherwise; (c) presuppositions of competence: in meeting someone, I assume that I know how to use the words and phrases in my language, the sounds needed to produce to render them intelligible, which gestures are appropriate, when to speak and when to remain silent.

In this regard Goffman has catalogued a range of interactions with others for which having presuppositions or background expectations is indispensable.

I will give only a few examples: (I) if I say at the cinema ticket box 'two', I can assume that the cashier will take this to mean 'two tickets'; I might also ask the cashier 'When does the film start?' or 'How long does it last?' but probably not 'Is it worth seeing?'; (II) I assume that police officers, doctors, judges and at times bosses or supervisors can ask me questions about my identity or life, but that a stranger randomly encountered along a street cannot; (III) if I witness a traffic accident, I assume that I can say at once without any preamble, 'It was that Fiat's fault'; but if someone stops me on the road I assume that some sort of preamble is necessary, such as 'excuse me': (IV) I assume that I can ask for directions to a nearby place but not to ask 'How can I get to Milan?' or for that matter, 'What day is it?' Things of this nature make up obviousness, which is the background of all actions, words or images, forming a set of instructions that can be employed in varying degrees depending on the circumstance. This should at least raise a few questions. For example, when going to the cinema, do we speak directly to the mind of cashier to find out when the film starts? And if this is the case, why does the cashier know certain things? But this again is obviousness and not its description. Cashiers know certain things, but we know that they know them, just as they know that we know them, and that everyone else too knows that we know, and that we know that they know. Whose mind then is it that knows all these things, these infinite minutiae, all the knowledge necessary to navigate the external world?

When going to the cinema, we do not speak directly to the mind of the cashier. We speak to an anonymous source of information, which is however also a means of access to a horizon of presuppositions. Essentially, we pose questions to a state of things; to space prescribed by what is taken or not taken for granted.

We pose questions to the external world, in that it is a space for prescribed operations of the mind.

The same thing happens when others speak to us, even if only to ask 'Where is the carton of milk?' because we too are a means of access to a horizon of presuppositions. Comments of the sort 'Of course', 'It's clear', 'Obviously', together with apparent evidence of the surroundings in which we find ourselves, reveal to us the boundaries of this horizon; the boundaries of a ritual order.

II.

Now I will instead speak of what can be recounted of the external world, or of certain kinds of events that are not taken for granted.

To start let us try to imagine what must happen for an event not to be taken for granted; to be distinguishable from the usual panorama, it needs to be 'put on' as if it were a show. For example, historical events are events put on as shows. This is to say that, unlike other events, they have a focal point, a point that two or more people determine, by way of an agreement or semblance of agreement, to consider essential.

To be staged in this manner an event must be recounted and made worthy of mention, and whose focal point must be agreed upon by two or more people.

Of course, the everyday events in which we are absorbed also have a focal point, but events of this sort do not necessarily require staging, but rather regular maintenance. Some of this maintenance of ordinary events takes the following forms: greeting, agreeing, conversing, courting, insulting, joking, giving instructions; such tasks require skills no less specialized than keeping account books, or being a mechanic or a computer expert.

For example, greeting one another. All greetings are composed of sub-compartments, as are conversations, telephone calls or courting rituals, and all our moves must fall into the correct sub-compartments. When I meet someone, I can hardly say all at once, 'I'm fine'; I have to pass through at least one sub-compartment: 'How's it going?' At the same time this operation involves specialized choices, because in a language there exist various repertories of greetings, composed of formulas of both tone and voice; the operation involves strategic choices because an adult and a child do not greet one another in the same way as two adults, a supervisor and a subordinate do not greet one another as do two members of the same group, a man and a woman do not greet one another as do two men. Now let us try to imagine what would happen if someone were to ask me 'How's it going?' and I were not to respond at all. A rift would crack open, not only in the relationship, but in the enveloping event. Things of this sort can happen, but they are not generally so obvious as to weaken the routine maintenance. It is rather that the continuous threat that things of this sort can happen, that rifts can open within events, which renders maintenance problematic. A mistaken glance, an inappropriate gesture, a tone of voice that is out of place, are always possible; not only this, but it is always possible that someone will make a mistake and misinterpret these rifts as resounding breakdowns of an order.

For this reason, everyday relations are full, at every moment, of reparative interventions, of repairs to and remedies for possible errors or mistaken interpretations of what we do. For example: 'Hold on now', 'Yes, but', 'Excuse me', 'I'm sorry to say', 'Have some patience', 'Don't misunderstand me' – without taking into account the reparative interventions of gestures and tones of voice.

Seen at close range, our everyday activities appear very complex, full of potential incidents. It is for this reason that there emerges a type of story, based on assumed evidence that someone has erred or misinterpreted something, or was simply overcome by panic. For example: 'Today that person made me so nervous that I had to leave'.

We see the underlying cause of these stories: routine maintenance must be carried out all the same, but it must be done so with a certain nonchalance.

This type of narratable event has a broader horizon, that of biographies. Biographic episodes are not interesting because they contain striking scenes, but because they recount simple cases in which someone managed to pull off an unexpectedly difficult job of routine maintenance, in spite of all the hazards. Biographies all for the most part speak mainly of this; only nineteenth-century novelists, however, such as Balzac managed to fully exploit this extraordinary narrative possibility.

I will now turn to another narrative possibility, one that is completely inverted.

In the external world there are collections of things that can be thought of as large machines that produce ordinary events: roads, stations, corporations, cataloguing and sorting systems, hotels, restaurants, newspapers, calendars and thousands of clocks. These ubiquitous machines produce, together with their ordinary events, masses of leftover and uncontrollable residues: for example, clocks all tell the same time, but it is exactly for this reason that the end of the workday is so hectic; stations serve to regulate the running of trains, but around stations circulate pimps and prostitutes; buses serve to move people around, but on buses pickpockets can be found.

Everywhere there exist leftovers of ordered events, exploited by other orders or networks of exchange, used for other purposes, described or presented in unforeseen ways. This results in a set of discontinuous events: discontinuous because not produced by the same machinery, without the same purpose and lacking clear distinctions between ordered events and leftovers. These webs of discontinuous events represent absolute randomness, which all the same cannot be told apart from ordered courses of events, because the two things interpenetrate one another at every moment.

At any point in a set of discontinuous events of this sort it is possible to encounter someone who asks themselves 'But why did this have to happen to me? Why today of all days? Why now?' Although this is an imaginary example, it allows us to distinguish a type of event that we consider narratable. It is indeed after events of this sort that, coming home, we can say, 'Guess what happened?'

Before moving to consider how events are enacted by way of their narration, I want to first pose the question: why do certain types of events seem interesting, and therefore more narratable than others?

It is relatively clear that events that can be considered accidental bring back into discussion several background expectations. If I assume that I can go home around 6 pm but then get stuck in traffic for two hours, this prompts me to revisit or redefine certain assumptions. This is what happens in every moment of social crisis: some, or many, explain to others how it was wrong to take certain things for granted, to have had certain expectations. And in stories, as in social crises, accidental or chance events take on meaning by way of comments or axioms. For example: 'Traffic has become impossible', 'Everyone in Italy has gone crazy'. Generalizations of this sort are clearly for the most part exaggerated. And yet consider how for us it is impossible to clearly distinguish at first glance an ordered course of events from an accidental one. This task becomes impossible without words, without using words to abstract a rule from scattered facts.

With these stories we thus carry out a difficult operation but one necessary for conforming to a usual panorama that defines and redefines that which falls within the ritual purview of an assumed order, and that which instead falls beyond its limits, within the chaos of dim, senseless events.

The task that narrators of biographical facts and of episodes of event maintenance must carry out seems to me an inverse and much more subtle operation. They find themselves having to necessarily begin from the expectation of an ordered course of events and having then to attempt to justify it with episodes found at hand, which consist however mainly of obstacles within the events. Their subtlety lies in passing over these difficulties, in stories of their own self-possession. Our own sense of composure in everyday encounters depends largely on an operation of this type – on the ability to minimize what we do not understand or know how to face, starting with the principle that it is not necessary to find an explanation for obstacles, given that events continue on in their usual way.

With these two examples I have tried to show how facts that seem narratable appear so because they constitute practical problems to resolve, and not because of some supposed representational 'content' that they offer. I will now speak about the fundamental practical problem of maintaining events, that is, of being able to speak to someone without feeling unrelated or alien.

III.

There are various recognizable stages in conversations: stages of exchange and contact, stages of reciprocal exploration, and stages in which topics to talk about are introduced, leading us to stories. The shift from the stage of contact to that of stories however doesn't always take place. For example, in certain shops shopkeepers allow customers to talk about themselves; in others, shopkeepers will engage only in brief asides or jokes; in still others there occur only transactions.

In this problematic shift to stories there are two types of difficulty to overcome: the first is linguistic, in that we must control the language in which we express ourselves; the second is ritual and depends on where we are, the time of day or night it is, and the person with whom we are speaking.

All of this is much more evident if seen from the point of view of an outsider or foreigner than an insider. An insider always has the usual panorama in front of their eyes and has no desire to linger listening to stories that are difficult to understand or cause too much thinking. The foreigner, rather, does not have the usual panorama in front of their eyes and must depend on an insider for a sense of this usualness. The verbal representation of the external world, if this expression ever meant anything, must pass through practical difficulties of this sort: for an outsider or foreigner it is a major feat to pull off inserting a story into a conversation. But all of us, as soon as we find ourselves in the company of someone who is a bit of an outsider, examine the situation to find a way to tell a story – except when we prefer to keep a ritual distance. But the question of foreignness is endless; for example, it might happen that someone, feeling the urge to tell their spouse something that would surely cause controversy, discovers a chasm between the urge to tell and the act of telling. Clearly this matter concerns us all.

It is at the moment of telling a story that an event is turned into a spectacle or is staged. Staging an event means presenting it for observation, but also in a way that two or more people find within it some meaning; in this way the event is transformed into 'the thing that we are examining', 'the object of our discourse', and thus the centre around which all verbal activities revolve.

The identification of 'the object of our discourse' allows two or more people to observe the event from the same point of view, or: it allows tellers and listeners to show that they see the same things in an event. If this occurs, tellers and listeners have the right to no longer feel separated and alone, at least for a few moments, because soon after come other events, and everything goes back to the beginning.

Given that the horizon of assumptions and its ritual order always (re)count infinitely more than we do, with every new encounter we attempt to define a small space, a more controllable frame; we then, after having brought what we know and what we expect into relation, can demonstrate that we speak with satisfaction from the same point of view.

In our everyday stories descriptions usually recur when locating events to stage. If what is usual is given by continuous, undifferentiated sequences of points in space and time, the unusual, or tellable, will be a precise point at which a discontinuity has been located. In fact, in stories there is always a panoramic part that provides an overview of sequences of usual events; then there is a scenic part, in which a precise point in space and time is located. Localized discontinuous events are usually announced by narrators with indications such as: 'all of a sudden', 'one day', 'at that moment', etc.

From this point on there comes into play descriptive ability. Here the narrator must give evidence that the event is tellable, leaving the listeners to imagine the scene in which the story takes place. The narrator must show that they have noticed certain details that the listeners, in similar circumstances, would have also likely noticed. The descriptions can be expanded up to a certain extent, but the narrator must not include descriptions outside of the recounted event. For example, in telling the story of a car accident, they cannot begin to add that at that moment the clouds were close to the horizon and a flock of birds was passing by in the sky, because one assumes that, in similar circumstances, the listeners would have paid attention to the accident and not the flock of birds.

Comments too must be conventional and suited to the evidence given by the description.

In telling the story of a friend's death, after having described the hospital room, the narrator cannot say, 'And when he took his last breath, I felt like eating some strawberries'.

I have given two examples of narrative error in order to highlight the conventional value given to the evidence that a narrator is compelled to provide. The motive for all this convention will soon become clear. For the moment, I will only add that in the course of a day we continually give conventional evidence for what we say; for example, 'I read in the newspaper', 'Aristotle said', 'someone who knows told me', or 'look for yourself and tell me if I'm wrong'.

In all these cases there reigns the principle of conventional narrative descriptions. Meanwhile there is taken for granted an equivalence of our observations, leading to the idea that in similar circumstances we would have read, felt, seen or thought the same thing. What is more, we are talking of something specific and identifiable, talking exactly about 'this' – and both of us know what it is.

This is the conventional process of staging events, turning them into 'the object of our discourse'.

Every story should have a clear point, message or moral that is comprehensible and ideally acceptable to the listener. For this to happen it is necessary to show that you are talking about something specific, about a precise topic embodied in a precise argument. Secondly, the event recounted must seem a special experience of the narrator – an experience that, containing unique aspects, qualifies it to be told.

And so, the question is this: how can it happen that the uniqueness of an experience be adequately evaluated at the moment of its telling? The question could also be posed in this way: how can it happen that the event absorbed the attention of my listeners, just as how did it absorb my attention? To begin with, the narrator or whoever is speaking, likely finds themselves in the position of having to throw at the listener a message of this sort: 'I'm also part of your group, of where you're from, of your people'; or, if the listener is a foreigner: 'I'm also a member of the human race'.

The narrative should resolve with an agreement on such messages, each of which involves a particular affective filter. However, to agree on something one must be able to identify it as the gist of a discourse, the focal point of an event; one must therefore know what 'the object of our discourse' is.

In narratives such as in conversations a central topic of a discourse does not really exist; there exist an infinite number, because the topic changes with every phrase, almost every response, every new tack in direction. More generally, if we did not have book titles or book chapters, we would never know exactly what a discourse were about.

For this reason, we very often refer, by way of various expressions, to the 'object of our discourse', to the 'this' of which we are speaking. For example: 'This means that …', 'All this leads me to say that …', or: 'This theme that the author engages …'.

The possibility of identifying that which we are talking about is always very uncertain. Moreover, in a conversation, when more than two people heatedly struggle to define the 'object of the discourse', the entropy of language becomes all the clearer. Also, when we attempt to identify the 'this', the less we understand what is being talking about. Labov saw in this a tendency inherent to much academic claptrap.

Good narrators adopt an opposite strategy, that of insouciant detachment. The principle is that events must continue along as usual, without any hiccups or jams. The ability of the narrator then lies in passing over any reciprocal incomprehension, above any obstacles to communication, above the gaping distance across which we speak, often with delays, deviations or reparatory formulas such as 'Forget about it', 'Let's not talk about this anymore', or 'Let's move on'. Narrators of this sort are endowed with a proficiency of the conventional, and most of all a proficiency in providing conventional proof of 'this', of 'the object of our discourse': proof that others can take for granted.

Thus, by focusing our attention up close over a staged event, which should also be a localized and represented point of the external world, the narrator and their listener can demonstrate, one to the other, the signs of a formal understanding: the formal demonstration of a possible agreement.

Considering all the difficulties in understanding one another, the difficulties of connection in a space in which every ritual framing is always incompatible with other framings, with the onus of the horizon of presuppositions, always beyond us, always enormously more important than us, one can also understand why this 'formal understanding' is often accompanied by signs of satisfaction with the successful outcome of the enterprise. Thus, very often people who are talking will say something such as, 'This chat is going so well'.

Moreover, by this very circumvention of obstacles through insouciant detachment, storytellers attest, with every story delivered, to the infinite accidentality of understanding and the entropy of language and communication.

This brings to mind much else: the precarity of narratable elements; the perishability of the so-called 'real'; the complete lack of a sense of experience, unless organized into little drawers or frames, unless held up by links that need every day to be reconnected, like the threads of a spiderweb.

Conclusions

In this discourse I have attempted to understand what a representation of the external world by way of words might mean. Of course, this is another 'this', a point of formal agreement. This however begs clarification.

The culture of factual literature, from psychoanalysis and sociology to anthropology, has spread the idea that cultural representations of a place or the external world can be extracted from reciprocal relations between people and described as a particular mental 'content'.

But why should there be a mental 'content' and not instead an endless, heterogeneous series of practical problems to be solved at any given moment?

That which exists out in the external world might be described as a gathering of states of things. But this holds little or no meaning for us. What is meaningful, and is the only thing that can have meaning, is the fact that out there in the external world is an order, with boundaries everywhere, beyond which there is a horizon of incomprehensible events.

The same idea can be expressed in another way: out there is emptiness, but this emptiness is the space that contains the operations of the mind.

I believe that it is necessary to be insouciant like the oral narrators I have described – given that what sets us apart, what isolates us, what disables us or drives us insane, is not the other, the unfathomable, the perverse, but the space we always have before us.

15
'Desert crossings' ('Traversate del deserto', 1986)

Max Frisch writes in *Stiller* (*I'm Not Stiller*): 'How much desert there is on this planet whose guests we are; I never knew before, I'd only read about it; I had never experienced how very much everything we live from is the gift of a small oasis, as improbable as grace'.[1] Between this insight and the storm surge that has recently struck the Adriatic coast, suddenly revealing that 30 or 40 kilometres of coastline, already devastated by tourism and development, are pure shelterless desert, between these two revelations, is a line of thought, which, if developed, leads us to recognize the desert on the threshold of every inhabited place, of all of our homes, and eventually also leads us to recognize the illusory character of every domesticated corner of the planet.

This line of thought also states that we are not masters of the planet, even if this is our most profound conviction. It tells us that our place of dwelling is always precarious, even if the drive of modern civilization is to cause humans to forget the precariousness of their existence. And lastly it tells us that, at this late stage of history, there is no meaningful path of study without reference to the sign of the desert.

This is a sign not only of our epochal misery, but also of the enormous imaginative effort required by any crossing of space, of the void, of the desert. Because in the void that surrounds us, misery and imagination are mutually recognizable, aiding instead of reciprocally negating one another: and in this way we will have deserts that are images of fullness, the grace of a small oasis in an endless expanse of sand, a word found in the middle of a silence, people who seem plants, mythical eras that appear in ordinary landscapes, and the gusting wind that crosses the valley.

But how much misery and imagination, desert and fullness, words and silence, are forcibly separated in order to carry out 'clear categorizations' (what would one ask of experts if not to carry out 'clear categorizations'?) thus initiating the shelterless devastation of the land, air, water and mind?

Unconscious misery begins to see itself as richness, substituting imagination with symbolic surrogates, in which the desert and the void are incrementally negated and forgotten as the desertification of the world increases along with the evidence of an enormous precariousness – such as the Adriatic coast. Thanks to so much unconsciousness, little by little precariousness is no longer remembered as an original quality of our place of dwelling, but rather considered as a temporary and remediable inadequacy, and thus loses value: because what Frisch calls the 'improbable grace' of a 'small oasis' is taken for granted like the functioning of a washing machine.

These are the signs of an epoch in which the desert becomes more and more the path to take, the way to rediscover, the silence to cross to be able once again to speak with others. In the work of the writers and photographers in this book,[2] the desert is this path: it is the way of silence, the celebration of the small oasis, the discovery of some mythic trace, glimmering or blinding or moving, the presence of a flower, of an animal, of a stone, in the indifferent planetary desert – or what we call Nature.

Notes

1 Max Frisch, *I'm Not Stiller*, trans. Michael Bullock (San Diego: Harcourt Brace, 1994), 22.
2 *Traversate del deserto* (Ravenna: Essegi, 1986), with texts by Giorgio Agamben, Jean Baudrillard, Gerald Bisinger, Gianni Celati, Jean-Paul Curnier, Max Frisch, Gabriel Josipovici, Gilles Lipovetski and Giuliano Scabia; and photographs by Olivo Barbieri, Paul David Barkshire, Jean-Paul Curnier, Vittore Fossati, Carlo Gajani, Luigi Ghirri, Guido Guidi, Klaus Kinold and Manfred Willmann.

Figure 15.1   Gianni Celati, 1985, by Luigi Ghirri. © Eredi Luigi Ghirri.

16
'Translating Jack London'
('Traducendo Jack London', 1986)

I.

The Call of the Wild (usually translated in Italian as *Il richiamo della foresta*) is Jack London's best-known work, recounting the various adventures of the dog Buck and set in the Klondike during the late nineteenth-century gold rush. I went about translating the book a bit at a time, carrying it around for months, with the idea that the work would come easily.

The first problems became evident the day that I managed to find a photocopy of the original edition, and after thinking it over, realized that I had to start all over from the beginning. In the original 1903 Macmillan edition there are surprising lexical archaisms and syntactical reversals, which in later, more common editions were either removed or smoothed out, because they had too literary a taste or were likely to pose problems of comprehension for contemporary readers. The fact is that the simple language used by London to describe Buck at times changes, with elevated phrasings and in certain passages taking on the appearance of a poem about the beginnings of the world (as in the opening pages), with poetic syntax, alliteration and repetition that produce the tone of long-ago, mythic fabulation.

II.

London's writing seems naturally inclined towards poetic devices – verses, stanzas, caesuras – with a panoramic fluidity that immerses us in an expansive, indeterminate time that rapidly courses through events. His approach to narration is of the simplest kind: one found in epics and fairy tales, without complicated structures or psychological stratagems. In reading *The Call of the Wild* it is hard not to detect an American intonation in the syntax of its phrasings, voice and patterned tonal accents that carry the story forwards. There arises in every image something emblematic of some legendary endeavour, at times giving rise to a song that unfolds into life and death struggles.

This problem of the translator then arises: how to bring to the text that panoramic fluidity, that expansiveness, but organized in simple phrasings. Producing a translation that 'objectively' corresponds to the original of course will not do. There is no easy path forwards in any translation. But perhaps there is a way to approach the linguistic bent from which a book is born by keenly pursuing its words to eliminate from the text purely functional readings and instead to restore to it an unpredictability that it had in the beginning, as a single, singular thing.

III.

In the writings of figures such as Jack London, Ring Lardner, Dashiell Hammett and Ernest Hemingway there arises an American prose style with certain similar traits – informal phrasings that brush aside psychological rhetoric and sentimental posturing, together with laconic mannerisms and intuitive rhythms that follow the curt phrasings of straightforward sentences. The basic American sentence of this sort is composed of a subject and a predicate, without subordinate clauses or other syntactical loops – a linear sentence that tends to repeat the subject instead of relying on relative pronouns. This boils down the language to a series of automatic phrasings or brief sequences of end-stopped words that in their linearity have little need of internal punctuation. These are well-known characteristics, especially evident in the style of Hemingway's stories with their series of short, self-contained sentences with an unmistakable American iambic cadence. Translated into Italian, however, these sentences start to sound affected because our literary tradition lacks an equivalent model and because our syntax is always more complicated.

IV.

Writing built of short phrases in Italian has a very different effect than one in American English, because in Italian we can elide the subject, something that is impossible in English, and we can invert the order of the subject and predicate without causing the phrase to seem rarefied, as can occur in English. It soon becomes clear that the framework of our syntactical patterns is not readily analogous to any variety of English, American or otherwise. When London repeats the same subject again and again in short sentences ('He … He … He … He …'), it gives a rhythmic motion to the narrative and at the same time keeps it on the level of the everyday, since it is common to repeat the subject in ordinary conversation. On the other hand, in Italian, given that eliding the subject happens so frequently, its repetition often produces a heavy or quirky effect.

Secondly, in English repetition rhythmically traces a tonal arc, creating a musical beat to which the phrases are set – and whose syllables if many are compact and if few are long, always following the same beat. In our tradition musical rhythm stems from a more fixed syllabic nature, and finding the beat is a matter that constantly shifts and is often left to a deft use of tonic accents. But this level of detail has little sense – what matters is a general idea, a linguistic style that emerges from reading.

V.

The writings of London, Lardner, Hammett and Hemingway all share some basic stylistic similarities: simplified syntax, speech-based rhythm, compact phrasing and repetition of the subject. And then the problem of the simple, yet not-so-simple past tense arises, something virtually impossible to match in Italian, since it can indicate everything from our past perfect to a remote past, from our imperfect to a historical present. And when the simple past tense is thrown into a fast-paced, monosyllabic sentence, it has the sense of something absolutely definitive, as if in some epic, aorist tense – a curt and decisive-sounding means of expression that stamps out any useless verbal excess.

I find this type of prose one of the most difficult to translate, above all for its dependence on the simple past tense, usually rendered in Italian systematically as the remote past, which often sounds off, such as in translations of books by Hemingway, Hammett, Chandler and Carver, because the Italian remote past has literary connotations that conflict with the 'cool' style of these authors.

VI.

The most delicate issue with London: his language has not yet reached either Hammett's characteristic dryness or Hemingway's stylized laconicism. London's American English, predating these other writers by some 30 years, indulges in non-linear digressions, relative phrases, meditative digressions. It is when it ranges out towards the horizon that the object of its aspirations become clear: the long song, the epic. The sound of American speech underlies London's writing, with his sentences coming across as a sort of lingua franca that shifts between simple and elevated registers as the situation demands. The problem of translating such a language lies mainly in the danger of mixing it up with pedantic phrasings, expressions considered official or correct. Translating *The Call of the Wild* necessitates avoiding such a flattening out, maintaining the singularity of its style, coming up with an Italian that is younger than the present one by a good 40 or 50 years.

VII.

In my translation I sought a tone from an earlier time in which the form of written Italian was not yet held in subjugation by the standards currently in force – and I seem to have found it reading London's first translators. These may have at times twisted or condensed the text, but still had a sense of the language as a delicate instrument. They never attempted to reproduce American or English syntactical patterns, but tended instead to combine sentences into longer, more complex, less linear constructions, placing value on the subordinate, the aside, the hidden relative phrase.

These syntactical patterns are very common in written Italian, for issues of modulation in our language. These issues of modulation also concern punctuation, which poses other problems, given that in London's American English there is a tendency to rid writing of all possible commas, in that the linearity of sentences defines a curve of intonation without uncertainties. In London's book punctuation is sparse at best and often employed inconsistently (corrected in recent editions) and had to be entirely reinvented. Here too the older translators suggested a less standardized use of punctuation, with subtle modulations, regarding end stops, commas, and so on.

VIII.

At the time that London wrote *The Call of the Wild* he was aware of a process of increasing standardization, evident too in the social automatisms in which obviousness was becoming the central rule. From this perspective, a good introduction to the adventures of Buck seems to me to be found at the beginning of London's 1904 story 'The Unexpected', in which he warns of a human society in which life is becoming transformed into a mechanized system of predetermined certainties:

> It is a simple matter to see the obvious, to do the expected. The tendency of the individual life is to be static rather than dynamic, and this tendency is made into a propulsion by civilization, where the obvious only is seen, and the unexpected rarely happens. [...] The effect of civilization is to impose human law upon environment until it becomes machine-like in its regularity. The objectionable is eliminated, the inevitable is foreseen. One is not even made wet by the rain nor cold by the frost; while death, instead of stalking about grewsome and accidental, becomes a prearranged pageant, moving along a well-oiled groove to the family vault, where the hinges are kept from rusting and the dust from the air is swept continually away.[1]

IX.

In Buck's adventures there is a liberatory urge, connected to visions of escaping the automatisms forced upon the human environment. The ideas do not lead to didactic discourses, but rather fleeting motions by which the dim trail of evolution can be traced (London was a reader of Darwin) down to a primeval origin: the dog pack's howling at the moon. The tale is one of unexpected escapes from which there emerge Buck's marvellous exploits over the expanses of icy deserts.

The title of the book evokes the call of open space wherein the unexpected and accidental reside. But this call plays out not within a closed-off text, but by way of a slow approach of words in the form of a song. The meaning of the song is first described at the end of the second chapter: 'And when, on the still cold nights, he pointed his nose at a star and howled long and wolflike, it was his ancestors, dead and dust, pointing nose at star and howling down through the centuries and through him.' This is the song of the boundless space in which we exist, the song of time and of the composition of space, including the cold, the darkness, emptiness and the indefinable silence of the stars, the sovereign death that prevails over every growth.

All that which for the functionaries of standard language is meaning, text or message in need of an explanation, has little in common with this extraordinary book in which the meaning of the story blurs into mute song, the silence of absolute death that dominates the space around us. Beings exposed to space, we – like the dog Buck – venture forth into the void and the desert, rising back up through the course of time, as we leave behind 'the pretences of men'.

Note

1   Jack London, *Love of Life, and Other Stories* (New York: Macmillan, 1907), 126.

17
'The frontal view: Antonioni, *L'Avventura* and waiting' ('La veduta frontale. Antonioni, *L'Avventura* e l'attesa', 1987)

After many years it seems to me that Michelangelo Antonioni's *L'Avventura* has become one of those films whose influence can be seen everywhere, having become a form of awareness no longer individual but collective, without which the cinema of directors such as Wim Wenders and Jim Jarmusch would be unthinkable, as well as many other films in which slow descriptive shots and lingering unhurried moments have been allowed admittance. It is in this sort of cinema that a form of epochal comprehension comes forth, a manner of waiting no longer at the mercy of expectations, no longer duped by expectations.

These ideas came to me while watching *L'Avventura* again at the moment in which the young woman goes missing on the island. The barren island, the wandering or immobile characters, the low sky, the grey and boundless vision, together reveal the realm of the indeterminate (like all deserts) in which cultural pretences begin to unravel. The views of the island are never descriptions fully carried out, but rather pauses in the landscape, moments of drawn-out lingering in place. The characters aimlessly wander back and forth, compelled simply by waiting. The varying expectations that the young woman will be found, that the truth will be revealed, that her disappearance will be rendered easily comprehensible by some form of explanation or reason, have often been discussed in a type of critical discourse that speaks of a 'collapse of values' in European culture. But clearly this sort of discourse presumes that before the collapse, the so-called values of art, culture and morality had a foundation. The simple awakening to values such as an empty order, without determinations, and outside of a justifying and controlling critical discourse, becomes a truth of experience which culture can never accept. All the attempts to verify the 'collapse of values' are nothing but anxiety over the definitive ascertainment of our culture, and modern conceptions of the world are marked by the growth of this anxiety.

If *L'Avventura* had embraced this sort of reductivism, it would have become unwatchable. It would have contained only the expectations of a critical discourse, a conception of the world, and a set of assertions that tell us what we must understand.

But at the moment at which the young woman disappears on the island, there begins a gradual extinguishing of expectations: expectations produced by the narrated facts together with those produced by cultural, artistic and moral values, which are discussed at length in the film. That the talk of these values is little by little substituted by a listless inertia seems to me a liberating aspect of this new type of adventure in which characters are no longer able to cheat time. Adventure in the past was conceived of as a dangerous race to cheat time, to cheat waiting by way of the expectations produced: but what happens when time proceeds along as something that can no longer be cheated?

To make note of one aspect of this form of comprehension, in the films of Antonioni, as in those of Wenders, the frontal view allows lingering without anxiety, in shots that are often stretches of 'dead time' in the narrative thread. The frontal view makes use of orthogonal symmetries, resulting in an ordered and simple way of observing things. In the photographs of Walker Evans, as in the films of Antonioni (the two seem to me to have much in common), the frontal view is at heart the preference for a low threshold of intensity, for a mode of narrating that avoids commotion and instead tends towards a calm practice of representation. This is in contrast with oblique or partial perspectives, which always have an air of instability, and thus introduce expectations that abolish the simple form of observing, lingering and pausing without anxiety.

L'Avventura ends with a lingering pause of this sort, a frontal view that makes use of orthogonal symmetries to order its gaze, with a young woman standing in profile and a man sitting on a bench, at dawn, while in the background the white tarp of the sky is visible. There is a type of comprehension here that begins to locate its characters, bringing them to the sensation of the ineluctable present, the actual time of waiting. This ineluctable present, time that cannot be cheated, is the opening with which the film entrusts us.

If the essence of an era is revealed in the way in which an era believes in time, we must say that the essence of our era lies in the dream of being in another 'more advanced' and 'future' time, the incessant dream of modern visions of the world. Our era thus is an era in flight from itself, an era without an era, because its waiting for another time is entirely cut through by expectations that cheat time, that render the present always more mysterious within the headiness of knowledge and culture. To perceive the empty present of an era that dreams of another era, seems to me to be the sole focus of a form of environmental comprehension – the only means of understanding that does not depend on the pretences of culture, and that tends once again to trust time without cheating it with expectations.

What waiting awaits is the awakening of time. But time is rendered ever more mysterious by modern visions of the world, all projected on other eras, and thus lacking conceptions of a time that makes of us living beings, or mortal ones. In *L'Avventura* there are in fact dead spots, gazes and gestures of a purposeless waiting, the fixity of frontal views, that reopen this comprehension for us.

I believe that this idea of waiting first came to mind while looking at a photograph by Luigi Ghirri that, in some ways, can been read as a comment on or homage to Antonioni. In it there is a frontal view of a grassy soccer pitch, with the distant dead ball line traced by the shadows of the dense trees that delimit the view, at the centre of which is an empty goal in a sort of large silence: is not a soccer pitch the locus of expectations, here mysteriously suspended in a present without expectations?[1]

With this type of open comprehension, all places become observable, beautiful and ugly alike. All places become possible places of lingering, with the very act of pausing to linger in places becoming a sign of our inhabiting the earth, in the realm of the indeterminate. When we stop sensing the landscape as the realm of the indeterminate, and thus beyond description, it means that our environmental comprehension has gone to pot.

Last year on a cloudy day I was wandering along the levees by the Po River in the direction of Porto Tolle, in places still nearly the same as when *Il Grido* (*The Cry*) was shot, the film in which Antonioni began to broach one of our indescribable landscapes. A few days later I watched Luchino Visconti's *Ossessione* (*Obsession*), which recounts the same landscape and is the last Italian film to speak without hesitation of death and of destiny, of death as our destiny. Immediately after this period, the idea starts to spread that death is the fault of society, and that we fall sick not because we are mortal, but because economic conditions are not what they should be. There then also begins a totalitarian propaganda, according to which everything in the life of a person depends on ideology and social welfare. Then politicians and administrators, assassins of the soul, and frenzied advertisers follow to conclusively impose on this country the dream of being another country, with always more expectations of a 'future', one that will, however, turn out to be catastrophic, with more and more cars and performances and cultural discourses to cheat time.

A few months ago, I met Guido Fink, and we spoke about all of this. He asked me to write down my thoughts, and so I did.

Note

1 This photograph, which appears in Luigi Ghirri, *Kodachrome* (London: Mack Books, 2012), can be viewed here: *Various Small Fires*, April 24, 2023, https://vsmallfires.files.wordpress.com/2013/09/kodachrome-031.jpg.

18
'Comments on a natural theatre of images' ('Commenti su un teatro naturale delle immagini', 1989)

May 10

Ghirri has often likened photography to science fiction.[1] He says that the seen world is not the same as the photographed world, just as the world of someone crying is not the same as the world of someone laughing, and that the world of a person who lives in a place cannot be the same of as a scientist who manipulates models in which no one can live. If there are analogies in details, passing from details to various comprehensive accounts, analogies become all but illusory.

Ghirri describes the landscape as a *scarto* (swerve, deviation) related to the moment of photographing. He mentions the science fiction stories of J. G. Ballard, which begin with the semblance of a normal situation. This is immediately disrupted by a small deviation that determines an altered perception of normality, which then causes us to come to terms with a world entirely different and fundamentally unnatural.

In Ghirri's photographs the small deviation (*scarto*) can almost always be traced to a question of light. There can never be the same light on things in two different moments, and thus things can never have the same colours. It would be impossible to take the same photograph in two different moments, and the slight deviation is established by this state of contingency that leads to taking a photograph.

Roland Barthes paid particular attention to this irreversibility, identifying it as the death of everything that a photograph represents at the moment at which it is taken. To this Ghirri responds by saying that it is also possible to conceive of time as something that renews, that every accidental deviation renews perception, instead of being only the tombstone of life's moments.

He says that every photograph, despite being tied to a contingent moment, in truth carries us back to another photograph already taken or to be taken, or to other images already seen. The situation is that of a story, which is composed of states of contingency, passages from one moment to another. But if each moment is a deviation from the previous one that renews our expectations, each moment renews the perception of the overall narrative.

There is an attitude of sufficiency that the representatives of artistic mentality have long held with respect to photography. This hinges on the fact that every photograph is mechanically tied to a contingent circumstance and is thus viewed as a gesture at odds with the eternality of art. Ghirri responds by underlining in affirmation this contingent element, and the applied instead of the artistic use of photography, with the added benefit of sidestepping unbearable aesthetic pretensions.

He has often said that in the last ten years his efforts have been focused on exactly this:

> To open the landscape, to dislodge (*dislocare*) ways of looking, to escape from the wall of art. To free ourselves a bit from cultured lingo, from critical apparatuses. Photographs are only images for remembering something, notes to put into an album. This after all is a common use of photography and different from the use of either art or documentary photography. When someone has artistic pretences, they end up thinking about the wallpaper without realizing that the problem is that they keep banging their head against the wall.

May 12

Ghirri explains: 'You are in a room, the light through the blinds casts shadows on the ceiling. A car passes by on the street, and you see its outline on the ceiling. Here is photography, its basis resides here. Then come rolls of film and lenses, but first there is this experience of images reflected through an effect of the passage of light.'

We are talking about the Sanvitale Castle in Fontanellato near Parma, in which there is a human-scaled camera obscura. Ghirri says that in entering it you feel as though you are walking into a film camera. In an exterior wall is a hole through which light passes, projecting on the facing interior wall an upturned image of the outside piazza. There is nothing unusual in the photograph, except for this inversion of the prospective lines caused by the passage of light through a tiny hole. Ghirri says, however, that whoever looks at this image suddenly finds themselves spying on the world, watching from a place of hiding, causing it to seem a backwards double of the visible.

The tiny hole imposes a monocular vision, which while very precise also lacks the depth of lived space. The high resolution of the image is a result of the restriction of the threshold across which it passes to our sight. This has little to do with the ordinary act of watching but rather with spying, which would seem to clarify what a point of view is, including in literature and philosophy. Those who watch from a point of view that is precise because it is narrow, find themselves spying on the world as if it were something alien.

Ghirri continues:

A photograph is only a nebulous image that gives you a nebulous sense of the world, akin to the shadow of a car on the ceiling. Perspective is not our natural way of observing, but a way of making you see better. There is a sort of utopia in seeing everything clearly. Modern photography is dominated by this tendency of bringing into heightened focus all details. And yet, to take one example, looking at recent American photography that relies on an extremely high definition of the image, brings to my mind one of Shakespeare's jokes, of what a shame it is to see so well and yet end up in a blind alley.

In looking at a few of Ghirri's recent photographs, I see that in some the foreground is slightly out of focus, because they take in various scattered appearances in the landscape. Ghirri says that we do not usually see scattered traces at the margins of our attention, that we do not espy things from a narrow angle. We are always inside of something akin to an enveloping embrace and need to use our peripheral vision. For this reason, he uses a wide-angle lens, which is closer to ordinary human vision. On the other hand, a telephoto lens takes away the feeling of the enveloping space in which we live. Ghirri comments:

All the devices devised to narrow and lock in our point of view could only have arisen from an urban context. Urban culture has a need to see the world backwards, as a double of the seen world. In rural culture no one feels the need to create a backwards world, because it is visible everywhere, in the ditches, the wells, the ponds, the shadows. It was part of the common way of seeing.

June 27
After studying Ghirri's arrangement of the photographs for this book, I find it striking that he has ordered them in a sort of game of snakes

and ladders, by way of analogical landscapes from one photograph to another. He responds that the effect of a montage always occurs with photographs, even when we are looking at them in random order. Photographs always end up together as if in a family album, accompanied by a narration that appears as you leaf through its pages.

I insist on the fact that normally a photograph, as with a painting, is presented to us as an image that is of value in and of itself. We are tasked with seeing something in that single image alone, separately from references to other images that lead us to see it. In other words, we feel the need to unfasten images from the contingency in which they always appear to us; only this impossible operation would be capable of giving meaning to so-called aesthetic evaluation.

Ghirri responds by saying that this is a convention, one that appeared between the end of the sixteenth and seventeenth centuries, but that it has not always been the case. He calls to mind the expansive narrative paintings by Giotto, Beato Angelico and Sassetta, in short the use of images common before the height of the Renaissance. In work from this time, one image leads to another, and the overall sense of what you see does not depend on an aesthetic evaluation, but on the comprehension of a story that speaks of events to remember.

Beginning at a certain point, however, the images in Italian painting were no longer indications of events to remember, but evidence of the eternality of art. For this reason, one assumes that these paintings should be viewed separately, in a fixity of contemplation that is never possible to achieve. And even with a photograph, often one assumes that what we see is only what is in front of our eyes, independently from all the shapes and movements that lead us to see it. But this is an idea that applies mainly to the use of photographs in art and documentation, and not more common uses. Photographs are only detached moments that are gathered in albums and fall into a story, based on the fact that there are events to remember, such as confirmations, weddings, trips and similar things.

I continue to insist on the impossibility of isolating a seen image from the totality of movements that lead us to view it. It would be as if, when having come to see something following certain guiding signs, we were to summon someone else to view it for us. The act of approaching is part of the act of viewing, and the arrangement of Ghirri's photographs helps me to understand that we approach images by way of rhythms. Perception takes part in a process of musical unfolding, like a dance.

Ghirri is understandably pleased to hear talk of this, given that he often thinks of his photographs as song tracks. Besides, the act of photographing is a sort of dance for approaching things, and Ghirri often insists on the possibility of falling into moments of astonishment, or trance states.

September 3

Ghirri's photographs in this album of his have as a central theme the Italian landscape that stretches out around the Po River as far as the Adriatic Sea. They are not arranged according to a thematic list, or in keeping with a geographical itinerary. They are scattered moments gathered together by an analogical lattice, in a plot whose myriad inter-weaving threads cannot be summarised.

Once the word '*trama*' (plot, weft) indicated exactly this kind of weaving together of various narrative threads, as for example in Ariosto. And it is in this way that Ghirri seems to have intended to compose his photographic album, precisely because this narrative principle allows for the dislodging of our gaze in the direction of various stories that travel in company.

September 4

On the threshold of the album, we encounter a painting by the photographer's uncle, Walter Iotti, reminiscent of many aspects of the figurative approach of Ghirri's photographs, for example in the colours and the use of the sky, with the horizon that cuts midway through the image. We are suddenly faced with questions of perspective.

We begin with the large bed in the hotel in Boretto, on the bank of the Po River, adorned with two headboards as monumental and symmetrical as buildings, and then pass to an analogous figure of frontal symmetries, of the two columns at the edge of the beautiful piazza in Pomponesco. These carry the gaze towards the openness of the levees, on a clear winter's day. Instead, on a foggy day, two common pillars arise at the edge of a country estate, displaying the analogical tendency of perspective framing by way of a frontal symmetry.

All of this is part of an environment in which perspectives sprout up like mushrooms. For example, in traveling across England it is rare to encounter anything similar. But perspective framing is also a means of suggesting and guiding a movement towards something to see, and it exemplifies an idea that resides at the source of these photographs. This is the idea that there is always a way of observing that is already expected, or guided, by the thing that we observe.

Ghirri says that a neoclassical construction can never be photographed as a baroque construction, because each demands a different type of vision, frontal or oblique. But all things require being observed in a certain way, according to movements and points of view that help us to see them more clearly. Ghirri's work consists largely in this attempt to adhere to a way of looking that is determined by the thing photographed, relinquishing as much as possible one's own point of view.

It is relatively clear that an old bed with two headboards calls for a frontal view, giving prominence to its monumental symmetry. This symmetry is then analogous to the symmetry of the two columns at the edge of a piazza, which call for being viewed similarly, because our gaze can thus depart towards the openness of the levees. And it is by following the fabric of similar analogies that Ghirri is able to narrate the various tonalities of a landscape.

This is not a photographic documentary on the historic situation of an Italian landscape, but rather a study of the ways of looking that are already determined in a landscape and their affective resonances. It is an album of things that can be seen, indicated in the way in which they ask to be seen.

September 5

When we arrive in this album at the grand arch rising from the landscape paired on the opposite page with a beautiful neoclassical villa, two constructions that call for being seen in the same way, I think one of the basic tonalities of this landscape becomes apparent. Doubtless much depends on the architecture, given that this is one of the most architecturally determined landscapes in the world. However, this type of Italian architecture that Ghirri shows us has always carried within itself an essential tendency towards theatrical vision.

A theatrical tonality is richly apparent in the stage set designed by Aldo Rossi, an extraordinary Italian architect, in which the distinction is clearly visible between the staging for the opera being performed and the architectural forms that envelop it. A theatrical tonality is also called for by the villa on the outskirts of Bologna, presented as a distant melodramatic backdrop, as if emblematic in some way of a diffuse illusionism ubiquitous in this landscape.

September 6

I would say that the overture has come to an end. A vast assemblage of messages embellishes that listing of landscapes in the manner of certain Venetian urban landscape painters, from elevated perspectives. Ghirri says that these landscapes call to be seen from such perspectives, and those who are familiar with these areas know that often the little towns here make their first appearance with a bell tower, with the rest of the buildings coming into view at our feet once we climb to the top of a levee.

With some knowledge of this way of looking, the music can start to come through more clearly. It is the music of the piazzas and streets and walls of old towns across the Po River plains, seen at night. From the piazza in Luzzara to those in Fontanellato and Brescello, to the street in Sabbioneta and the wall in Montagnana, there is carried a song celebrating the architecture by way of the night's colours. Among them the photograph of the piazza in Brescello could appear on the cover on a manual on the ways called for in looking at public spaces from the Renaissance, with a steadiness adhering to the memory of the grand model evoked.

The celebration, however, would have an entirely different flavour, had it not been achieved by way of the colours of the night and twilight, that is, the hues of a modern artificial splendour. This is because, if the streets and piazzas had been photographed by day, they would presumably have appeared as monuments to the past, taking on the guise of historical documents. Instead, with all the artificial colours, the perception of these places as historical monuments is muted, and everything becomes contemporary, as in fact it is.

Everything becomes part of that timeless form that is the world co-present with us, as we perceive it in the passing moments of our everyday lives, as long as we do not start acting knowledgeable. Those walls and piazzas call instead for a fablelike air, being as they are part of an atmospheric vision, one wrapped in colours and tones that lend a sense of haziness to their architectural forms.

The next landscape in the album brings us to fully recognize this atmospheric vision, by way of the murky colours that loom over distant horizons. And this atmospheric vision is in itself a celebration of phenomena, compared to which any historical documentary becomes a vain display of knowledge.

Ghirri's work, as it so intensely emphasizes the contingent character of photography, also makes of it a means of achieving a sense of floating time dislocated from historical coordinates, akin to what we encounter in fables. And yet it can be said that the time that we experience passing by every day is also floating, like the clouds that make their way across the sky, changing shape in strange suspension.

September 11

In our conversations, Ghirri has often spoken of a closing of the landscape, of landscapes that close in upon themselves. Hence the phrase: '[t]o dislodge ways of looking, to open the landscape'.

One day while talking about Ferrara he said that that city gave him the shivers because the orthogonal layout of its streets causes all gazes to run in channels towards vanishing points, even in the way that they must go around the edges of street corners. Then, showing me a photograph of a fisherman's hut on a bank of the Po, near Brescello, at the back of a poplar grove, he pointed out that here too was at play this same game of chessboard symmetries, which is in the end reproduced in all poplar groves.

Certain places in those areas come to mind. For example, the more chaotic the spaces there become, full of utility poles, billboards and new constructions, the more the illusory order of orthogonal symmetries come to the surface. They reappear in way billboards, sidewalks and little geometric houses are arrayed along the roads, the prefabricated little gardens, in epidemic games of geometries as in no other part of the world.

Studying the ways in which it tends everywhere to structure our way of looking, this landscape can at times seem obsessive, because it is a prisoner of its own illusionism, as is Italian culture. There is a perspective and architectural illusionism at play along low-lying horizons, and there is a melodramatic illusionism that leads us to think of all landscapes as more or less absorbing backdrops. And it seems that for us the perception of open space can take only this form: a fissure between two monuments.

When I was at work in this environment taking notes, I often complained with Ghirri about the difficulty of finding some sort of slippage or deviation and sense of wonder with which to move ahead. Doubtless: monotony is nothing but the deluded feeling of those who constantly expect new illusions, as if they needed to be seduced to take even a single step forward.

But it is only from such a place that there can arise the strange idea that there is 'something to see', as some unconditional quality of places, quantifiable by a list of values. While, in reality, there is never anything to see, but only things that we happen to see with greater or lesser zeal, independently of their qualities. A state of mourning attenuates all the colours of a landscape, and one of falling in love reawakens them.

From Ghirri I learned that in situations in which you feel stuck because everything seems monotonous and expected, it is necessary to turn your eyes to the horizon. This is to say: '[t]o dislodge ways of looking, to open the landscape'.

Here then are those distant and barely perceptible horizons under hazy skies – photographs at the edge of the possible that generously open our vision, moving it away from the idea of 'something to see' and instead bringing it back to an animated motion that widens the eyes. As with many other photographs by Ghirri, they simply shift our gaze towards the open and bring us back into contact with the horizon. They bring everything back to an atmospheric vision, to an account of the phenomena that envelop us.

September 15

Atmospheric vision widens the aperture of our outlook, attenuating the isolation of our point of view, and is above all a celebration of the colours and the tones of the sky. In Ghirri's album there arise colours with diffuse light of all sorts that seem capable of unleashing everything. It is their song that is heard everywhere, at a racetrack, on a highway, at an ordinary petrol station. The colours are what lead us to look even as far as the wiry streetlights of the outskirts, or the red and white striped smokestacks that rise up along the Po, from a point of view that is anything but seductive.

Ghirri's narrative is one of phenomena, akin to Robert Flaherty's extraordinary documentary on the Aran Islands, *Man of Aran*, or Joris Ivens' beautiful *Rain*. Atmospheric visions, whose protagonists are not people, but the things and the phenomena in whose company people find themselves.

With such an approach everything seems observable. Something has already occurred in this landscape which releases us from the old pretensions of judging the world as it is, and from determining whether it is dull or interesting. This is because in these photographs it seems as if people have departed, turning the space over to things.

And the things have remained there under the sky, teeming with their colours, neither ugly nor beautiful, but at last observable without interference. What is that glimmer on the horizon, in the direction of that sliver of a crumbling house in the fields? And that motionless geometric house, built in the standard boxy way, next to an old church, it too only partially glimpsed? And what are all these Madonnas up to that I see just about everywhere? The landscape seems a storehouse of leftovers, in which everything continues to have a meaning even if not a use.

There are monuments to unknown soldiers, rooms in which Garibaldi slept, the workshops of mechanics who love to listen to opera and collect portraits of Giuseppe Verdi, and strange obscure museums in old villas that no one visits anymore.

In this setting with a hint of science fiction, in which leftovers continue to have meaning even if not uses, everything truly seems in a state of suspended reality, as in fables. Here one loses track of the old difference between what is obscure and what is familiar. There is no longer any grand journey more stirring than a stroll to see the colours of the world. Perhaps now we are coming to know this little theatre with its vast proscenium, closed only by the curtain of the sky, this storehouse of the forms of art and illusion that is the Italian landscape.

October 1
In looking at the photographs again, I now understand that not even melodramatic illusionism has been left out, the kind that causes us to view all landscapes as if they were painted backdrops.

The image of the yellow church comes to mind, with a bell tower and carnival ride to its side, viewed from a town piazza like many others. The photographer has hewn closely to the architectural staging, pulling from it the tonality of the already seen and the obvious. But with a trace of extreme lightness, given the sky that seems a watercolour.

Herein is a point regarding photography and observation that I have reflected on with others. First, as Ermanno Cavazzoni was saying the other day, these photographs are small theatres that give a sense of an observed world – of a baroque theatre in which an actor sits on the stage facing away from the audience and watching the play unfolding and in so doing showing us that what is occurring is only the observed world. It seems as if these photographs show the photographs of someone attracted to stereotypes of obviousness, which as Ghirri reveals to us, resemble many others taken out of habit, from points of view and framings that seem predetermined.

To this Ghirri responded that he attempts to adhere to the way in which things ask to be seen, but that this way belongs in part to the inhabitants of a place. He said that he is not interested in disguising obviousness, but rather in finding common affective elements. For the rest, I would add, the observed world is not what appears from the point of view of an individual person. It is, according to him, what is already common in various observations and representations, because it belongs to a form of life.

And yet Ghirri's photographs seem to contain a challenge to common biases against obviousness that leads him to photograph even what could be called stereotypes of this melodramatic country. My first impression of the photograph of the confessional in a church that seems a *trompe-l'oeil*, even before fully realizing what it was, brought to mind Stendhal and his theory of Italian melodrama. And the small Verdi theatre in Busseto – is it really possible that it is so pink, so neatly kept, so reassuring? And then the nod to Ariosto, in the image of the fresco from the Mauriziano in Reggio Emilia, the poet's childhood home, in which emphasis is given to the frame because the painted landscape within it starts to resemble a common theatre backdrop.

Ghirri unearths backdrops of this sort even hanging in a farmhouse garage in Casinalbo. Pictorial finds that recall habits and ways of looking, the effect of which is not unlike that of certain still lifes and mannered images in which the obvious and the familiar become sensations of lightness. A country house between two Japanese pagoda trees, a wall brushed by the shadow of a branch, the entrance of a villa in the snow, are facets of an observed world no longer in need of disenchantment.

October 2

In this search for affective elements, Ghirri's photographic staging displays things that resemble stereotypes, but does so by transforming the stereotypes and obviousness into phenomena of colours, reminiscent of the shades of the atmosphere.

You might say that everything lying in corners and closets has been drawn out into the open to be presented on a grand stage that spreads further and further out, like the outdoor theatre that not unsurprisingly attracted our photographer. This effect without doubt depends on the use of light, which is always enveloping and never shown as a partial source, except in a few cases. But this depends too on something else, which leads us to perceive the vast heterogeneous variety of residues and appearances as entirely observable. And this, I believe, can occur only thanks to an extraordinary appetite for looking.

More than teaching us to observe this or that thing, I would say that Ghirri's photographs work by way of contagion. They produce a contagious hunger to observe, which is in essence attention to the splendour of all things enveloped in light. This splendour is their glory, which unsurprisingly does not appear to the disenchanted or sorrowful. It appears to those who for one reason or another find themselves in good company with the horizon and the sky, these two outermost edges of the vast natural theatre of images.

October 3

There is something active, a sense of arduous continuous construction, that I often find in Ghirri's photographs. I see it, for example, in the interiors of houses, which always seem images of a continuance. I also see it in the views of shops, of workshops, which are presented to us as little workshop theatres. Giorgio Morandi's studio too seems a small workshop theatre, with whispered allusions that leave you guessing at something.

The fact remains that all of these are little performances staged with art and illusion that carry us always back to a crafted dimension of the spectacle, such as carnival rides, wedding banquets, town fairs. And these too are night photographs whose fablelike effect is in part produced by artificial light.

One particularly intense narrative thread in the album conjures a Hesiodic 'works and days' vision, perhaps summed up in the perspective view of farm buildings at the far end of a ploughed field: an extraordinary melancholic moment in which the sky, earth and buildings seem to have achieved an extreme harmony, in the vast natural theatre of phenomena.

After these traces of labour come evening, after-work celebrations. Some of these photographs, such as the two taken in Scandiano, produce in me a sense of longing for a film that I will never be able to see because it does not exist, calling me back to moments of enchantment that perhaps were only dreamed. And a story by Robert Walser suddenly comes to mind, about a dogged reader of Gottfried Keller's novels, who one day breaks down crying and saying, 'The world isn't like this.'

In Walser, as in Ghirri's photographs, it would seem that only a laborious effort to make good use of the inauthenticity, the artificiality of all words and images, can redeem the moments of the world, transforming them into phenomena of the vast natural theatre, closed only by horizon and the curtains of the sky. All the artificiality of art and of life then are no longer faults from which we should redeem ourselves but are, above all, signs of good will. The weeping of the woman Walser describes is but the affective base of all this, compassion for the world.

October 4

I now have in front of my eyes the long series of landscape views near the Po Delta, the apex of this imagistic intertwining. Atmospheric vision and song of the horizons at their highest point.

I know these places are almost impossible to approach photographically, because where there is only sky and horizon, photography feels ill at ease. And yet it is exactly because of this difficulty that I find these photographs the high point in the album, because of all the tenuous resonances that have been so as to help render observable this infinitely diffuse space.

There is, however, something else. In speaking of a vast natural theatre of phenomena, I believe that I had in mind Rilke's eighth Duino elegy ('We never even for a single day, have before us / pure space [...] It is always the real world, / never a nowhere void of negation'). We never have access to the open because it lies always on the other side of the threshold of the world. With the term 'world', Rilke intended the obviousness of things and appearances, already understood as being named in a certain way, as being seen in a certain way, and on which are based our indifference or normality.

It seems to me that the profession of the photographer, perhaps more than any other of our era, bears witness to this limit of the representations that underpin our sense of normality and indifference. And this is not a social or historical limit, but a spatial one. It is the horizon as a final proscenium of all possible apparitions, and the sky as an ultimate backdrop of the colours and tones that give an affective quality to the phenomena all around us.

Ghirri leads all appearances and apparitions towards that ultimate backdrop, towards the limit over which open space becomes the world. He manages this through an atmospheric vision, or, in other words, through an affective taste of colours and tones, permitting him to present all the appearances of the world as floating phenomena, and thus no longer as documentable 'facts'.

Every moment in the world is redeemed by the possibility of giving it back a vagueness, that is, of bringing it back to the feeling we have of phenomena. This, it seems to me, Ghirri does in a most extraordinary way, in the final series of images of the Po Delta. Here we are called to a basic attention to the phenomena of colours and lights that are so undefined and undefinable as to destabilize the very notion that there truly exist documentable 'facts'. These images are artifices of vagueness, to borrow an old term from Italian art, to indicate something resembling the phenomena of the clouds, the sky and the horizon.

October 6
Rereading what I have written, I find myself as someone seemingly lost in interpretations, fully aware that all interpretations float about in the air, and nothing will ever bring them back to earth. And then suddenly that someone is overcome by the opposite urge, to pose only pragmatic questions, to look only for precise facts.

For example, how can a photographer assemble all these artifices? Ghirri responds that just as a writer cannot help but put trust in words and sentences, a photographer cannot help but put trust in a way of framing things. But how can things be envisaged in a frame, in landscapes that are not designed to guide the eye, such as the Po Delta?

Ghirri responds that even in the delta there are foreseeable ways of looking. For example, along levees, along valleys as they open up, or lengthwise across cultivated fields. But, first of all, one must find viewpoints that are comprehensible to others. You must reject the notion of an individual viewpoint, because otherwise you end up spying and not looking. Photography is unnatural for this reason, in general. But in working at framing the camera, one can reach certain approximations that evoke a collective vision and a spontaneous way of looking.

He continues:

Everything that we see, lives only in a frame. Even the sea – how can I photograph it if I don't put it in a frame? It is something like having a window through which to view phenomena, and like a child you must write an essay on what you see. You look through the window, but who is looking? A story by Calvino comes to mind: it is the world looking at the world.

Note

1 Some of the photographs from Ghirri's *Il profilo delle nuvole: Immagini di un paesaggio italiano* [The profile of the clouds: Images of an Italian landscape] mentioned in this preface to the book by Celati can be viewed here: *The Atlas of Places*, https://www.atlasofplaces.com/photography/il-profilo-delle-nuvole/; *Nadir Magazine*, https://www.nadir.it/libri/PROFILONUVOLE/ProfiloNuvole.htm; and *Archivio Luigi Ghirri*, https://www.archivioluigighirri.com/artworks/il-profilo-delle-nuvole.

Figure 18.1   Gianni Celati and Luigi Ghirri, 1990, by Luigi Ghirri. © Eredi Luigi Ghirri.

19
'Swift, prophetic treatise on the modern age' ('Swift, profetico trattato sull'epoca moderna', 1990)

I.

What many consider to be Pieter Bruegel the Elder's last painting, *The Storm at Sea*, features a tempest-wracked ship whose sailors have tossed a barrel into the water at a menacing whale. In one of Jonathan Swift's most compelling works, *A Tale of a Tub* (*Favola della botte* in my translation), we find the same image enlarged and offered as an explanation of the title. When the sailors are attacked by the whale, they 'fling him out an empty Tub, by way of amusement, to divert him from laying violent hands upon the Ship'. It is possible that a rendering of Bruegel's painting found its way into an old printing of Swift's book, given their shared moral allusion. In Bruegel's image the barrel thrown at the whale to distract it can be seen as emblematic of human folly – or of the common tendency for one's attention to be arrested by the nearest attraction, as in another of Bruegel's paintings that depicts a little monkey captured when distracted by a peanut. Swift's title alludes to something similar, because the expression 'tale of a tub' carries the connotation of a tall tale or fish story: one meant to dupe and poke fun at fools.

The book's preface tells us of the meeting of a grand committee to investigate the dangers associated with certain intellectuals of the era whose criticisms threatened grave injury to both Church and State. And here is the nature of the whale: this imminent threat – namely Thomas Hobbes's 1651 *Leviathan*, the source 'from whence the terrible wits of our age are said to borrow their weapons'. Hobbes's book becomes a monster that disrupts traditional political thought, due to its proposing of a materialist theory of the State and its identification of ethics as simple rules of convenience. The ship here represents the ancient

Christian consortium threatened by the mythic Old Testament whale (the Leviathan in Hobbes's title). And what can we make of the barrel thrown at the whale? It is the book we are reading, written to be thrown at the terrible wits of the age to distract and beguile them with words, to buy time for the arrival of reinforcements to hold off their assault on Church and State.

This explanation gives an initial sense of the book we are reading – a yarn or tall tale that amuses by means of fatuity and new ideas, in keeping with many other books of the time – modernist treaties stuffed with erudite digressions and panegyrics that lead nowhere. Our book is indeed presented as the work of one of those prosers of the era, compilers or authors of books written to exploit a fad. It is also a compendium of calls to modernity, an acclamation of the attractions of the new, an avowed imitation of forward-thinking authors of the time, written for 'the Universal Benefit of Mankind'. It is a parody of many future books to be written with the objective of saving the world with a fabrication – and a prophetic treatise on the modern world as an era of shapelessness in which things fall into a state of complete disorder.

II.

A Tale of a Tub was Swift's first book, published in 1704, anonymously, as were all his books. With its attribution to an anonymous proser and even more so its bountiful flourishes of bookish eloquence, the text seems written with the desire to be mixed up with the mass of useless chatter of the popular press, to sink into the cauldron of literary vanities, the aping of toploftical speeches, headless hodgepodges. There is something quite special about this treatise: as a project of talking in endless circles, of revealing its own absolute inconclusiveness, with a swarm of discourses that circle a hole inside of which one espies not the famous Void, but rather Chaos. One espies the shapeless hubbub of an age that prides itself on being modern out of parti pris.

The book achieved a certain European fame, with eighteenth-century French, Dutch and German translations, but remained all but unknown in Italy until recently. I came upon it while at university in a collection of Swift's writings that included a few of its chapters; I suddenly felt the urge to translate all of it into Italian, since no one had done so. Even in England the text had remained shunted to the side, considered by the critics to be too violent and contrary to moral and religious precepts. Included in a miscellany of Swifts writings in 1720, it was then reprinted in Temple Scott's 1814 grand *Prose Works of Jonathan Swift*; in 1920 a critical edition appeared, and then only in 1986 a paperback edition, issued by Oxford University Press. I later hazarded a first translation, laborious and badly done, but could access the book only in libraries in the 1814 edition, whereas the collections of Swift's work I managed to find had at best only snippets, but often excluded it entirely.

I remember my impressions at the time: being staggered by his sarcasms that spared nothing; feeling admiration for his serio-comic vivaciousness; being continually surprised by his way of entering disorder without then seeing it from the outside. William Alfred Eddy wrote that if Swift was admired and feared more than loved, it was because he did not write from the heart. It was exactly this unlovable, anti-seductive aspect of his, unreconcilable with the fictions of goodness, with all novelesque and humanizing veneers, that most attracted and struck me. Swift writes as if he were an alien seeing humanity as a race doomed to falseness, duped by all possible deceptions. His tone is so unnaturally detached that it can leave you stunned – but also uncomfortable, with sudden invective or sarcasm, especially readers in search of solace in common forms of print media. Swift indeed does not write from the heart. But the effect of his work that sticks in the mind is that of a clear and unmistakable discourse in which the words lose their discursive and prosaic quality, causing our imagination to take off. His is not the flight of novelesque imagination, but one of a pure style that moves sentence by sentence into another space, an indefinable space, in which our opinions and analyses no longer count for anything.

III.

In looking over the range of Swift's work, it becomes apparent that almost all his writings mimic various forms of popular print media of his day, such as almanacs, astrological predictions, open letters published in newspapers, proposals of political reform, treatises on new discoveries, pamphlets and manuals on etiquette. Reading his work as it appeared over time, one passes through an encyclopaedia of common, low-prestige genres, imitated with great precision. Not only amusing genres, but also pedantic ones, and most of all publications of London's famous Grub Street, the home of various hack writers who worked for the printing industry – a tribe whose members included the supposed author of *A Tale of a Tub*. These are true Swiftian heroes, scribblers who lived hand-to-mouth in the boom years of the book market, rewriting old novels, assembling compilations of selected passages, or composing apocryphal 'second parts' to famous books by authors such as Cervantes, Boccalini and La Bruyère. Apart from a few cases, Swift's texts are falsely presented as having been written by drudge writers of this sort, or by promotors of political projects, almanac merchants, tradesmen who decided to take up the pen and by others in one way or another involved in the trafficking of the illusions of common print media. There is always in Swift's work the taste of the vacuousness of the popular press, of the typographical world as an unnatural one, alien and populated by aliens.

Question: how long can the world in print be surprising or perturbing as in Swift? Response: I would say as long as printed words remain anonymous discourses, not yet marked by the humanizing figure of the author as we understand it today. Like Swift's works, so much of the print media of the period was anonymous or apocryphal; when you manage to remove the obscuring figure of the writer, the words form an apocryphal world, like the graffiti we read on walls or obscene messages in public toilets. They appear to us as utterances that have become things, without a re-constructible relationship to the person who thought them up, lacking any sacred justification. They are simply pieces of our world, scattered and strange, whose origins remain always murky.

This is true too of the book here translated, in which it is easy to lose one's way amid the tangle of discourses that seem haphazardly pieced together, with frequent ellipses to indicate missing sections. The digressions are particularly amorphous, each a sort of stylistic exercise that takes off on its own flight. Everything seems tossed together, with leftover pieces put in an appendix, as if they had been lost along the way. And then, in the footnotes that shift and at time overflow the page, the sense of a stable authorial identity is further undermined, as the notes are by an anonymous editor attempting to decipher the meaning of the text – or even notes by hostile critics added to spice up the book. The book's general structure, as reconstructed by Angus Ross and David Woolley in their 1986 Oxford University Press edition, reveals a mosaic of fragments that are held together as if by a miracle:

1. The book's backbone, which recounts the stories of three brothers, Peter, Jack and Martin, who respectively represent Catholicism, Protestantism and Anglicanism. Their stories are of the religious conflicts that followed the reforms in Luther's wake, imagined as sort of puppet theatre. These five chapters are interspersed with

digressive chapters, but these often roam off on fanciful digressions on Catholicism and Puritanism.

2. The alternating five digressive chapters are like rhetorical flowers. There is the acidic 'Digression Concerning Critics', the extraordinary 'Digression in the Modern Kind', the entertaining 'Digression in Praise of Digressions', the mad digression in praise of madness – and so on.

3. The book opens with a list of the extravagant treatises penned by our 'Author', followed by an 'Apologia' of the book addressed to the Right Honourable John Lord Somers, the Bookseller's 'Note to the Reader', the 'Epistle Dedicatory to His Royal Highness Prince Posterity' (so as to render the book immortal), the preface in which the title is explained, and at long last, the real and actual introduction. All these are imitations that mock the interminable prefaces of the most reputable books and the rancid eloquence of panegyrics.

This jumble would never hold together without the fiction of an anonymous compiler, our modernist littérateur. This person seems a true alien among the living beings of the normal world, or a crazy person, taken over by the illusion of writing a book that will be translated into all languages, including Chinese (as he says). As happens with the insane, with him we are unable to have any comprehensible human relationship, and his pages are words wandering about in some ethereal realm of erudite references, or a performance of puppets manipulated by an unknown puppeteer who does not need to be original to draw us into his disjointed universe. All this then is a sign of the era: these are the last bizarre traces of old baroque treatises, at the dawn of a new, more scientific and pragmatic era. After Swift the problem of the literati will be to find humanizing veneers, the inventing of the author as an original and humane wellspring of words. But if things had remained as they were in Swift's time, there would be no need to invent the alien worlds of science fiction.

IV.

Let us look at a few of Swift's books so as to have a sense of their contents. Let us take up his proposal to reduce Christianity to a purely nominal religion in which all moral scruples would be eliminated apart from certain useful religious precepts, such as the piquant taste of sin, the political exploitation of the bishops and the profitable trade with pagan peoples. Or let us consider another serious discourse proposing that the English nobility add to their diet a particularly tasty new dish – the meat of Irish children, stewed, roasted, baked or boiled – with detailed explanations as to how this would be an enlightened way of resolving the problems of Irish impoverishment. Or take in hand another piece on the possibility of scientifically determining whether the excrement encountered on the streets of Dublin originated from either English or Irish behinds. Or consider *The Tale of the Tub*, the book at hand.

Would Swift have been able to write texts of this sort had they not been published with the anonymity of the printing press? Certainly, it would not have been in his best interest to have claimed them as his own. However, as the compiler notes in his 'Apologia', anonymity is no disagreeable diversion, neither for the author nor the public. Swift indeed plays much with anonymity. He makes the most of the effect of printed words that come to us by way of an anonymous means of support, such as a stretch of wall, an inked sheet of paper. Their meaning erupts forth as if seeming to lack any trace of a common enunciation, as a vertigo of overwhelming meanings that rise over and beyond us. In the writers who come later the sense of this vertigo will be lost, and of the myriad accompanying shams. The taste of that deception is still fresh in Rabelais, who mocks as he plunders popular almanacs and erudite books. It is also fresh in Cervantes, who discusses it a length in *Don Quixote*, and for good reason invents a hero who does not understand the difference between the world of people and the world of the printed word. You can say what you will: all possible words, as soon as they are touched by the alienness of printer's ink, seem to acquire the right to demand attention from us. This magic certainly comes to play in *A Tale of a Tub*. If all printed words can demand our attention, they all become similar. It does not matter whether they are futile, false or plagiarized, or even if they spin in circles. In fact, at the end the author states that this is 'an experiment very frequent among modern authors, which is to write upon nothing, when the subject is utterly exhausted to let the pen still move on; by some called the ghost of wit, delighting to walk after the death of its body'.

In the conclusion it is also said that a book is a journey where anyone can stop whenever they want to admire the landscape, choosing the path they like best, but also a journey on which any fellow travellers in a hurry to reach the destination are nuisances to be given the slip as soon as possible. It is a parable that brings an air of freedom from the obligations of sensibility, of openness to pure diversion. But there is more. The book wanders like an aimless journey, written about nothing, letting the pen move of its own accord, forming a hole from which there arises a whirl of words that no longer have a centre, no reason for being, no foundation.

They are words from which one can no longer tell whether falsehood and futility can be subject to indictment, or whether they are instead of the mercurial nature of all things on which all our concepts must rely. In this loquacious and volatile universe, one no longer knows where a morally guaranteed truth might dwell, in books or elsewhere. Swift was a reader of Cervantes, a fact that brings to mind an episode from *Don Quixote* (Part 2, Chapter LXX), with its strange descent to the gate of hell, where Altisidora witnesses devils playing tennis with modern books stuffed with wind and rubbish. This seems emblematic of Swift's image of society as an immense theatre of forgeries, in which all printed books, as social pathways, can be nothing but balls full of wind and rubbish.

V.

A Tale of a Tub is the serio-comic exaltation of a new era of social life: the era of volatile words capable of pronouncing nothing anymore except instantaneous and contagious falsifications. The Introduction expounds upon oratorical machines that spout competitive words in a war of opinions. These words have no meaning, only weight, for it is according to the weight of printed matter that the merits of various political factions are assessed. In the Epistle to the Royal Highness Prince Posterity, it is said that words are now like elusive clouds of a windy day, already replaced by differently shaped clouds after a minute, all destined to float a moment and be lost in nothingness. By now there is only the volatile word, the wit that is worth only a moment, the anecdote that makes sense for a day, the book that tomorrow no one will remember. In this vision, printed matter becomes the vehicle of a shapeless inchoateness; printed matter is in and of itself the creation of the world, of a virtual world made of momentary breezes that are lost in nothingness, in which it is clear that words can no longer spread credible messages.

But we must delve deeper into the situation Swift recounts to us. His 1710 pamphlet *The Art of Political Lying* recounts the great upheaval that took place in the world with the entry of Fame, understood as the triumph of newspapers. Fame becomes the fundamental weapon, wielded no longer by the Devil but by the modern figure of the political liar. The political liar is the representative of the parliamentary regime, who speaks according to the interests of his party; by combining information and lies, he can 'make a saint of an atheist, and a patriot of a profligate' or 'furnish foreign ministers with intelligence'. But, the author adds, the political liar must have the gift of a short memory: that is, he must be able to instantly forget every lie he has told, believing each time that he has told the truth, and lying again when he must tell it again, with a lie that in turn will become a truth to lie about. He is able, in so doing, to always swear 'to both sides of a contradiction', lying either way, but in addition rejecting any criteria for distinguishing the true from the false. If then, says the pamphlet, one abandons logic and accuses politicians of perjury because they always invoke God and morality, one is wrong again. For they do not believe in either, so they cannot be perjurers. And if by chance a lie is publicly exposed? If a lie is told at the appropriate time, it has already fulfilled its function, for it has pure strategic value according to the place and the moment in which it is spread: 'Falsehood flies, and truth comes limping after it, so that when men come to be undeceived, it is too late; the jest is over, and the tale hath had its effect.' The old motto, that truth always triumphs, has gone out of fashion.

VI.

To sum up: in the scenario Swift recounts, a 'truth deficit' has arisen. Any attempt to verify some correspondence to the truth is futile, precisely because we are talking about the lack of truth, its deficit. We are very far from the satirical authors who condemn the vices of the world as if they were looking at them from the top of a hill, with a manual of moral precepts under their arm. With Swift, such a trick no longer works to put one's conscience at peace. In his writings, one is at the mercy of volatile words, thrust immediately into the ephemeral, inside the 'truth deficit' and the canonical formulas of the printed page. In reading his work we find ourselves suddenly without the lifesaver of a moral truth at hand, because everything flows by in a mercurial stream of language.

With this in mind, I can attempt a sketch of Swiftian theatre, his *theatrum mundi*, with the first question that comes to mind being: what kinds of plays are being performed? Swift's interest in mental asylums can be seen in his service as a governor of the Dublin workhouse and as a trustee of several hospitals; he would leave a large part of his estate to help build the Dublin mental hospital, intending it to be charitable and more humane than Bedlam. Of particular interest here is a custom of those times, when members of the public went to watch the mad in their cells, as a form of paid entertainment. In his *Journal to Stella* (13 December 1710), Swift notes that he and a group of friends, on a winter afternoon, went to see the lions in the London Tower, then the madmen in the asylum, then the Royal Society at Gresham College and finally a puppet show. It strikes me that those four types of entertainment are presented together in the space of a sentence as similar entertainments. Swift's theatre is inspired by these kinds of amusements, which are in the end facets of a sort of world theatre: the zoo shows, the scientific *Wunderkammer*, the puppet theatre and finally the theatre of the insane.

In particular, the association between the spectacle of madmen and the spectacle of scientists in the Royal Society seems to me to be at the heart of Swift's theatre – for knowledge is seen as inflated and represented by characters in the grip of galloping prideful madness: scientists, astrologers, philosophers, pen-pushers, reformers. Here is the source of the most provocative proposal of his *theatrum mundi*, to see all institutions as inflicted with prideful bloating whose activities resemble those of insane asylums. This is the gist of Chapter IX of *A Tale of a Tub*, in which he advocates the use of madmen from asylums to perform administrative, political, scientific and military tasks. And to show what advantageous contributions lunatics would bring to the commonwealth, our author cites cases of monarchs, preachers and philosophers who accomplished great feats precisely because they were 'crazed or out of their wits'. The chapter ends with a description of an insane asylum, doubtlessly inspired by the spectacle of the insane in the London asylum: each in their cell making strange gestures, talking to themselves, squinting, mucking about in their own faeces. It is an image that seems emblematic of Swiftian theatre – this enigma in humanity that is madness, which reduces us to a spectacle of pure bodily matters, tics, stenches, agitations, faeces and urine – here is humanity at its natural end. But it is precisely Swift's 'heartless' language that makes it the extreme spectacle of all proud bloatings, and at the same time the allegory of something hiding behind social adornments: the disorder and formlessness of the brute body. This is the ultimate nature of a *theatrum mundi* affected by a 'truth deficit', one that cannot be judged from the outside.

VII.

One of the favourite targets of *A Tale of a Tub* is the rationalized inspiration of the Puritans or Calvinists, presented as a modernist development. Calvinists claim an individual contact with divinity, without the mediation of a religious bureaucracy, as in Catholicism. Swift presents this new idea as an invention of the brother Jack, a figure of Calvinite or Puritan fanaticism, 'a person whose intellectuals were overturned and his brain shaken out of its natural position' by his brother Peter – representing the

Catholic dogmatism of Rome, inventor of other *mirabilia*. In exposing the brother Jack's invention, Swift elaborates a theory of inspired language, wherein Calvinist knowledge and inspiration are figured as intestinal or other bodily gasses.

The doctrine of Jack's sect rests on a syllogism: 'Words are but wind, and learning is nothing but words; ergo, learning is nothing but wind' (Ch. VIII). It is thanks to this quip that inspiration becomes a modern convenience accessible to all; for all one has to do is to carry around a bladder of air to put into one's body, rectally or otherwise, and the learning that once descended on the apostles will enter any fanatic. Moreover, the inspired words will be able to be measured and evaluated according to the breeziness with which they erupt, by posterior or anterior ways as belches (sacred in Jack's sect, 'the noblest act of a rational creature'). Swift reduces Calvinist inspiration to an aeriform phenomenon, like that of volatile, flighty words: states of turbulence in a man's bowels, or tumefactions of his rod that excite drivel (other signs of holiness in Jack's sect).

The key phrase that descended from God in moderns becomes 'individual inspiration', which takes the form of mechanical impulses arising from vapours in the brute body. Here Swift reveals the oddity of the individual, a typically modern invention: the individual who claims his own originality of thought, but then follows recipes that are in vogue and suitable for anyone. Typical is the modern habit of rapidly acquiring knowledge, set forth in a digression (Ch. V), wherein knowledge already seems to be a mass convenience. The core of the explanation is this: moderns believe it is possible to extract the contents of the various discourses of knowledge, to concentrate all the knowledge of mankind in a few small volumes, putting it within everyone's reach. One of the recipes suggested the brilliant fifth chapter is this: distil in a bain-marie 'all modern bodies of arts and sciences whatsoever, and in what language you please', evaporating their volatile elements; redistil the resulting condensation 17 times, reducing it to an elixir to be stored in a vial; drink a vial of this elixir on an empty stomach, and immediately the knowledge will expand in man's brain, allowing him to compose as many books as he wants, on any subject – proven by the fact that the book we are reading was born in the very manner, the author assures us.

VIII.

At the heart of Swift's *theatrum mundi* are clothes and fashion, apparent at the very start of the fable concerning the three brothers Peter, Jack and Martin. The fable tells us that the representatives of the three branches of Christianity went astray because they could not help but follow fashion trends. But the theme expands into an allegory, which harkens back to the Kabbalistic theory that the things of the world are garments of divinity. The author then explains that the universe is 'a large suit of clothes which invests everything', in which the soul is a garment and religion is composed of nothing but more items of clothing. And the Mayor of London? Nothing but a gold chain, red gown, white rod and great horse. There is in this passage a striking stylistic expansion worth quoting at length:

> Look on this globe of earth, you will find it to be a very complete and fashionable dress. What is that which some call land but a fine coat faced with green, or the sea but a waistcoat of water-tabby? Proceed to the particular works of the creation, you will find how curious journeyman Nature hath been to trim up the vegetable beaux; observe how sparkish a periwig adorns the head of a beech, and what a fine doublet of white satin is worn by the birch. (Ch. II)

And man? Man is nothing 'but a microcoat, or rather a complete suit of clothes with all its trimmings'. And the achievements of his mind? A suit of clothes to cover his shame:

> To instance no more, is not religion a cloak, honesty a pair of shoes worn out in the dirt, self-love a surtout, vanity a shirt, and conscience a pair of breeches, which, though a cover for lewdness as well as nastiness, is easily slipped down for the service of both. (Ch. II)

These last lines illustrate a divergence in stylistic movement in Swift's prose with respect to the previous passage. The first is a simulated allegoresis, high in tone; the second points to specific examples, often with tremendous sarcasm, repulsive figuration and a slaying of fine sentiment. It seems to me to be well summed up in one oft-quoted example, which takes us right to the heart of Swift's fashion show:

> Yesterday I ordered the carcass of a beau to be stripped in my presence, when we were all amazed to find so many unsuspected faults under one suit of clothes. Then I laid open his brain, his heart and his spleen, but I plainly perceived at every operation that the farther we proceeded, we found the defects increase upon us, in number and bulk. (Ch. IX)

There is no dramatic unveiling of the shapeless mass of ventricles and nerves, hidden behind social adornment; there is, however, the cruel realization of an incongruity between an outside and an inside – between the organ-stuffed darkness of the human body and the *mise-en-scene* of the outside world filled with passing fashions. This is Swift's peerless art: a rapturous stylistic piercing of human faults with a velocity and intensity that proves disturbing to many. The quartering of the young man seems a dismemberment of the living body of social simulations – and leads to volatile associations of ideas: between the ephemerality at the heart of all fashion and the dead substance of which a corpse consists.

IX.

Swift's last pamphlet from 1733 is entitled *A Serious and Useful Scheme to Make a Hospital for Incurables*. Here the author calculates the expense of admitting all manner of insane people into an asylum and makes a list of the types to be admitted there, including incurable fools, knaves, scolds, coxcombs, scribblers and liars, as well as the incurably envious and vain, not mention prime ministers and governors, who – given their office – accumulate multiple qualifications for admission among the insane. But then the author himself asks to be accepted into his dreamed asylum:

> My private reason for soliciting so early to be admitted is, because it is observed that schemers and projectors are generally reduced to beggary; but, by my being provided for in the hospital, either as an incurable fool or a scribbler, that discouraging observation will for once be publicly disproved.

In Swift's writings, there is never anyone left off the list of lunatics; everyone is included – even the author of *A Tale of a Tub* eventually requests that privilege. The asylum begins to resemble a place where one is removed from the dangers of the world, with everyone in their own cell, alone with their own follies. All the regurgitation of passing fads ends up here, going about in a peaceful and sensible way. Swift's way of grappling with social lies is not that of pompous condemnation, but rather stems from listening to the voices in the public square, sensing that all are words in the wind, words that in a moment will mean nothing, but that also comprise the theatre of the world – a world in which everything, being as volatile as words, is always on the verge of losing meaning and vanishing over the horizon like clouds on a summer day.

In this sense, everything Swift wrote serves to compose a view of a world of ruins, over which the scythe of Time triumphs. In 'The Epistle Dedicatory to His Royal Highness Prince Posterity', the author speaks of the mythical figure of time, armed with a scythe, under whose blade fall modern works like his own:

> I beseech you to observe that large and terrible scythe which your governor affects to bear continually about him. Be pleased to remark the length and strength, the sharpness and hardness, of his nails and teeth; consider his baneful, abominable breath, enemy to life and matter, infectious and corrupting, and then reflect whether it be possible for any mortal ink and paper of this generation to make a suitable resistance. [...] His inveterate malice is such to the writings of our age, that, of several thousands produced yearly from this renowned city, before the next revolution of the sun there is not one to be heard of.

In this allegorical parody, the modern age is staged as one in which the new and the ruins of time are one and the same. The proliferation of ever-new volatile words marks nothing but the daily grind of death, a panorama of mortality accelerated by the rapid turn of fashion. (It is worth pointing out the similarities with the dialogue between death and fashion in *Operette morali*. But Leopardi had not read Swift, to my knowledge.)

20
'The sentiment of space' ('Il sentimento dello spazio', 1991)

A conversation with Manuela Teatini, occurring shortly after the release of the film *Strada provinciale delle anime* (Provincial road of the souls), a 'pseudo-documentary' that recounts the crossing of the Po River Valley by Celati and a group of friends, relatives and collaborators in a blue bus, revisiting many places earlier encountered in *Verso la foce*, as well as *Narratori delle pianure* and *Quattro novelle sulle apparenze*.

When did you first become interested in the landscape of the Po River Delta, which in addition to *Strada provinciale* is the topic of a number of your books?

After I had returned from the States, in 1979, I decided one day to go see the little village where my mother was born. I believe that it all started there, my return to thinking about these areas, and I began to dedicate myself to explorations of the delta that have continued for a number of years.

What is the relationship between this video story and your writing?

I wanted to revisit these places in another way, together with other people. And so I thought of bringing my relatives from Ferrara together with friends on a journey to the Po Delta and to film the stages of the journey. Stories are born in this way, when you are able to find a rhythm and a logic in something that you have seen or felt.

How did the project come together?

Luckily, I found some extraordinary collaborators, who wandered with me for many months over the delta flatlands, attempting to piece together my ideas. We studied ways to shoot takes, but I still wasn't very convinced. Only when we came to editing the film did the sense of a coherent vision come through.

What aspects of documentary filmmaking interest you the most?

I don't have much faith in documentaries because the idea that images are able to convey a true sense of reality belongs to a way of thinking that is not mine. It seems to me that documentaries are stories like all other stories. And yet neither does the idea appeal to me of a 'fiction' in which cinema is inextricably trapped.

Are there films or directors that have particularly influenced you?

In the end I feel closest to the documentary tradition of Joris Ivens, Flaherty, Murnau and Rossellini. There is a short documentary by Joris Ivens about the rain that I wouldn't trade for all contemporary cinema. I'm also very attached to Visconti's *Ossessione* and Antonioni's *Il grido*, but I don't see these films having much to do with what I've done. On the other hand, the roving sequences shot along the streets of Naples and elsewhere in Rossellini's *Viaggio in Italia* often came to mind while we were shooting our story.

What distances you so much from contemporary cinema?

I don't feel at ease with the idea of 'fiction', because this necessitates a sleight of hand that I can't stand. I feel a profound fatigue for the all staging needed to dupe viewers, all for the sole objective that the spectacle triumphs. If spectators need this staging, it only due to their emotional flaccidity.

What sort of story is able to escape from the trap of this sleight of hand?

I have always preferred the most archaic sort of storytelling, fables and epic poems, the pictorial cycles of Giotto, Sassetta and Piero della Francesca. Here the principle is that everything is memorable only for the fact that we recount it, or in other words, what counts is that something emerges in images and words, and that which emerges is a collection of stories about the world. For example, documentaries that I have seen about the last world war made from clips of amateur films have this sense of memorable things, only because they were captured by a movie camera.

How much does painting have to do with this video story?

I once went to the museum of ancient art in Vienna, and it was a remarkable experience. There are dozens and dozens of rooms dedicated to Italian art, and this brings about a sense of near suffocation. In Italian painting, beginning at a certain time, space is closed, being only a matrix of lines that lead towards the centre of the picture. And this is the type of space that I also see in cinema, a space in which everything exists only with regard to the action represented. Instead, when at the museum in Vienna I arrived at the room containing Brueghel, it was like exiting a nightmare. In his work, space becomes something in which you become lost, where every object carries on along its own path in the light and is not a collection of perspective lines that carry the eye towards a prede-termined point.

How would you describe images?

Images are only appearances – that is, phenomena of light, nothing of substance. All that we can ask of images is to leave things and people in their space, to make us feel their distance. This is the sentiment of space. Space has a unitary sense, an affective tonality, because it is the tone of nearby things and distant things, and it is in this way that we orient ourselves in the world. When you lose this sense of distance, images take on the sense of things to capture, and are used to annihilate the space around things and people. And this is the current use of images, in the news and in cinema.

Was Luigi Ghirri's participation key to the filming?

I learned much from Ghirri. Yet when it came to working with the film camera, I realized that I had tendencies different than his. He prefers the frontal view, such as in the work of the great Venetian painters, and I instead tend towards an oblique and obstructed view. I am drawn to elements in the frame that distract the view, in order to have a contrast between the point of observation and the thing observed. I prefer that space is left to wrap around the thing observed, treating it with tact and leaving it in a state of its own vagueness.

What changes in shifting from writing to using a movie camera?

I don't know how to precisely explain the difference between writing and using a movie camera. I believe it all depends on a type of vision, and vision is not a technical factor but a state of spirit, a state of body and of mind. In vision there is no clear separation between voice and image, because voices become images and vice versa.

How were you able to carry out the practical matter of turning this state of vision into a film without a script?

Our project was an intuitive one, a project of the eye and ear. It takes a certain effort to forget the theories, to put aside academic cleverness, with which the pavements are clogged. For example, in studying music you realize that everything is entrusted to your perception, to the readiness of your ear. And it is in this way, I believe, that we carried out the film.

In terms of the landscape, how would you define what the provincial means today?

In his introduction to *Racconti della bassa*, Antonio Delfini writes that the true provincials are those who consider a province an isolated phenomenon, something that can be observed from above. As a matter of fact, current intellectual culture, especially the type found in universities, is very provincial for exactly this reason. This is because it views everything from above in a Tower of Babel that is, in fact, a very limited province, made up of stereotyped jargons and ridiculous terminologies. Living in this Tower of Babel, one enters into a state of amnesia in which remembrance fades of what life is like down on earth.

There are a number of younger directors interested in the provincial, including Mazzacurati and Luchetti. Do you think that the provincial can be of more interest than the urban?

The idea of recovering the provincial is of no interest to me, because it often seems only a sociological or news-like discovery. I think that the provincial is above all a state of spirit. It is that limited horizon in which each of us lives, and where we can all let go, living in a sort of floating enchantment together with others. This is the effect of habits, a sort of floating enchantment of which we are rarely aware. And then there is all this modern anxiety to overcome the banalities of life, to be stunned by something extraordinary, something never seen before. All this angst over avoiding our inadequacy has the air of the reparation of an error. But the error is simply that of existing in the world.

Where does the title of the video story come from?

We found the title *Strada provinciale delle anime* during our second location scouting trip. It is the name of a road just outside of Portomaggiore, currently closed where it meets a level crossing. From there grew the logic behind our story, beginning with that road and with that name.

The name is dense with mystery and is evocative of an exploration. Did you choose it for this reason?

In the name there is, above all, the idea of a journey. And I was thinking along the lines of something like *The Canterbury Tales*, that is, of a sort of pilgrimage in which the travellers all tell stories. I had many stories ready, but then I realized that all that was necessary were phrases and thoughts with which various voices would reveal themselves. And then in the name there is the notion of the provincial, which is dear to me. And at last, there is the appeal to souls, which is an ancient way of acknowledging what connects all people, each to everyone else.

21
'Introductory note', *Narrators of the reserves* ('Note d'avvio', da *Narratori delle riserve*, 1992)

I began gathering the pieces that make up this book a few years ago while editing the story section of a newspaper. Afterward I continued the collection on my own, reading a bit of everything: stories of occasional writers, manuscripts of people who lacked audiences, work of little-known and isolated authors, and work by others better known. I sought out writings that were not shaped by external pressures: writing not out of the pressure to publish a book, but in those moments in which it becomes possible to write for the sake of writing, for the thing itself, without having to prove anything to anyone.

In this book all the writers make their own way, travelling beyond any category that could contain so many divergent callings, and thus the collection should be seen as an album of distinct cases. The only common element running through all the pieces (it seems to me) is the fact that writing can be self-sufficient, in the sense that it need not resort to external stimuli, to social problems or current events, to some sort of wittiness or exciting revelations. This is a sign of absorption in the experience of writing, absorption in the thing itself, when writing lacks pretences. Rhythm and the tonality of the words are enough – the only essential things.

And yet there is another comment element in many if not all the texts: an attitude in writing that is similar to that in reading, a way of looking that retraces things as if reading a pre-existing text. This might take the form of mental hospital protocols (Ermanno Cavazzoni), of news of a turn-of-the-century giant (Nico Orengo), of common toys (Sandra Petriganane), of ordinary everyday words (Mara Cini), of an artist's work (Massimo Riva) or of an old trail (Marianne Schneider): all are ways to rediscover reserves of things to read by way of writing, always with the sense of something already experienced or felt, or in other words, not revealed for the first time. The visible is always already seen, the expressible already expressed.

Writing brings us closer to reserves of things that were already there on the horizon, ahead of us. And from now on we can also live without new visions of the world.

Figure 21.1 Gianni Celati during the filming of *Strada provincial delle anime*, 1991. Reprinted by permission of Gillian Haley.

22
'Threshold for Luigi Ghirri: how to think in images' ('Soglia per Luigi Ghirri: Come pensare per immagini', 1992)

Two trees form the threshold of the image, like the wings of a stage, beyond which there is nothing particularly extraordinary to see: two rows of more trees that extend outward in the direction of a motorway. Luigi Ghirri photographed many thresholds in his life: thresholds of small farms, rural houses, piazzas, palaces and theatres, and thresholds represented by the empty goals of soccer pitches.[1] He was always going about in search of such things, which give a sense of order to the framing, create a stage effect and double the photographic threshold across which our vision passes.

And as we stand before these thresholds, looking into the distance, we always see something very ordinary. In the distance there is the full order of the visible world, which we can at last read like a printed book, because the threshold positions us in such a helpful way. We are on the near side of the threshold, with all the disorder of our thoughts, and on the far side is the vast order of the visible world, that is, a habit of seeing order in everything. This gives us a sense of trust, and perhaps for this reason Ghirri's photographs are comforting.

To describe this order of the visible world is not something that can be easily done. Perhaps it is only a sort of trust, a patient waiting. And yet this order, which Ghirri has studied for his whole life, allows us to think in images.

I.

I come across a photograph I recall by Ghirri from his first collection, from 1974: two Sunday cyclists wearing racing jerseys pass along a country road, in the background a truck is parked on the side of the road, in the sky are little clouds, and the only movement in the image comes from the centre line running parallel to the outline of the truck. Everything here suggests a weekend photograph, one that seems amateurish: firstly due to the theme, then the framing, which is carefully but hastily done, and finally the colours, which are those of a photograph printed using standard processing.

This is one of many examples in which Ghirri brings photography back to the very common practice of snapping images without much forethought during outings to the countryside. This frees the head somewhat of all the questions regarding the meaning of an image and instead is indicative of a simple interest in what is occurring in the external world. Unsurprisingly, however, photographs of this type, when placed together in a series, can seem to mimic or parody a photographic practice generally considered not particularly sophisticated.

There are many similar images in collections of Ghirri's work from this period, such as a series showing people in the act of snapping photographs during trips or visits to touristic places. Here it is the very practice of taking photographs that is brought to light, with our attention drawn neither to the environment nor to the circumstance, but entirely to that gesture which can be seen as automatic or stereotypic. Other work focuses on repertoires of common uses of photography, such as postcards, snapshots and oleographs. Another beautiful series, from between 1972 and 1974, is of local photoshop window displays of confirmation, baptism and wedding snapshots.

All these are examples of common uses of images (such as hanging oleographs in homes, or arranging snapshots on pieces of furniture) which are often simply viewed as examples of bad taste, in so much as they contrast with so-called works of art. But similar attitudes can be found in a tendency, just as forced and stereotyped, that renders vision compromised by what Ghirri called an 'aesthetic mania' – bringing to mind Cézanne's comment: 'They are no longer able to see things, they see everywhere only pictures in museums.'

The distinction between works of art and oleographic copies has rested on the idea that works of art are 'unique and original', whereas other things are reproductions or imitations of the already seen. Photography has long been considered a simple 'reproduction of the real' and thus incapable of having 'artistic originality'. Celebrating the role of photography as a reproduction of the already seen, Ghirri sheds these burdensome judgements, turning a limit into a strength, that is, the revelatory quality of the act of taking photographs.

II.

In the early 1970s, Ghirri photographed patterned sweaters and shirts, old pictures, pieces of statues, domestic and public oleographic decorations, and 25 square metres of advertising posters covering a wall of the Modena speedway, creating an extraordinary sequence with (as he points out in his notes) certain similarities to the narrative frescoes in medieval churches and palaces, such as the sequences of Giotto, Sassetta and Piero della Francesca. Such images must recount not only the already seen, but also a known and widespread experience as a point of reference. After all, as Ghirri says, this is the most common use of photography: photographs are usually put in albums, and albums recount moments in life that we want to remember – trips, weddings, confirmations or celebratory events.

What is Ghirri doing? He is shifting attention from the so-called (indecipherable) quality of images to their uses. Photography takes on a revelatory quality because it reveals how people use images, how they need arrays of images to organize their spaces, highlight their preferences, direct their gazes, decorate their dwellings, celebrate their rites, remember moments in their lives. This is a shifting of attention akin to that produced by literature, when we stop attempting to define the unique and original characteristics of a certain author, because we realize that what is more important is a commonly held language, and that the great resource of this language lies in the use of a shared capacity that connects us and allows us to understand each other.

And yet photography can never be only a document that informs us of these uses, as if an alien intelligence were contemplating us from above in a Tower of Babel. The manner in which Ghirri offers us an observation of the already seen has nothing to do with a documentary vision and is uninterested in informing others of some unique discovery. It is rather in his way of constructing and framing images that he evokes a use of the already seen and pays homage to the already seen, often painting. Far from being theoretical or discursive, his is a thinking in images, a disciplined learning of how to order the seen.

A series from 1972 comes to mind of storefront gates, closed or semi-closed, with nothing special to draw the eye. But Ghirri's elegant images bring to light an order envisioned by the craftsmen who built these shops, one based on very few geometric lines and a few shades of colour, in an extraordinary abstraction.

Thinking in images needs this ability to read. Just as when reading a book, I need to be able to trust something which I perceive as an orderly form, a rhythmic form, but which I don't understand well because it is only appearance and semblance. A reading of the visible always presupposes something such as a text that we follow with our eyes, being able to see only a few lines at a time, some semblance at a time, knowing that every appearance has an imponderable sense of the order that guides us.

III.

There is another series that especially appeals to me, shot between 1972 and 1974 and dedicated to a distinctive aspect of our landscape – those little geometric country houses, painted bright colours, with rolling shutters and Arizona cypresses planted out front. Ghirri's approach to photographing them, in frontal views, with a rigorous balancing of visible components, without perspective escape hatches, does not cut far into their surfaces but deeply enough to allow glimpses into an entire mode of decorating everyday dwellings. It is a mode of expression made up of infinite repetitive symmetries, for example in the placement of the windows, the flowerpots and the Arizona cypresses, even the TV antennas. It is a very deliberate way of ordering every object, which can also seem nauseating, and which Ghirri has made even more evident, going so far as to create of it a pictorial opportunity.

Early critics focused on these images as merely examples of bad taste, interpreting them through Ghirri's irony as evidence of the isolation of the lower middle class. In his notes Ghirri responds to this view, refuting the idea of a 'critically merciless' gaze and calling attention to the fact that the houses are collections of traces of attentive care for spaces that require reading before judgement.

It is typical that critics tend to judge the quality of the things photographed, while Ghirri is instead interested in the distinctive ways in which these things are decorated. Nothing in his photographs allows us to develop a complex interpretation: the eye traverses something to the front of it, with a vision that is always partial and fragmentary because it cannot embrace everything in one glance, in a world in which all that appears is enveloped by emptiness and muteness. One might say, 'it's there and that's enough'.

In his notes to these early collections, Ghirri underlines that photography can record only fragments of the visible, and that we are able to see only one thing at a time; each thing remains in a state of indeterminacy, because the framing that renders it observable is also what eliminates all other space. And yet, Ghirri says, 'It is thanks to this elimination that the image takes on meaning, becoming measurable'. The framed image becomes a measure of our vision, a measure of our experience. And in this sense, 'within what is visible of an image there are also traces of this elimination, inviting us to seek out what is not represented'.

For example, in one series there is an image of a door with a street number, two pots to the side, a little overhang that gives a bit of shade, a wall covered with boards, and everything wrapped in radiant light. What can be said of this? What is most striking is the visual precision of the framing that isolates the door from everything else, and the extreme muteness within the translucent light, producing the effect of a vast silence, which is exactly what brings me back to it, enchanting me, interrupting the disorder of my thoughts. It also has an additional effect, very familiar to me, and common in Ghirri's work: I know that when I see a door of this sort, I will tend to recognize a similar image, likewise serene and silent. The sensation will last perhaps a moment but will give me a visual scale, a bearing in space, a sense of the possible uses of the world.

IV.

The shifting of attention that Ghirri helps us to undertake, from an undecipherable quality of images to their uses, seems to me to be nothing other than a decisive shifting of attention to the ability to read. Celebrating the reproduction of the already seen, he places us in front of a world already observed, to which we return in order to read. It is not a world revealed or seen for the first time, and much less a creation or invention of what does not exist, but a world already given, that already has meaning, its own customs for organizing experience, and for this alone it is rendered visible.

A 1973 collection is dedicated to atlases. The photographic atlas is one of the most affectionate homages to our ability to read: it is the reading of a world-book (Ghirri says: 'The atlas is a book, the place of all the signs of the earth') that allows us to 'find where we live and where we would like to go', following the lines of conventional signs on paper. It is also a characteristic way in which Ghirri undermines the idea that vision leads to some awakening, to something that the eye uncovers and captures like prey, making of it a discovery. What the eye discovers is always a representative use of the observed world; but it is exactly for this reason that the game of reading can never be substituted.

Within reading, vision is not only an optic phenomenon but also a means of perceiving how all signs and images are accompanied by parades of other signs and images in which the world comes to life thanks to our attention. Behind every image, Ghirri says, there are many others, all re-echoing one another, forming a lattice of the uses of the visible, the 'visions of other people that I cannot overlook'. To be inside a book, inside a thing that is read, is to be inside 'the history of images', a comment referring to a series of images of his own house, his books, objects and images of affection. The return to home is a return to the world-book, the world already observed through its representations.

A woman and a man holding hands walk towards a distant mountain, and the landscape rises up as all appearances rise up. Every aspect of the world here seems beautiful and sorrowful, and I have the impression that the two wanderers (tourists?) are returning home. We see them from behind, in an astonishing opening of space – and we see that their house is the ordered aspect of a representation.

V.

Ghirri's first book (*Kodachrome*, Modena 1978) ends with a strange photograph of a newspaper (where he found it, I don't know) with an article headline that reads 'COME PENSARE PER IMMAGINI' ('How to think in images'). In his notes, Ghirri states that this phrase expresses the meaning of all his work. There is something that discursive thought is unable to clarify for us, with its explanations and valuations: an edge, a threshold, where what counts is not so much what we think but what we are able to see, a way of thinking in images, which is also a meditation on limits and measures.

If there were not a scalar measure for what we see, defined by a threshold of our vision, we would be like those people who cannot see despite having fully functioning eyes. The entire visible order that appears in Ghirri's photographs seems to me unusually sensitive to this scalar measure that establishes each object at a certain distance, the distance of things from us. And it is this, I believe, that allows us to take indeterminacy to heart, to entrust ourselves to appearances whose meaning is often unclear, but which at times can become a gauge for seeing everything else.

I wanted to arrive at the threshold in Ghirri's work, so well represented by those two trees planted in the fog, beyond which rows of other trees lead to a motorway. There is order despite the fog, his idea of photographing the breathing of the earth, the extreme search for a sense of measure, one of his very last images.

Note

1 For a selection of Luigi Ghirri's photographs, some of which Celati discusses in this piece, see *Archivio Luigi Ghirri*, https://www.archivioluigighirri.com/.

23
'In praise of the tale'
('Elogio della novella', 1992)

From a discussion with Silvana Tamiozzo-Goldman at a conference on the novel held at the Fondazione Cini in Venice in July 1999. Celati was asked to comment on what he saw as some key differences between older and more recent modes of narration, what he thought of Pirandello's work, to what extent older Italian storytelling traditions come to play in *Narratori delle pianure* (*Voices from the Plains*), and if with this book he had begun a new type of storytelling.

Early collections of stories, from the thirteenth-century *Il Novellino* [also known as *Le cento novelle antiche* (One hundred old tales)] to various later examples through the sixteenth century, are bazaars packed with stuff. Every time I go back to *The Decameron*, it gives me the impression of wandering through an old Arab souk, with perfumes, jewels, spices and fabrics from all over. In many Tuscan stories this memory has a local origin: Sacchetti, Sermini, Fortini, Sercambi, Grazzini. But others come from far away, like precious goods. The first tales in *The Decameron* are about Florentine merchants in Paris, while others are set in various parts of the Mediterranean, or India or Persia, by way of Venice. Much of what constitutes a traditional story depends on the ceremonial opening that serves as a context. Boccaccio expanded this convention by way of the frame in which all the various tales in *The Decameron* are set.

Boccaccio's system gives an immediate sense of joining a lively conversation. In the earlier *Il Novellino*, it soon becomes clear that the book is concerned with 'flowerings of speech, of good manners and lively responses'. The tale is born from 'flowerings of speech', an outgrowth of the rituals of conversation. But what remains fresh in our minds in Boccaccio's work is the most memorable point, which has been set in a frame through the contextual system alluded to in the opening.

For example: at the end of the first story of *The Decameron*, what we remember most is Sir Ciappelletto's false confession on his deathbed. Expectation in the story rests on our understanding of Sir Ciappelletto as a liar, cheat, forger, thief, blasphemer, assassin and sodomite, whereas surprise comes at a point of paradoxical excess, a culmination of all the expectations. And thus comes the marvel: that the culmination of the story is that Sir Ciappelletto manages to pass himself off as a saint thanks to his deceitful confession, feeding a crock of lies to a friar.

Of Sir Ciappelletto we know all there is to know, with no information withheld. But during his confession to the friar, with each of Sir Ciappelletto's quips, our expectations are breeched; and each time our jaws drop lower and lower, until we are told that upon his death, he even became a local saint. Surprise with wonder can be likened to an overflowing in which something transforms under our noses, initially following our expectations, then going beyond them to the very edge, that is, to a point at which anything can happen, as in dreams. The story can have an unexpected culmination point and then instead end in a more conventional way. But the effect of the marvellous always has the character of a metamorphosis that happens right in front of us, without special justification. The second tale in *The Decameron* is about Abraham, a Jewish moneylender whom the French merchant Jehannot de Chevigny wants to convert to Christianity. Here even the idea of Christianity is transformed in an unexpected way, by way of Abraham's final decision and the effects of a paradoxical culmination.

Yes, there has been a change in the way we read stories from older to more recent times. In traditional tales the listener is always kept abreast of the subject at hand by way of the introductory ritual, whereas in modern stories things are turned on their heads, with the introductory ritual all but cut out, leaving readers, who find themselves suddenly immersed in unknown territory, to discover on their own the nature of the plot. Take for example Giovanni Verga's 1889 *Mastro-don Gesualdo*, one of the most important novels of its time. It begins with a fire in the Trao family house, screams, and neighbours running to help. But we know nothing of the Trao family, nothing of the setting or the story. While it is true that these details will eventually come to light, readers, when faced with this beginning, find themselves struggling with the quandary of being outsiders, cut off from the innerworkings of the story. They have no ceremonial guide but are instead thrown headlong into the narrative as it unfolds, as if suddenly falling into some predicament.

I mentioned *Mastro-don Gesualdo* because it is useful for understanding the methods of naturalistic and realistic narration. However, the situation of the fire in the Trao family house into which the reader is tossed is representative of a hellish life in which everyone has become estranged from everyone else. It is a sort of requiem, a dreadful premonition of what is to come, hinting at the final image of don Gesualdo, alone in this room, sick and listening to the voices of a world in ruins.

One of Moravia's novels, to cite a more recent example, begins with this short phrase: 'Carla came in.' Who Carla is we have no idea. It is as if we are taken by the shoulders and pushed directly into the action, skipping any prelude or lead-in. Moravia coolly employs this technique, as at the start of his *Racconti romani* (*Roman Tales*): 'Slowly shutting the door and staring at his lover, the young man entered the room …'. Here too we are thrown straight into the action, lacking any introduction, as a standard means of capturing the reader's attention. This is not my approach. But what I want to say is that when readers are put in the position of an outsider, as is the case here, confronted by the 'bare facts', they are left to await some relief from the unknown, finding interest in the story from the intensity of its voyeuristic tension. This is the normal scenic mode of setting the stage for the unfolding of the story, the details of which the reader seems to be spying upon from the outside. This is a realistic approach, based on scenic modes of narration.

There are some differences between realistic or scenic and panoramic modes of narration. When narrating a story, you can recount something that occurs in a specific place and time in the form of a scene that unfolds under the eyes of readers. This is a scenic mode of narration, with a precise centre of attention. Or you can fashion a panoramic summary of certain events without a precise centre of attention, using indefinite times and referring to the vagueness of far-away places. Fables, tales and chivalric poems always start with indefinite times – the imperfect tense so characteristic of fables, as well as of tales: 'there was of yore in Florence a gallant named Federigo di Messer Filippo Alberighi, who for feats of arms and courtesy had not his peer in Tuscany'.[1] Tales always begin with panoramic devices of this sort that serve to slowly carry readers to a somewhat more definite sense of time, for example: 'One day it happened that …'. But in tales, even successive events almost always occur within a foreshortened, summarizing and panoramic temporality – until the reader reaches the memorable point, which is staged in true scenic fashion, such as Sir Ciappelletto's final confession.

Take for example the beginning of one of Pirandello's short stories, 'Scialle nero': "Wait here', said Bandi to D'Andrea …'. Having no idea who these two characters are, we are outsiders facing a scene that captures our attention because we are not privy to what will happen.

Scenic modes of narrative, precisely because they put us in the position of an outsider or voyeur, amplify our attention to events that are occurring. And it is always scenic devices that reveal through dialogue backstories or the so-called psychology of the characters: 'He said', 'She replied', 'He responded'.

You ask if I prefer panoramic modes of narration, with their slow, imperfect cadences? Yes, I prefer panoramic modes, because they are closer to daily usage, which does not begin with a precise centre of attention but with an ambiguity, giving a wider margin for linguistic nuances. This helps to avoid falling into the trap of a plot, and to open up new paths and to hear distant voices. A lovely story by Antonio Delfini comes to mind, 'La modista' [The dressmaker]. In it everything is kept suspended in the imperfect, in the indefinite past of fables – so much so that it is impossible to determine, judging from her past expectations and dreams, what happened to the dressmaker. Unexpected voices from the past can thus come into play, recollections that have nothing to do with wrapping up the plot. Here, for example, is an exceptional, unexpected passage: 'Oh! Elvira, oh! Elvira, the neighbourhood children were singing. She would go to the shop in the morning, her footsteps resonating loudly on the sidewalk. That little man who would likely still be asleep, up there, had he been able to listen, would have understood with torment and delight whose legs were producing that rhythm … .'[2] Everything is an evocation. The evocative power of indefinite time transports you to a sort of indeterminate *illo tempore*, a space of ambiguity that stirs the imagination.

Yes. The tale, if we go back to the traditional sort, is understood as a story of an already heard story. In Bandello's *Novelle* we are also told where and when a tale was told, or where the author claims to have heard it. In this respect, tales celebrate something overheard, which suddenly materializes from out of the stream of words flowing from mouth to mouth. A tale can be anything: fable, rustic yarn or short anecdote as in *Il Novellino*, or St Bernardino's sermons. These examples are interested not so much in the laying out of narrative facts, but rather in the act of engaging in clever or fabulist conversation. Consider these titles: *Motti e facezie del Piovano Arlotto* [Piovano Arlotto's quips and maxims], Fiorenzuola's *Ragionamenti*, Basile's *Lo Cunto de li cunti*, Straparola's *Le piacevoli notti* [The pleasant nights], Fortini's *Le piacevoli et amorose notti dei novizi* [The pleasant and amorous nights of the novices] and Grazzini's *Le cene* [The suppers]. One can see that the inspiration or bent behind tales stems from performance in a place of friendly conversation – giving rise to the sense that the heterogeneous world of stories is one in which there circulates an endless repetitive stream of things already said, of overheard fabulations. Modern stories instead are primarily interested in people who believe only in so-called reality.

A realistic-naturalistic story more or less takes for granted that it is a recording of a real experience, with the following assumption by the reader: 'If you had been in that place as the facts of the story played out, you would have seen and heard exactly what I am telling you.' In traditional tales the conventional rapport with the reader seems rather like this: 'Let me tell you something talked about in these parts.' Tales present themselves as wellsprings of voices, from which there arises the particular telling at hand. For this reason, it is never a closed circuit, as in modern novels or short stories, which are fixated on their own textuality and have no need of being retold to others who haven't read them, or of being rewritten, as doing so would be seen as an act of plagiarism. Shut within the margins of the text, it is as if they are extractions from the uncontrollable stream of words. The impetus behind most literary activity today no longer lies within the circulation of language in its various guises, but rather always the story of some meaning to be discovered: the novel as mirror of supposed reality.

What do I make of Pirandello? Well, his *Novelle per un anno* (*Stories for a Year*) is a collection of parables on the dreariness of ordinary life. And there is always some sort of judgement on the forced normality in which most people live, as a blind routine of drudgery. Pirandello can't do without judgements of this sort, and his is a game of intelligence that never manages to escape from the hell of its own thoughts. For this reason, *Il fu Mattia Pascal* (*The Late Mattia Pascal*) remains his masterpiece. It is my impression that for Pirandello, the naturalistic or realistic idea that the story is a kind of lesson to make the reader aware of reality remains an underlying limitation. This is the idea of administering thoughts to others, so as to carry them towards a complete rationalization of so-called reality. All the rationalism of contemporary stories and novels tends to move in this direction, towards a censuring of socially useless fabulations, things to be eliminated.

You say that this is a frightening prospect. Yes. And the more readers become accustomed to this rationalizing literary regime, the more fabulation is incriminated. Lastly: not only have rationalizing productions become more and more filled with realistic 'truths', but their meaning is also tied to a tension that must always rise, with ever new intensive effects. The modern reader tends to put up with words less and less and increasingly seeks out the bare 'meaning' of facts, to be read quickly. From Zola to twentieth-century writers, naturalistic narratives have increasingly adopted a standard, purely grammatical language. So too is the language of Pirandello a 'repeated' language, as Corrado Alvaro used to say.

With *Narratori delle pianure* (*Voices from the Plains*), at a certain point I realized that a means of escaping this trap was to return to the form of the tale. I had almost nothing to say apart from half-remembered, overheard, scattered echoes. What is essential is that a story causes you to imagine something, even only glimmers of images. Think of Dante, in whose work voices crop up from all over, with just a few lines at times being enough to serve as a story. In the circle of thieves, a voice rises up: 'Cianfa, dove fia rimaso?' ('What's become of Cianfa?'). We know not who Cianfa might be, but this single phrase causes us to imagine something and in doing so is already a story.

When someone starts to write, where do they begin? Well, it's best to start with deictic words, such as 'here', 'there', 'this', 'that'. For example: I am someone sitting here, who at this moment is writing, not knowing exactly why. There is no obvious purpose or goal in view, only an endless path to come. The mind can wander around exploring or hearing voices, something akin to Dante's afterworld, or to a personal madhouse carried about wherever I go.

Notes

1 The *imperfetto* (imperfect) tense in Italian, roughly meaning 'inexact', is employed, among other ways, in narration to describe situations that unfold over an indefinite period of time in the past and that is not identified with a clear beginning or end. The quotation is from *The Decameron* (Fifth Day, Novel IX; J. M Rigg's 1903 translation).
2 Antonio Delfini, *Autore Ignoto Presenta*, ed. Gianni Celati (Turin: Einaudi, 2008), 72–3.

24
'Last contemplators'
('Ultimi Contemplatori', 1997)

Our region is a depression of the earth slightly tilted towards the sea with plains so flat that the line of the horizon is never that far off, at most usually a few dozen miles. Travelling across the countryside of the Po River and along the Via Emilia, one always feels close to the ground, and if you happen to see some small rise in the land, it is more likely than not to be a levee bordering a watercourse or a setback levee that often delimits an area of poplar trees. Every so often a bell tower appears in an open area, the only point of elevation visible for miles and miles. It often happens that while approaching a small town protected by a levee, simply climbing the few feet to the top is enough to produce a bit of a rush at gazing off into the distance, over the absolute flatness of the landscape surrounding you.

In flat areas our thoughts tend to sink, with few flights of the imagination. The saying that in the mountains comes a sense of freedom is a fantasy that has little to say to people of the plains, with sight always bound by a narrow horizontal encircling. Here in every direction fields planted with wheat and other crops stretch as far as the eye can see, usually in right-angled geometrical shapes and with nearly completely uniform surfaces. Scattered along the roads are farmhouses or farmsteads that have the shape of giant huts with rectangular bases: buildings lacking decoration but beautiful in their essential forms, with a style conspicuous even from far off. The side roads that border the tracts of farmland are all straight, tending to intersect with other roads at right angles, and are often accompanied by ditches that run along the ends of the fields to carry off water brought by either rain or irrigation.

One must become accustomed to this rigid geometry of flat space invaded by right angles, to this monotony of uniform agricultural lands, lacking any trace of the picturesque nature found in other places. Here, for thousands of years the picturesque has been substituted by a grid of divisions and subdivisions, of endless geometric demarcations that go back to the first Roman settlements. Viewed from above, our plains often reveal the reticulum of ancient Roman land partitions, which have remained intact for 20 centuries. From Piacenza to Bologna, and then along the Via Emilia to Rimini, the Romans subdivided arable lands in the same way that they demarcated outposts that then became settlements: by simply dividing the space into four equal parts with intersecting grid lines, the same basic urban pattern underlying New York and almost all other large American cities. For this reason, while travelling by car on country roads in the Po Valley, almost everything that you can see is evidence of a systematic linear order that guides the eye towards fixed points. One's gaze never strays too far in open space, is never taken by surprise by unexpected shapes in the landscape, and little by little comes to recognize a vast and abstract, nearly architectural order. Houses and farmsteads come into view, scattered and isolated in the distance, but all within a grid of straight roads that situates them in space as if on a chessboard; and only when a canal or watercourse of some sort interrupts the symmetry of the chessboard do you come across a road that meanders for curved and irregular stretches, giving you the sense of unexpected adventure.

This urban and architectural order, with its straight-lined roads and furrows running off into the distance, creates a perspective illusion that plays off the low-lying profiles of the horizon. So too within the geometric style of the houses, the parallel alignments of the trees, the habit of demarcating the entrances to farmsteads with two-pillared thresholds, an order is repeated in which one's gaze cannot easily wander among things but is instead continually guided by symmetries and perspective views. Take for instance the poplar groves scattered everywhere, arranged in diagonal rows that intersect in squares such that from whatever angle you view them, you will always see a line of trees disappearing into the distance – one example of the architectural style by which our landscape has been organized for centuries, reducing space to a checkerboard of linear plots and erasing all the formlessness of nature not subject to human control.

Furthermore, open pasturelands no longer exist here, having been eliminated years ago, and so no grazing animals are visible. Together with farmyard animals, they are now confined to industrial breeding facilities. If you thus make your way across the countryside of the Po Valley, from Piacenza to the Adriatic Sea, what you see of the encircling environs may produce a sense of emptiness, of stagnant, lifeless fixity, wherein it is unclear what to look at for a modicum of visual relief. It is difficult to say if anything here is 'beautiful'. Other adjectives are needed. And yet if you happen to meet an older resident, perhaps a lone elderly cyclist, or someone resting in the door of a small-town bar, an entirely different impression of these places will arise. Hazard speaking to certain old country people, and you will discover a fabulist spirit, a kind of congenital extravagance that tends towards comic or surprising digression. In country bars almost every conversation is but a series of ludicrous jokes with which outsiders can hardly keep up; they can only observe these interactions as a form of theatre from which they are excluded.

Certain country bars are infamous for the jokes told there to make strangers feel ill at ease. One example (from near Piacenza) consists of telling an absurd and comical story, then surprising the laughing stranger with the following: 'Why are you laughing? Do you think I didn't tell the truth? Do you take me for a liar or a clown?' In which case the other customers make serious faces to show that the story is really true and that there is nothing to laugh about, until the stranger retreats in good order. I witnessed such a scene, which I found very embarrassing. It is hard to understand this tendency to crack jokes with the intention of making outsiders feel ill at ease, this tendency to isolate oneself from others, this fabulist mood that replaces the pleasantries of sociability.

When I think of the great authors of our plains, from Ariosto, Boiardo and Folengo, all the way to Zavattini, Delfini, Fellini and their contemporary heirs, especially Cavazzoni and Benati, I am reminded of a fabulist extravagance that I do not find in authors from other regions. I cannot explain this tendency, probably because it is not clear to me, but I do know that traditionally there were various forms of local madness. There was the famous madness of Reggio Emilia (due, it was said, to the fact that the people there drank barley water), the gloomy melancholy of Ferrara (because Ferrara is sunken below sea level), and then what was called the 'matàna del Po' of Cremona. Here the word madness ('matàna') was understood as individual extravagance, almost a form of boasting. For example, the 'matàna' of the men of the Po from Cremona indicated an unshakeable independence: a person not subject to social rules imposed from above.

I believe that the saying 'la matàna del Po' referred to the 'madness' of certain people as being inspired by the water of the river, its turbulence ?lentless floods within a stable bed. The river and its waters are ly the opposite of the stable, geometric order visible everywhere in the countryside – the opposite of the age-old project to organize all of nature's formlessness into a regulated space. Only for the past few decades have people channelled the entirety of the river into a solid cage of sloped levees to prevent it from meandering down new paths opened by floods to pool in dead, swampy branches, ponds, aquifers, sloughs or other unforeseen outlets. But this is an unresolvable tension, because the more the Po is enclosed by stable levees with no freedom of outlet, the more unpredictable and dangerous its floods become.

'Because the Po is like a snake that goes crazy', a lonely old gentleman, whom I met along an oxbow lake on Serafini Island near Piacenza, told me a few years ago. And the same gentleman told me, with the usual quirky sense of humour of those areas, that he considered himself a *tarabusino*, that is, a bird that hides in reeds and oxbow marshes. He meant that, as an old retiree, he could find nowhere to go to feel comfortable, so he often came to take refuge on the riverbank. But his idea that the Po is like a snake that goes crazy when it is blocked in its natural movements makes me think that in our parts the image of nature has always been very different from that of other areas: that is, not related to vegetation, but only to the turbulence of the waters.

Our plains must have been almost completely cleared at the time of the Roman appropriations, so it was never vegetation that suggested the worship of nature, and it is on this that the complete absence of the natural picturesque depends. Absent altogether is that taste for irregular green patches cultivated in Switzerland, England and elsewhere. In our pictorial tradition, so-called nature has always been an abstract presence, where the picturesque tends to fade into the theatrical. The same is often the case in the countryside between Reggio and Parma, where two pillars stationed on either side of entrance roads to farms focus the view of fields and farmhouse into a theatrical perspective. The fact is that in our plains the image of nature has nothing peaceful about it, because it has always been linked to the tremendous flooding of the Po, the destructive exuberance of the waters, and the enormous amount of groundwater, which easily penetrates the clay soils and can spring up at any moment in pools, ponds, swamps or resurgences. Until the last century there were swamps nearly everywhere, with the Po continuing to open new branches across the countryside and the basin of our plains showing its face more clearly as an island suspended over uncertain terrain, with rivers circling in sinuous and extravagant paths almost at ground level, and the land always threatened in its surface arrangement by water.

That is why in our parts, I believe, there is no restful and idyllic idea of nature as in other lands. Here water is evidence that nature is not subject to complete human control; it is an unpredictable exuberance, a madness to which people must adapt, good or bad, much as one must adapt to eccentricity in the family. Almost all the older people of the Po I have met have boasted only of this: that they knew all too well the 'madness' of the waters, that they knew that the river is a 'mad beast' to whom one must adapt in order to live, allowing it its necessary outbursts, without which all environmental balance is thrown off. But in talking about these things, they always showed a tendency for fabulist invention, with dialectal and bizarre idioms, with a stunning visionary listlessness – as with the old gentleman I met on Serafini Island, who, in telling me that he considered himself a *tarabusino*, only pointed me to the inspiration of his extravagance as a solitary contemplator of the waters.

Now suppose you travelled through our region, entering by way of Piacenza to the north-east, then following the path of the Via Emilia, visiting the ancient cities that the road passes through, perhaps even with a detour to Ferrara, a north-west threshold to other territories with their various dialects and customs. You may have noticed that even in the cities there survives a linear order resembling that of the countryside, although one often disturbed by curvilinear paths, usually indicating where a now silted-up waterway once passed. The cities of our plains were once rich in canals and rivers, and it was once again water that disrupted the symmetries of the urban checkerboard, interrupting or diverting the flight of perspective lines. But it must also be said that in Bologna, Modena, Reggio Emilia and Parma, the areas crossed by watercourses were mostly working-class, artisan, mercantile neighbourhoods, where water was necessary for work and movement, whereas the upper-class areas were located along the streets of the city centre and within the perimeter of its oldest walls, with the palaces of the wealthy creating impeccable vanishing perspective lines punctuated by the regular rhythm of Italianate windows.

Our ways of using space are the reverse of what you find in England, where aristocratic mansions are always in the countryside, completely hidden by picturesque nature, so much so that nothing is visible from the outside. Here instead the constructions of the wealthy have always accumulated at the heart our cities, within scenes of ostentation and centralization, wherein one's gaze is at once channelled and impeded by fixed perspectives. And even if this urban landscape has been altered by widenings, churches and piazzas with a more unpredictable Baroque spatial order, there remains in our cities a sense of despotic centralization, where local political power is manifested by a conspicuous ostentation that precludes all other contemplative possibilities.

The ancient linear magnificence of the aristocratic thoroughfares in our cities is still visible today along those stretches of the Via Emilia that run through Reggio, Modena or the centre of Bologna. These grand avenues have never failed to chase down their destiny as centres of ostentation and have in doing so turned into concentrations of banks, luxury storefronts, advertising glitz and other displays of wealth, where anything that does not allude to profit has lost any meaning or appeal. City centres have now become little more than a parade of merchandise displays, and people who are not driven by frenzied wealth feel like fish out of water in such places, much more so than in countries with different political-religious traditions. Having become concentrations of commerciality, with canals and waterways now buried, besieged by maddening traffic, our cities now allow one's gaze to wander only at night. It is only by visiting them at night that one rediscovers the sense of their linear geometry, but less and less the traces of a fabulist extravagance, a distracted musing that for centuries was an antithesis and a release, in contrast to the overly geometric, despotic and artificial external order.

I would say that the pastime of fabulist musing is now a thing of the past, and that here new generations are largely driven by ideas of what constitutes normal life that are derived from advertising. A few years ago, I went with a group of students from the University of Reggio Emilia to conduct interviews in the countryside with elderly people who had left their old farmhouses; the students were asked to transcribe the interviews and then comment on them. From what I remember of their comments, it seemed that the old humour of the speakers was taken by many students as an odd mannerism of 'people who didn't go to school' because it didn't resemble anything found on television or in the urban regime of forced normality. That humour (similar to Zavattini's) is now an unintelligible irregularity even in the countryside, which is increasingly invaded by industries spreading haphazardly, imposing a parcelled-out, urbanized and commercialized order of life.

Together with this shift has come the systematic abandonment of old farmsteads, and the collapse of the accompanying social organization that developed alongside their rural architecture. Now it is common to see stretches of the countryside almost completely devoid of human presence, where the only perceptible movement is that of the traffic on busy roads. Old, abandoned farmsteads collapse little by little, year by year, along roadsides or in the fields. These areas are fast becoming no man's lands marked by the ruins of a highly stylized rural architecture that carried with it the memories of an agricultural way of life whose traces are disappearing.

If you visit one of the few remaining country bars today, you will often find old people playing cards or reading the newspaper, while the young people fiddle with some new gadget or stand around discussing vacations, cars and money. Old retirees ride bicycles and the young drive cars. Increasingly isolated from the advertising clamour that sings nothing but the praises of youth, the older, more independent and imaginative tend to retreat to seldom-visited places, as if they were a species of animal on the verge of human-caused extinction. You can often spot them at sunset on a levee, riding their old bicycles, extraordinarily absorbed in thought along the banks of the Po, motionless contemplators of the waters. They are witnesses to modernization's disastrous advances: the cementing of levees that trap the river's movements, the spreading of asphalt that seals off the water table, the fouling of the river with industrial waste, the triumphant sprouting of weeds that thrive in acidic soils, the swarming of seagulls that feed on toxic mountains of garbage. I have seen so many such musers, lonely retirees on bicycles, old people defending their isolation with comic dialectal jokes, or locked in their thoughts with no desire to respond, pondering some widening of the river. They are the true experts of place, the most attentive observers, the last fabulist spirits of our region.

Figure 24.1 Gianni Celati, in Milan, 1993, courtesy of Vincenzo Cottinelli.

25

'Italo's death' ('Morte di Italo', 1997)

A few days after Italo Calvino's funeral I jotted down the notes that follow, in order to remind myself of the situation and the feelings of the moment.[1] I had just returned from France, and that evening Calvino's wife (Chichita) called to tell me that Italo was dying. I left that night by car for Siena together with Carlo Ginzburg's wife Luisa, while Carlo arrived by train from Rome.

Luisa and I made it to Siena at half past midnight, just as Carlo was getting out of a taxi in front of the hospital. Chichita had gone to sleep at a hotel. Italo was in intensive care, where we were not allowed, being kept alive with drugs 'as stipulated by the law'. We called all the hotels in Siena without finding a place to sleep, and so we ended up sitting in front of the hospital to wait. We were able to enter only at 4.00, when Chichita arrived together with Giorgio Agamben, Giovanna, Aurora, François Wahl and Italo's brother. They had already arranged Italo's body in the coffin, but in a ridiculous way, it seemed to me, putting lace around his head.

Later we all sat around a table in the hospital director's office. Chichita needed to make arrangements for the coffin and other things, but when she returned she began to recount what had happened to Italo. While he was in a state of semi-consciousness the doctors interrogated him at length, and Italo answered back, but always in a novelesque way. He pronounced phrases as if he were still mulling over something to write, and at a certain point he said: 'The eyeglasses are the judge', then a pataphysical joke, in French: *'Je suis un abat-jour allumé'* (this was due, according to Chichita, to the fact that the aneurism had caused a terrible burning in his head).

In another moment Italo woke up, asking if he had had an accident. Then he told the doctors that he was 30 years old and lived on Boulevard

Saint Germain (where he would go for walks almost every evening, when I was in Paris). Before falling into the stupor that precedes a coma, he began to speak as if he were reading a book, pronouncing these words very clearly: 'Vanni di Marsio, phenomenologist … straight lines … parallel lines …'. After this he stopped speaking.

Later they placed his body in the coffin in the middle of a huge room in the hospital. In the coffin he seemed shrunken, his face disfigured by a large lump on his forehead, where they had opened it in order to operate. His hair was all cut off, and this too rendered him different. His lips still had a trace of his old smirk, and when I looked at him from the side opposite the lump it was easy to recognize him. The large room was full of frescoes, with velvet-upholstered chairs lining the walls, and a long narrow carpet that led to the marble table where the body had been laid out. There was a ridiculous strip of lace around the coffin that every so often was blown out of place by the wind and had to be readjusted. It was already 6.00 in the morning, and there was a beautiful light in the valley outside the window.

At 7.00 the patients in the hospital began to file in to see the famous dead man, of whom all the newspapers had been speaking. Then many women carrying shopping bags arrived on their way to the stores. These women never wavered in their path, circling around all sides of the coffin with a humble and respectful air. Even the stores around the piazza were dominated by talk of Italo. It was a beautiful day and tourists began to appear on their way to visit the cathedral. Towards 8.00 the town prefect arrived and greeted Chichita with a very stiff bow. Then the commander of the military police came to greet her in a very humane, almost apologetic way, then left looking upset. The prefect, in contrast, walked away as stiff as a piece of dried fish.

People of all sorts came, including a restaurant owner who greeted Chichita with affection. Military policemen, priests, nuns, patients and nurses all came to see the body of the famous man. Children from an elementary school came accompanied by a nun, and while the nun said a prayer the children stood up on the tips of their toes in order to see the dead man. Then Natalia Ginzburg came, the person dearest to me in all that traffic. François Wahl seemed a tortured man: he muttered that a year ago his mother had died, then Foucault, and now Italo. *Sic transit Gloria mundi*, I wanted to reply.

At 11.00, Carlo, Luisa and I went to a hotel. I slept until 4.00 and had a dream. In the dream there was a road under construction, and a sort of tractor was spreading gravel before laying down asphalt on the road bed. Italo was sitting on the tractor, with his arms wrapped around himself in a habitual pose, and his lips in their old smirk. Then when

Carlo came to wake me up, I had been dreaming that the road connected two distant cities, and Italo was involved with the construction, as if he had been a supervisor of some sort (I thought much about this dream, and of the road in it connecting two distant places).

When we returned to the hospital, the atmosphere of mourning still seemed pleasant to me. A delegation from the Communist Party had arrived, with many wreaths, many ordinary people. I liked that so many had come, everyone mixed up, priests, communists, nuns, pale provincial intellectuals who peeked timidly at his death. I liked that there was an unplanned yet still funerary procession, and that everyone, little by little, exited the room into the piazza to chat sadly in front of the cathedral. I also liked when the President of the Republic arrived, and all the patients applauded him. I sat on the steps of the cathedral with Carlo; another character from the Communist Party arrived with a sympathetic air; a little rain began to fall but the sky was very calm.

Things went on in this pleasant way until 7.30 in the evening, when the hospital staff needed to close off the room of the hospital. Chichita said, 'I can't bear to leave him here alone'. Giorgio Abamben and I wanted to stay closed in the room all night to keep Italo company, but this wasn't allowed (rules!). And so we had to leave him there alone, after which perhaps Chichita told me other things. I don't remember what she said that made me laugh, but it had to do with the fact that Italo didn't care very much for so-called social life.

We had an enjoyable dinner in a restaurant, Carlo and Luisa, Giorgio Agamben, Ginevra Bompiani. I thought about Italo's last words ('Vanni di Marsio, phenomenologist … straight lines … parallel lines …'). Geometry for him was an idea of clarity, and he had little love for the hole in our souls, the darkness that we have inside. He spurned these things, he rejected them. He was drawn to *l'esprit de géométrie*, like an inverted Pascal. He had recently taken to studying Husserl's phenomenology. Vanni di Marsio is a name that doesn't exist: his last words are a summary of all this.

Now, however, I realize that I must have mixed up the time, because in reality the large hospital room didn't close at 7.30, but rather at midnight. And it was there that I began to feel uneasy. Precisely at midnight I saw emerge on the piazza four figures of high culture with the air of bloated parasites who are ashamed to be there, who are ashamed of death. They seemed like dogs with their tails between their legs, not out of sadness or mournfulness, but because grief embarrassed them. One of them even said these exact words to me: 'You know, death seems indecent to me, lacking dignity and unaesthetic.'

The next morning, at 8.00, everything took a turn for the worse. With every minute that passed the situation became less bearable. All the newspapers carried the front-page news of Italo's death, but not one article was worth reading. Calvino was becoming the symbol of a sort of privilege, the symbol of literature as an elite privilege, a mirage that for the first time since D'Annunzio had begun to spread again. Italo, who had for many years derided the mania of 'playing the writer', who had resisted giving in to the comfort of a 'famous name', was now becoming a decoy. In a return to an industrial form of D'Annunzio-like mythology, literature is officially conjoined with the host of advertised consumer goods, turning into a montage of 'famous names' flapped about by the newspapers, followed by aspirants to the privileged role of 'writer' who pop out like mice in search of cheese.

By 11.00 they had all arrived, one by one – to do what, I couldn't tell – all embarrassed by grief. They came to look at Italo, slipping past as fast as possible, our men of culture, representatives from the upper classes, the bloated parasites. And then immediately after this they gathered to chat about fashionable topics in front of the hospital. It was clear that each one had an orbit to follow, each making an appearance to a series of notable personages. I saw that Italo was now completely in their hands, a death of the Upper Caste: he was their celebrated representative, at whom they had come to peek out of duty, before returning to buzz about in their orbits.

I wandered here and there, listening to the orbiters in the piazza. They were speaking about books, their books, their successes, their important acquaintances, their articles in newspapers, things that must be read, things that mustn't be read. I heard someone say, speaking of a book he was about to publish, 'It's going to be a big success'. Then someone said, 'And we'll have it translated into French right away'. They were so absorbed in their dealings that grief didn't even distantly occur to them. In a bar I met Umberto Eco, who, seeing me eat a pastry, greeted me with this joke: 'Shall we hold a feast in honour of the dead?' He had to leave in a hurry – they were waiting for him in Bologna.

Around noon I too felt like leaving in a hurry, but I couldn't because I was with Carlo and Luisa. There in the piazza I watched the orbiters circulating, all puffed up with the gas of culture, all carrying on and feeding on judgements, all constantly trading judgements, this being their main incentive. The judgements echoed in their orbits, with those aspiring to make a name for themselves compelled to imitate the others so as to gain access to the orbits, this being their main incentive. In the meantime, the coffin was being carried out of the hospital, and patients who wanted to leave were being held back by nurses. Apart from the representatives of the cultural Upper Caste, there weren't many other people in the piazza, which was strangely empty even of tourists.

I travelled by car with Carlo and Luisa to the cemetery near Roccamare, through a hilly landscape full of muted colours. On the road to Grosseto, among freshly ploughed fields and on a beautiful September day, we felt a strong desire to talk about Italo. We thought about when he had introduced us, 16 years ago, with this compulsory order: 'Become friends!' From that point on Carlo and I didn't stop arguing, until that moment in which we started to feel like true friends.

The Castiglione della Pescaia Cemetery, on a high promontory. Here there is a clear division between the classes. The Upper Caste is clustered around the tomb's hole, which is being cemented shut, while the natives have climbed up on walls and are watching everything from afar. The mayor of Castiglione della Pescaia had fliers posted that paid tribute to Italo as a 'local author', but nothing of the funeral seemed local. Everything stank of publicity and elitism. A photographer snapped a shot of Natalia Ginzburg crying. All around me I heard many people speaking a sophisticated French, from the best circles of Parisian society. There was nothing left to do but escape in a hurry. Chichita could barely remain on her feet and didn't even recognize me when we embraced.

Luckily Carlo and Luisa were there, and as we left by car we felt very close. If I cried that evening it was because everything had gone, with nothing left to do but leave that cynical and deceptive place. All of so-called high culture had at last found a dead man who could lift it up from its baseness, and personally I felt my own misery to be no different from Italo's. What comes to mind of Italo are his quirky expressions, those of a young boy, that often revealed how he never felt at ease in life, and how he could play the fool when he wanted to, things that do not appear in newspapers and that lack interest for university professors: because our dark side, which at moments becomes our most radiant one, is not easily rendered in the language of high culture.

Note

1   An earlier version of this translation appeared in *The Massachusetts Review*, 61.1 (Spring, 2020), 24–8.

26
'Two years of study at the British Museum' ('Due anni di studio nella biblioteca del British Museum', 2001)

From 1968 to 1969 I had a scholarship that allowed me to spend nearly two years in London, sequestered in the library of the British Museum. Often, after having finished and stepped out, as evening was coming on, I would go to Foyles Bookshop on Tottenham Court Road, which had a room dedicated to anthropology books on the second floor. At the time I devoured many books by English anthropologists, often stealing them from Foyles, for want of money. I would read them quickly, stirred by the descriptions of distant peoples, primitive rites, mythological stories, fables and folklore. I found these books more captivating than contemporary realistic novels in which the sense of imagination was saturated with critical discourses or incurably focused on the Western belief of abolishing all illusions in the name of so-called reality. It was in this way that my initial interest in studying Western fictions was born, directed at identifying the origins of the practice of subjugating novelistic passion to the scrutiny of critical discourses, of censuring its imaginative excesses.

My hero was Don Quixote, martyr of romantic passion's excesses, who passes unruffled through the censures of critics or other experts seeking to coerce him to travel along approved routes. Lacking this passion for Don Quixote, what would I have done? I might have fallen into the moral enchantments of Hollywood films, with their prototypical allure for Western aspirations. I believe that herein lay the deciding impetus for my study of Western fictions, the passion of rummaging through libraries in search of something still buried under the piles of modernity's ruins. On the one hand there was a thrill of discoveries, with something naive and dazzlingly about it, and on the other, the illusion of dismantling the sterilizing conventionality of contemporary criticism. Here too lurked the trap of ambition as a sort of tax that I was compelled to pay.

Before this time in London, Enzo Melandri's teachings had had a deep effect on me. He had just published *La linea e il circolo* [The line and the circle], a book which has remained his *summa philosophica* and one which I believe proves an endless source of astonishment to those able to enter its labyrinths. At the time Umberto Eco gave it high praise, Jacques Derrida proposed translating it into French, and many considered it an absolute rarity in the field of Italian philosophy. Every so often I meet someone who came to know Melandri, either through his lessons or his books, and within this circle of people his teachings remain a singular, unforgettable experience. What most inspired me, however, was his style, with an extraordinarily modulated and rhythmic syntax, unusual in modern scholarly prose. His writing opened up in all directions, taking in everything, and continually revisited its own presuppositions. I would read and reread *La linea e il circolo* for this reason, more than for its philosophical theories, which I found very difficult. Melandri was naturally Rabelaisian and omnivorous, bringing to mind Carlo Emilio Gadda; his work still seems to me a high point in Italian philosophy. And yet for years his books have been impossible to find, and he died without anyone writing a line in mourning. Perhaps what most influenced me of Melandri was his verve for speaking, richly evident in his university lessons, in which he managed to transform the most complicated diatribes into a game of states of mind, at times comical or paradoxical, that would undermine all definitive assertions.

I now know that much of the thinking and writing in this book [*Finzioni Occidentali* (Western fictions)] stemmed from a desire to emulate Melandri as a master of shifting, mutable language. I am aware of having imitated him in the game of dismantling rationalizations, in the attempt to cast some light on the symptoms of a process of removal that tends always towards the abstract: 'always more abstract', he would say, 'always more artificial and schizoid, on the path of civilization'. Contemporary literature is one mirror of this process, becoming ever more abstract, more intent on removing all trauma behind a façade of professional words. But herein also lies the crazed ambition of going against the grain, simply because otherwise you wouldn't know what to do with yourself.

Among other influences of the time was Italo Calvino, who encouraged me to collect these essays into a book. Between 1968 and 1973, we confabulated, together with Carlo Ginzburg and Guido Neri, on founding a literary journal. These confabulations didn't lead anywhere in particular, but they enthused my various studies, increasing in particular my hunger for new French books, obscure and combative, or simply stammering and frenzied, which at the time were flooding the book market. I would buy them while passing through Paris on my way to London in an old, trembling car, stopping to stay at Calvino's house. Every time I showed up at his place on Square de Châtillon I was full of ideas, like a street peddler come to sell his goods, and I would show them to him as if they were the latest arrivals. Only later did I come to understand that if I always had a head full of swarming thoughts, it was because Calvino was ever ready to listen attentively to me, nodding his head in agreement, with the air of Kubla Khan listening to Marco Polo recount his imaginary cities.

I now find it tiresome to talk about our conversations, because every memory of a famous person turns into a sort of testimony before the enormously false tribunal of history. But I will try to make some sense of why Calvino was interested in my London studies, in part because of how they related to the journal project. One reason was perhaps his conviction of having 'to turn the page', as he would say, leaving behind a certain untroubled, routine approach to writing that he saw as typical of 'Sunday writers'. The tangle of new theories in circulation at the time, which I then mixed together, tangling them even further, seemed to offer him new and increasingly complicated intellectual perspectives. This seems to me more or less what was behind the drive to find a launching pad for the journal. Perhaps I appeared to him as a sort of messenger from an era in which everything had been turned topsy-turvy, infinitely chaotic and disorderly, in the storerooms of civilization's amassed and increasingly garish ruins and debris.

In rereading my work from the time, together with the materials for the journal that we were working on, what strikes me most is the unrestrained intellectualism of my proposals. Intellectualism often leads to some sort of *agon*, with an eye to knocking out rival systems of thought, similar to the instinct that drives roosters in their struggle to dominate the chicken coop. And yet at the time there seemed to be an abyss separating the implacable intellectualism of those of the cultural elite and the banality of ordinary life. The intellectualism rather seemed based on an implicit contempt for ordinary life, on the repudiation of everything that appeared obvious. The so-called intellectuals seemed strangely unaware of the fact that they were able to walk around thanks to banal habits, just like everyone else, and were furthermore generally more tedious and boring than other common human beings.

But then there began the era of fluctuating currencies, of politics as exchangeable as money, according to an exchange rate no longer guaranteed by a gold reserve. As soon as certain code words started to lose their grip, overtaken by more random enthusiasms, the obviousness of everyday life started to emerge as though it were a sponge capable of absorbing and blotting out everything in the repetition of inclinations and habits. And now intellectual models – or systematic models of other models – are no longer any help with living or even thinking, due to their having lost the ability to function as historical footing or stable awareness with which to confront the slippery, sliding terrain across which we must make our way every day. Everything appears on the surface as a residue of the general obviousness that envelops us, in everyday life, in the continuous process of casting aside and removal.

What I am trying to say is that there was a change in perception that occurred during the time of my studies, leaving in its wake a mass of detritus into which many certainties melted, including credibility in so-called high culture. For example, our journal was to be called *Ali Babà*, a title that called to mind an enchanted cave wherein were hidden the treasures of European intellectualism. But at a certain point that cave of Ali Babà's seemed to me more than anything else a storeroom of cast-off junk, of old tools and equipment, of leftovers of everyday obviousness destined to become banal, forgotten objects, like a can of Coke tossed in a ditch. I now see my studies of the time, with all those names and citations, as the jumbled dust of detritus in the grip of an unstoppable mutation, over which there looms a sense of oblivion, such as permeates prehistoric objects.

In September 1972 I left for the United States, where I remained for two years. As soon as I had arrived, I wrote a letter to Calvino criticizing certain parts of his project 'Lo sguardo dell'archeologo' [The archaeologist's gaze], in particular his use of semiotics as a means of tidying up some of the mess of the detritus. That was the only time Calvino showed signs of fatigue with my perorations, and he replied to me, writing that he wanted to pause work on the journal and instead wholly dedicate himself to *Le città invisibili* (*Invisible Cities*), a book that he had begun two years earlier and in which he brought to bear many of the ideas born during our discussions.

During my stay in the States, everything took a new turn. I too changed in those years, and in the Cornell University library I was able to focus on my work, with no more distractions. I finished the essay on comedy, enlarged the one on Beckett, began the one on *Don Quixote* and rewrote the last one ['Il bazar archeologico' ('The archaeological bazar')], which was meant to be a reply to Calvino. I remember the effect of a seminar with Michel Foucault in Ithaca (the little town where Cornell is located) and of Foucault as a person, his mannerisms, incomparable eloquence and extraordinary intelligence, sent astray by a maliciousness towards the *'petits prof de lycée'* (among whom he included Jacques Derrida). After that seminar I decided that I could no longer stand intellectual clashes, and that I no longer believed so blindly in intelligence, or simply that it was not my calling.

27
'Rewriting, retelling, translating' ('Riscrivere, riraccontare, tradurre', 2007)

From a conversation with Marianne Schneider in Florence on 2 June 2007. Schneider recounts that 'I came to know Gianni Celati in 1985 while translating *Narratori delle pianure* (*Voices from the Plains*). Since then, I have translated all his books that have appeared in German. Together with Michelina Borsari, Daniele Benati, Ermanno Cavazzoni, Ugo Cornia and Jean Talon, we later collaborated on the journal *Il Semplice: Almanacco delle prose* from 1995 to 1997. During this long and pleasant time, every so often I would ponder his way of writing; one frequently recurring question was this: why was it that in immersing myself in his stories, listening to their rhythm and their melody, his phrasings would come to me almost effortlessly in German? I still have no response to this question. Something else that I noticed while working on his writings: his tendency to rewrite things already written. Often this question has come to mind while translating his books: "why have you so often rewritten and continue to rewrite things already written in the past?"'

I don't believe that there exists any book that is simply 'written'. To write means to rewrite, an endless venture. A page that seems acceptable today changes appearance after a year, with parts that stand out in need of rewriting. Only the end of one's lifetime and editorial deadlines put an end to rewriting. Try to think of a definitively written text as if it were a solid, unchanging object, always with the same appearance, across generations and all the various ways of reading it – a ridiculous idea, an illusion tied to the mythology surrounding classic works of literature. All literary genres are better understood when they are viewed as collective modes of storytelling, of writing poetry, of imagining life. The idea that there exist static monuments of classic literature instead of a collective flux of words is not a fact but rather an old humanistic pretence.

Suppose we have read one of Boccaccio's tales. We then come to realize that there exists a story by Masuccio that reworks Boccaccio's and introduces something new, and that another story by Sermini reworks Masuccio's, and that there is yet another by Da Porto that reworks the lot into Romeo and Juliet. This is typical of the history of short stories, but it is also true of current modes of writing. There is no such thing as an 'original' work. There is always a pulsating tangle of motifs that stem from all over. There is always a tribe of authors at work within whatever you are writing or rewriting. Then the writer puts their own name on the cover as one who carves their own tombstone. Writers are always already dead because their ultimate function is that of filling in the burial holes in literary cemeteries, so as to give work to professors. This reminds me of one of Totò's jokes: 'Have you ever noticed that it's always the same people who keep dying?'

You want to know why I am rewriting *Comiche* [Slapstick silent films]? *Comiche* was published in 1972, after I had rewritten it at least 11 times. Yet when it came out, I no longer liked it, in part because Calvino had advised that I cut out passages that were sexually explicit and would have run afoul of the editors at Einaudi. And without the excitement of sex, to me the book seemed to have fallen apart, becoming an avant-garde production akin, say, to the work of Gruppo 63.[1] Then one day while in Turin I mentioned to Nico Orengo (who was working in Einaudi's press office) that I was rewriting it for republication. He reacted to this by opening his eyes wide and saying: 'But are you crazy? That's impossible!' And in this way the rewrite ended up in a drawer, half-done and half-undone.

Lunario del paradiso [Almanac of paradise] instead is the typical case of a book that reveals flaws after a few years that I didn't see at first. While writing it I was living by myself in a borrowed house (in Bologna) and would go walking all day long in order to tire myself out as much as possible, because when you're tired it feels like being a bit drunk and the imagination kicks in more easily. I went ahead like this, dedicating one hour in the evening to writing, only one hour, and everything came out effortlessly. And so, after a first and a second draft (written in Venice) I finished the book in a couple of months. In it I followed a syncopated jazz-like rhythm that became an elastic, swerving, erratic way of speaking with interrupted syntax. But after 15 years, when it had come time to republish it as part of *Parlamenti buffi*, I realized that the rhythm was off. And there were also frivolous and false slips, some due to youth. There was nothing to do but summarily rework it. When it came to preparing the book for a new paperback edition, I found many other defects, and so in a month I rewrote it entirely, adding some parts that had been cut out of the first edition.

There are writers who carry on writing their 500 words a day, a book or two a year, who are applauded by the public and held in great esteem by their publishers. They certainly do not have the urge to rewrite everything as I do. Why? Because they get by with their 500 words a day, while what I do has always been for free.

If you take a story as a well-defined object, enclosed within the boundaries of the written page, you will always be obsessed with undertakings related to profits, sales and the public. If instead you take a story not as a well-defined object but as an event – something that occurs, like a gust of wind that blows from one head to another, that crashes into you, like an imaginative wave carrying emotions and thoughts – then there is no doubt that the story will be intertwined with an expansive kinesis of contentment. And nothing good comes forth if there is not this contentment, which is the same sensation that arises when exchanging thoughts and fantasies with newly met people, or that arises sinuously and secretly between lovers. Rewriting is a way of prolonging the state of non-fixation that exists in imaginative gusts.

I have never written a book from beginning to end or with a plan or plot in mind. I have always written fragments here and there, without a guiding plot, preferring to write whatever comes into my head day by day, depending on my moods, urges or feelings of depression. The difficult part, the snag, has always been assembling all the scattered parts, the need to rewrite and adapt, to pretend that there is a continuous narrative. It is also difficult to maintain musical tonalities, whether comic and rousing or melancholic or depressive.

Yes. Depression is a gravitational force that pulls you downward and reveals things not evident before. Depression can bring light-heartedness, just as it can bring desperation. This was my experience with *Le avventure di Guizzardi* [The adventures of Guizzardi], my first experiment with narrative therapy: that is, recounting something, anything, in order to transform melancholy into comic, expansive states of mind. I would write bits and pieces, half a page or a page each day, but following a path similar to the one in *Pinocchio*, passing from one adventure to the next without stopping to think where I was going. Then I ended up in America at just the time I stopped having depressive symptoms; and it remains one of the few books that I have never rewritten at all.

With *Fata Morgana* I was also faced with a mass of little scraps, struggling to understand how they would fit together. I tried dividing them into chapters, according to the themes they had in common, but the results were not very convincing. Then in Berlin I met an American artist who painted little pieces of metal every day, as if composing a diary of images, which she later used to make vast collages. I understood that I had to do something similar, that is, make a collage and completely give up on chasing after a continuous narrative. I rewrote some of the fragments and gave a brief title to each, seeking to emphasize the discontinuous effect of a collage. The fact is that writing short, scattered passages in the way that I do makes it very difficult to give a sense of a continuous and complete story. The tale and short story pertain to a genre with strict rules. The reader must arrive at the end with the impression that all the narrative kinks have become untangled. The difficulty in creating this trick, this illusion, is the reason why the stories in *Cinema naturale* [Natural cinema] were in the works for so many years.

The story is perhaps the most fragile of narrative genres, always on a knife's edge, a bit like a sonnet that, as it approaches its last few lines, is obligated to come to a persuasive conclusion. It always comes down to a matter of emphasis and de-emphasis, of emptiness and of intensity. For example, this is the problem posed by the stories to be called *Costumi degli italiani*, at the moment coming to life from a notebook of bits and pieces written in the 1970s and 1980s. When I finally pulled the first of these stories together, called *Vite di pascolanti*, I couldn't make sense of how I had managed to keep it all from falling apart, with parts stuck in here and there and holes left everywhere.

L'Orlando innamorato raccontato in prosa [*Orlando Innamorato* recounted in prose] seems to me somewhere in between rewriting and translation. Translation seems to me a way of rewriting books, and for this reason I find translation very enjoyable. There is something similar between translating and retelling – the emotion of leaping into a stream of images that carry you forward, moment by moment. Faithfulness in such cases lies in maintaining the energy, the colours, the tonalities, of a certain flow. I felt very light-hearted while working on *L'Orlando innamorato* – happy to be chasing after his fantasies. I would imagine myself reading out loud to my father (a passionate reader of Ariosto), my mother and other dead people. In so doing I seemed to be among family for once, instead of uprooted and adrift as usual.

Manganelli was right. In our work as writers and thinkers it is necessary above all else to free ourselves from superstructures, or in other words from the tendency to write in a way that can be passed off as acceptable to anyone – because in reality no book is acceptable to everyone. Our writings have to do with the states of the body, the most unseemly desires, the strangest, maddest, most reckless flights of thought. Their integrity lies in escaping from the traps of mass communication, which demands a fake adherence to social consensus. Writing, rewriting and translating find their state of grace in being antisocial and in the joy of not having to answer to the tyranny of the majority – because without joy these activities have no sense.

Note

1   Gruppo 63 was a 1960s avant-garde Italian literary movement that included Edoardo Sanguineti, Elio Pagliarani, Nanni Balestrini, Antonio Porta, Renato Barilli, Giorgio Manganelli and Umberto Eco.

28
'Heading to the river's mouth'
('Andar verso la foce', 2008)

Verso la foce (*Towards the River's Mouth*), published in 1989 and written over time beginning in 1981, was a stack of travel notes that I had collected over the course of five years. It took me a long time to adjust the flow of the sentences and find a modulated form. What inspired me was the anonymity of the places, the sense of emptiness while crossing the countryside, the complete lack of topics considered 'interesting'. I had nothing to say, no theory to apply to what I saw. I knew nothing about the little towns I travelled through, marked on geographic maps but virtually unknown to tourists. I was drawn to the pure 'being there' of things and people in places that interest no one.

Twenty-five years ago, our dear departed photographer Luigi Ghirri and I, together with another 20 photographers, embarked on a project to study the new Italian landscape, which at the time was called 'post-industrial'. We pondered over many things, searching for a method of inquiry distant from social documentaryism. We understood at the outset that we needed to learn how to recognize the ways in which a landscape is imagined, because all landscapes are largely represented according to the imaginative criteria of their time. Through postcards, Italian Touring Club travel books, advertisements, art books and other means, fascism created a very codified representation of Italy. It was an Italy made entirely of famous monuments, churches, beautiful panoramas, famous beaches, couples in love, dove-filled Venices and marvellous mountains to climb. These were the postcard views that fascism bequeathed to us, creating a representation of the country as a backdrop suitable to a national rhetoric. Before the end of the Second World War, in 1943, Luchino Visconti shot his first film, *Ossessione* (*Obsession*), in one of those landscapes outside the ambits of these postcard places. He set it in an area near the Po River a few miles from Ferrara, in an old building called 'La Dogana' (the customs house). Beyond the road that ran along the levee with that isolated building, in all directions, there was nothing else, as can be seen in the opening shots of the film. When Visconti presented a selection of clips to the fascist censors, they told him: 'But this isn't Italy!' Indeed it wasn't, from the point of view of official fascist representation. The novelty of *Ossessione* was this landscape, which immediately gave the sense of places where you end up when you no longer know where to go, where misfits live, like the two protagonists, or wretched people such as the husband. Modern cinema has come to understand the meaning of evoking landscapes of this sort, beyond postcard images. These are spaces of an unpremeditated way of looking in which encounters are still possible because everything is subject to chance, to unfiltered events.

The work with Ghirri and the other photographers resulted in *Viaggio in Italia* [Voyage in Italy], one of the most innovative books of photography of its time, published by a small niche press. Evident throughout the book is the influence of Visconti, Rossellini, Antonioni, Fellini – not out of an intention to imitate them, but rather because we faced the same problem of evading prescriptive views. This is evident in the ways of looking of the new photographers who worked with and discussed a myriad of topics with Ghirri, often staying up late into the night. Theirs is an observation of scattered attentions, residues of worthless things, always with the sense of a vast enveloping silence. With this manner of perceiving, other worlds came to light, precisely in those places where 'there is nothing to see'. In truth these are places where there is more to see, with the countless traces of those who have passed through them, people like us. *Viaggio in Italia* was published in 1984, along with a piece that I wrote about the landscape. This began the gestation of *Verso la foce*, which emerged from a number of crossings of the Po River Valley that I undertook from 1981 to 1986, as far as the delta. This project would never have materialized had it not been for these photographers, whom I soon began to admire, including Guidi, Barbieri, Castella, Cresci, Battistella, Fossati, Leone, Basilico, Jodice, Chiaramonte and of course Ghirri, who was the driving force behind the project, inviting me to take part in it. Everywhere in *Viaggio in Italia* is evidence of what can be found beyond History's prescribed scenes and famous itineraries. The book is composed of views that cross over into chance and anonymity, with neither 'beautiful landscapes' nor the myths of social documentaryism. What comes to light instead is an element of ordinary randomness: the pre-categorizable nature of objects, before the judgements arise that we develop about places.

We drag behind ourselves an old distinction between subject and object, between the self and the non-self, that goes back to Fichte. And this antinomy is a true ball and chain, holding us back from cracks through which to glimpse the outside world. Vision is neither subjective nor objective: it is an inspection of things when we find ourselves disoriented in a place where our usual parameters of judgement no longer work. This is a response that causes us to observe things without a precise agenda, leaving us to wait to find clues with which to reorient ourselves. I bring this up because I believe that the innovative work of Ghirri and the other photographers consists precisely in subverting this antinomy between subjectivity and objectivity, tied to that other antinomy between the 'social' and the 'artistic'. And this was also my path, working with them. This said, at the time several critics dismissed *Verso la foce* because they saw in it a 'subjective' and eccentric vision disconnected from reality, while others dismissed it because they saw a naïve attempt to describe 'objective reality' without reference to socio-logical or economic data – that is, without those categories of judgement which I had sought to evade.

Vision is a way of taking part in the external world by way of certain traces, traces that are elements of the random ordinariness in which we can recognize something outside the categories of judgement that establish prescribed ways of looking. Ordinariness is neither meaningful nor insignificant, neither beautiful nor ugly, neither sophisticated nor base. Within this random ordinariness all antinomies fade away and what comes to the fore is the simple fact that objects 'are there', as they are, and that the entire world consists of things and habits that simply 'are there', as they are. This, it seems to me, was the way in which these photographers were working, and it was also my direction in *Verso la foce*. What was most important was no longer the distinction between the subjective and the objective, nor a specialized definition of 'reality', but the encountering of external situations through an adherence to vision.

The current idea that words can capture reality, making of it a sort of saleable booty of 'objective evidence', is mistaken. One may say that what words describe has nothing to do with what we see, and vice versa, that what we see will never become an accurate description. Descriptions in novels are stage directions that contain nothing 'visible' to us and that serve only to refer us to the idea of photographic representation. If there is a visual imagination that emerges from words, it is never the result of a clear description, but rather an altering of shadows that attract our attention and that lead to a suspension of lived time (thanks to which, for example, we lose track of surrounding noises).

In front of a tree, a house, a wall, a rock, words are only able to transmit the universal abstractness of a name. Saying 'over there is a tree' is only meaningful as a deictic indication, because that tree is different from all other trees, just as each thing is different from all other things within the same category. Once this diversity is eliminated, 'reality' has already been invalidated. So-called experience no longer has the support of the language which it had so long been presumed to have. It is not true, given an experience, that there are words ready to express it, in the same way that a camera captures an image. The reverse is true: first come the turns of phrase to express certain situations, after which every perception must be adapted to these pre-existing turns of phrase, in a written language or a way of speaking. *Verso la foce* was an experiment with some of these fundamental ideas in mind, including the fact that descriptions do not capture any reality. If anything, we invoke reality as something that always escapes us. While I was going around taking notes, wandering across relatively sparsely populated areas of the countryside, what came to the fore was the continuous need to find meditative reflections. What fell apart was the ideology of an adroit hunting down of so-called reality, the idea of a direct experience of the world, without reflection. This is an ideology with a vast retinue of ready-made phrases, such as 'lived experience' and 'lived places'. What was most memorable about those trips across the Po Valley was the discovery of not being able to describe almost anything. Descriptions worth making are those in which you pass beyond the specific thing seen, in which the words seem to fly, moving along on their own accord. In these cases, the words enact their basic function, which is to name things, but in lesser importance to 'calling to things' that are outside the self. *Verso la foce* was an exercise in attempting to detect an obstacle: if there exists an external reality, it reveals itself in the form of an impediment, a barrier, uncertainty, struggle. It is never something immediate or evident, nor an 'objective reference' to an explanation found in books.

The experiment of writing (or rather of taking notes) along the road, in country bars or on buses or trains, brought to light that there does not exist a world spreading out in all directions that waits for you to describe or photograph it as you like. Nothing of the sort exists. There were moments in which I was so tired that I could not take another step, others in which I found everything that I did absurd, and entire days when I had no desire to look at what was around me. So long as you are at home at your desk, it is easy to come up with a theory of how to write, conjecturing ways to complete your thoughts in a such a way as to fill all the holes, to replace all the questions with lovely answers. But if you are wandering around with your notebook, in a bar or somewhere else, you are always at the mercy of moments, of uncertainties, of obstacles. And thus, everything in space around you, far from a capturable reality, seems to be a zone of shadows to cross. These are all signs of colliding with something 'real' – that is, the external world as something always undone, never reducible to the calm comprehension of an informative fact, of what is already known, or of journalistic news.

An undertaking such as *Verso la foce* clearly only holds meaning if carried out in the company of a passion for the world as it is, not for the world as it should be, improved and advanced, but for the external world as we encounter it in its daily, ordinary aspects – a passion that comes to light in desolate places (such as the Po Valley lowlands, starting near Polesine), where there is nothing special to see, and where one quits rejecting everything that seems banal, negative, useless or outdated.

Within this residue of everything that the world of finance considers worthless resides the great power of *Stimmung*, as Benjamin writes. This is because the tonalities of desolate places in our times absorb everything that mass communication rejects out of fear that it would unsettle the tranquil mass sterilization of our brains. Every trace of desolation carries within itself this unsettling tonal element, like a thought that announces the failure of experience together with the necessity of other encounters.

During those crossings of the Po Valley, full of mistakes, bewilderment and the almost total inability to write, the most insignificant places transformed into adventurous scenarios, thanks precisely to their perpetual uncertainty and difficulty. I remember particularly well the feeling of crossing an absolutely desolate stretch of land (near Polesine) or approaching a *finis terrae* (on the delta). In those places I thought about old French knights' tales that spoke of searching for the grail and of wastelands (*terre gaste* in old French). Ghirri used to say that places are depositories of affective images that we reuse as an alphabet for our fantasy.

The moments of contentment, among the sightings transcribed in *Verso la foce*, are those in which I discovered the daily habits of a local population, for example the evening promenade in Comacchio, with young women parading along the main street, or the sunset in Scardovari, with people sitting in the doorways of their houses to chat while awaiting dusk. If, while wandering around, I felt all day in a void, isolated from other people, in front of those forms of daily ritual there was born instead the fantasy of a connection with others – a connection even without approaching them, out of the idea that one can be connected to others despite also being completely isolated. It is the idea that everything that we do or think is part of a web that ties us to others, and that determines my gestures, the ways that I behave, what I want and what I don't want. And the greatest link lies in the fact that everyone I see out and about, everyone with whom I speak, is moving towards death, as if we were keeping each other company on this path. That was the culmination of a type of cure or therapy, going towards the river's mouth.

Figure 28.1   Gianni Celati, in Mantua, 2001, courtesy of Vincenzo Cottinelli.

29
From 'In Zurich with Joyce'
(Da 'A Zurigo con Joyce', 2009)

A year in Zurich, on the trail of Joyce, struggling forward along increasingly entangled narrative paths. (September 9)

Zurich. Spring 2009. Routine for translating Joyce's *Ulysses* on the days when I am not teaching. Wake up in the morning at 5.00 and work nonstop until 5.00 in the evening. Then groceries at a nearby store and a walk down in the direction of the river or up into the hills of the area where I live, called Zürichberg. From here, walking uphill for half an hour brings me to the cemetery where Joyce is buried, not far from the zoo where animals from various lands are on display.

Joyce's grave is a simple stone slab level with the ground and bordered by a low, rectangular shrub. Behind the shrub there arises a bronze statue resembling our author. A thin and lanky body bent over in thoughtful repose, legs crossed, chin leaning on a hand holding a cigarette between two fingers, Joyce looks towards the shrub on his right. You might say he looks like a bendable man thinking up some acrobatic feat to perform while visitors arrive to pay him respects as a great literary acrobat, after having visited the zoo around the corner.

The idea of a literary acrobat seems well suited to the character portrayed by the statue, Joyce being like someone who flew from one trapeze to another under the big top, as in Kafka's story 'First Sorrow' ('Erstes Leid', 1922). This brings to mind a passion widespread among writers and artists in *fin-de-siècle* Paris: that of circus acrobatics soaring in exaggerated flight far above the prosaic world of the bourgeois masses.

Joyce came to Paris in 1902, and something remained in him of that manner of flying above the prose of the world in leaps of thought that lead to unsanctioned inventions. This happens in most parts of *Ulysses*, in which it is easy to get lost among the avalanche of sentences without explanation, whose sense must be grasped by way of the slightest of hints. For this reason very often readers become confused and tired, then set the book aside, with the inscrutable flights of thought leaving behind the greatest impression. And for this reason, readers such as these (who do not scorn the bourgeois masses, in part because today there are supermarkets, without such need for flights of thought), if the occasion arises while touring about the city, after a visit to the zoo, may pay a visit to Joyce's so very sober and charming grave.

During my year spent in Zurich I lived in hilly Zürichberg, full of money, psychotherapists and beautiful old villas. The street that I lived on was called Hochstrasse, and not far from where it turns, five hundred steps to the left, is the Universitätsstrasse. Here rises a large building with a plaque engraved in Latin script that informs you that J. J. once lived in this building and so on. The plaque seems a humanistic gesture intending to honour a foreign refugee (Joyce took refuge here during the First World War), as in the time of Zwingli's protestant reforms.

Joyce's grave is commonly advertised in tourist brochures, and summaries of his career are given in good guidebooks, such as those published by Lonely Planet. Over the past few decades, the vast number of references to Joyce's passing haunts in Zurich have made his name even more famous, with all the information necessary to declare him a local figure, one who has contributed to making Zurich a renowned city of the arts and culture. With great wisdom the Swiss have thus tied the name of a writer whose work is very difficult to read to a tourist industry in which everything needs to be easy to digest. This, however, does not help to orient readers lost in the Joycean disorder of words, generated by continuous shifts in narrative direction and bizarre digressions of thought.

During my stay, many people suggested that I pay a visit to Fritz Senn in order to resolve a number of the problems I was facing in translating *Ulysses*. Fritz Senn is an extraordinary non-academic critic, a life-long Joyce scholar, founder and director of Zurich's James Joyce Foundation, which offers 'a lively understanding, which does not resort to footnotes or the residue of academic apparatus'. These are words that meet with my own interests in Joycean matters, but in thinking them over there seems to be a catch. If this lively understanding were to work, it would be like learning a recipe for a marvellous dish, but one so stimulating that there would be a rule stating that it could only be tasted after a long fast – a fast as long as those suffered by the ancient saints of the desert.

Zurich, almost autumn. The translation of *Ulysses* struggles along. I have the sense of never managing to get to the end of it, even if I were to ask Fritz Senn for help. A few days ago, someone wrote 'Konsum totes Empathie' in large, sweeping strokes on a wall near my house on Hochstrasse. 'Consumption kills empathy.' The contrast between these two actions stands out to me. The consumption of words, the consumption of money, the consumption of food, the consumption of everything. The consumption of Joyce's *Ulysses*: what does this phrase mean? The image comes to me of a crowd of people who have bought a new translation of *Ulysses* (mine, for example) and take it home, carrying it tightly under their arms. Then what happens? I see that most of these people from the crowd, little by little, put the book aside, pick out another, a thriller or a mystery novel, and begin reading it with great pleasure. Has consumption occurred in such a case? Yes and no, because on the one hand the bookseller has made some money, and on the other, it is as if the reader has bought nothing, having thrown away their money, thinking that *Ulysses* is a rip-off.

In some sense this is true, because the bookseller has touted a famous book, but without warning customers that many people are unable to read it. Or this: as is the practice with pharmaceuticals, customers should be warned of a book's relative digestibility, according to mood, curiosity and taste. And yet booksellers cannot do this without negatively affecting sales of the book. Perhaps there are some booksellers who, with a bit of effort, might accept the idea of warning customers. And yet, because we live in a society based on the rule of competition (which means prevailing over others), all the means possible for selling that book would be put into action, and inevitably those with fewer scruples would prevail over the others. In all this, the idea of consumption would remain ambiguous, and to make matters clear it would be necessary to sell only guaranteed books.

Now the other term, 'empathy'. The dictionary defines it as coming from the Greek *empatheia* (passion), derived from *pathos* (experience, misfortune, emotion, condition). I can then rewrite the phrase written on the wall in this way: consumption kills or suffocates something for which we feel affection, passion or love. How does this matter? What comes to mind first is that the things for which we feel affection are generally those which have been a part of our lives, or of the place where we grew up. But this affection can also be something that grows inside someone while working at or learning a new activity that then becomes important. This has been the case for me with Joyce's *Ulysses*: there is nothing for me to expect out of this task of translation; I won't earn enough out of it to cover even a fraction of the years of work likely needed to complete it. But I don't feel cheated because what I am doing is like a mania or a love or like one of those acts of sacrifice carried out by saints from long ago. This seems for the moment to be the only plausible conclusion I am able to reach.

30

'On Jonathan Swift and the development of aliens' ('Su Jonathan Swift e lo sviluppo degli alieni', 2010)

An interview with Riccardo Donati, published in *Veleni delle coscienze. Lettere novecentesche del secolo dei Lumi* (Rome: Bulzoni Editore, 2010), a book that focuses on the interest writers in the 1940s and 1950s, such as Calvino and Sciascia, had for the *Lumières* (Enlightenment thinkers). But as times changed, devotion to the masters of (Diderot and d'Alembert's) *Encyclopédie* shifted to interest in more eccentric Anglo-Saxon models, along with modes of anti-romantic and mocking satire that increasingly seemed more suitable for recounting the present.

My passion for Swift, which began in the early 1960s, grew in fits and starts. I was 26, living in London and washing dishes in a Leicester Square restaurant, and one day bought a collection of Swift's writings, which to pass the time I tried translating. Later I met Giambattista Vicari, the editor of *Il Caffè*, and started publishing a few of these translations. When I met Italo Calvino, much of his initial interest in me came from the ideas I had gathered from Swift. With these ideas Swift turned out to be a progenitor of eighteenth-century culture (Voltaire found his way by reading Swift, who remained his literary guide up to *Candide*), but also an author who was not reducible to all Enlightenment discourse.

As for the two editions of your translation of Swift's *A Tale of a Tub*, the first in 1966 and the second in 1990 …

A Tale of a Tub is one of Swift's masterpieces that had never before been translated into Italian, and I dived into it with closed eyes, without being fully prepared for the task of carrying it into our language, with the result being a ludicrous translation. Many years later, in 1990, Einaudi asked me to republish it, and for this new edition I completely reworked the text, rendering it more closely to its late seventeenth-/ early eighteenth-century style and adding a new preface. And now, while rewriting the preface once again (for a collection of essays due to be published by Feltrinelli), I thought of my giddy youthful careening through Swift's merciless ironies, ironies irreconcilable with all the fictions of goodness and the profits of the religious upper classes, a group Swift mocks in one of his acutest satires (in which he proposes to transform Christianity into a purely nominal religion, such that, despite being emptied of meaning, it is allowed to continue its lucrative activities in peace). The impression one gathers from these satires is of an alien viewing humanity as a species of animal devoted to falsity, sordidness and feral violence, typified in the Yahoos Gulliver meets on his last voyage. Swift often brings to mind authors of science fiction such as Philip K. Dick in whose work I find a similar sense of being an alien in a world in which everyone thinks they are safe, in the company of a humanity bent on its own destruction.

How have Swift's writings influenced your own work?

Recurrent is this idea of an alien, like Gulliver, who is an outsider wherever he goes, even at home. The characters in *Comiche*, for example, were born from the idea of an alien or an alienated neurotic among people who believe that they are sane and normal. And neither in this book could there exist any fictions of goodness.

Are there other key eighteenth-century figures?

Candide is Gulliver's cousin, almost his appendage, sharing a certain lowering of expressive tone. These eighteenth-century aliens, including Tristram Shandy, are all closely related to us, anticipating the modern sensation of overwhelming disorientation, of the inability to associate with austere figures of authority, with seemingly mentally upstanding people—who are the sickest of all. Naturalism then attempts to right the boat, embracing a scientific point of view, which also gives us a rather clinical view of humanity. But in this clinical vision of life there is also something dictatorial and intolerant.

In the June 1968 special issue of *Il Caffè* dedicated to Swift, you write in the opening essay that Swift's is a high form of satire, built on archaic images of violence and apocalypse – a type of satire that has never flourished in Italy, the country of Horace. However, in the 1960s and 1970s various authors, moreover ones very different from each other – from Frassineti's *Tre bestemmie uguali e distinti* to Berto's *Modesta proposta per prevenire* – adopted modest proposals as starting points to confront then-current social and political affairs in a way that was also fierce and, indeed, apocalyptic.

Yes, but Swift's appeal did not stem from a call to current affairs. Topicality is a reduction of everything to a set of criteria established by a form of humanity that considers itself 'normal' while in the meantime an endless stream of cruelty passes by in full view as if part of some carnival attraction – from skeletal starved children to the various effects of a rampant capitalism untethered from any legal restraints, able to manipulate the masses through TV and gadgets of every sort. Among the writers who collaborated with *Il Caffè*, those I felt closest to are Italo Calvino, Giorgio Manganelli and the dear Augusto Frassineti, author of *Misteri dei ministeri* – which through ministerial scrivenings highlighted the existence of a hitherto little-known species of mutants or aliens.

Would it make sense, today, to write another modest proposal?

No, I don't believe that it would make sense to thematize Swift's ideas in this way, sending them to the gristmill of topicality, which grinds the sense out of anything it encounters, putting everyone's conscience to rest. Swift's proposing to English lords to procure from Irish children the meat for new succulent dishes, forces us to confront a condition in which there can no longer exist the hypocrisy of good intentions, the farce of goodwill, or the emblem of those who believe that they are 'in the right'. Swift is a gust of wind, filling our lungs as it sweeps away the falseness of all optimistic justifications.

In your introduction to the 1966 translation of *A Tale of a Tub* you trace Swift's influence to the heart of the twentieth century, from Joyce to Céline, and from Gadda to Manganelli.

The idea at the time, to view Swift at the beginning of a modern genealogy of thought, had been suggested to me by a scholar (whose name I don't remember) who had compared various aspects of Swift's thought to Baudelaire's. It still seems to me that Swift and Baudelaire, as well as Leopardi, the writers you mentioned, Beckett and others, together take part in a recognizable web of influence, each playing with expressions of one's state of being, carrying with it the signs of one's weakness, the acceptance of one's alienness – a state in which no one can any longer boast of personal achievements or virtues, bringing to mind one of Baudelaire's *petites poèmes en prose* in which a poet leaves home wearing his beautiful halo, which then falls into the muddy road, leaving him as much man as poet but without an aura.

This condition of 'alienness' sets Swift's writings at complete odds with dominant systems of thought, as much today as three hundred years ago …

Yes, but matters have become much more complicated with advances in genetics to the point that it seems possible to create a race of neo-aliens to replace us, the older paleo-aliens. I use the term genetics in reference to the pinnacle of various efforts to endlessly manipulate humanity – from the fanatical peddling of appearances to the daily brainwashing of the masses, to the impossibility of appearing acceptable except through corporate strictures. And above all the religion of the economy, which is talked about nonstop, among elsewhere on networks such as CNN in a swirl of delirious statements based on daily fluctuations of the stock exchange, but always leaving out mention of how massive concentrations of wealth exploit the catastrophes that miserable aliens face. Enough. What I intended on saying is that Swift's satire forces us to rethink our conception of the human as a political animal: such satire exists only by reactivating liberating means of expression, irreducible to that language of the dead that is topicality, means of expression that give us space to breathe, freeing us from the ghosts of success.

31

'The disorder of words: on a translation of Joyce's *Ulysses*' ('Il disordine delle parole: Su una traduzione dell'*Ulisse* di Joyce', 2013)

I began my translation of Joyce's *Ulysses* seven years ago. It had taken the editors at Einaudi five years to convince me to take on the job. In the end I agreed, feeling as though I were leaping into rough waters, lacking the certainty that I would stay afloat.

When in my 20s and a university student I bought a copy of *Ulysses* at a used bookstore in London. Tired from my job (washing dishes at a restaurant) I managed to read at most half a page a day, and often the dictionaries that I consulted at the British Museum were of no help at all. Something else that confounded me was the difficulty I faced in distinguishing between differing ways of speaking, whether from Ireland or England, or words that seemed endowed with sounds from a particular neighbourhood or a brothel. Something else stood out: one page of my book ended with a capital M outside the margin, and I took it for some sort of modernist gesture. Back in Italy my English professor explained to me that it was simply a typographical error. The first edition of *Ulysses*, printed in Paris in 1922, was a constellation of badly corrected drafts, with a few sentences gone missing along the way.

My professor of English literature, Carlo Izzo, was part of a group of experts who had revised the first Italian translation of *Ulysses*, and it was he who warned me of the difficulties I would come up against. Facing long hours of research in various libraries, attempting to read expressions whose sense I could barely fathom, brought upon me a feeling of uncertainty but along with this also the sense of a utopic venture. In the end it was Carlo Izzo's literary passion that compelled me to read that book, a book that now appears to me like an immense ocean in which you continually lose your way, with hazards in every direction.

The routine of twelve hours of work a day did not lead to much headway. Some days I managed to produce at most three or four pages of passable translation. And my doubts continued to grow, namely that there were problems of language that I understood only vaguely, even with the help of annotated versions of the text (such as Don Gifford's truly essential *Ulysses Annotated*). But it is in this respect that Joyce's book broke away from all others of the time, with its way of speaking being always a game, a juggling of genres or unusual or distorted pronunciations. And I came to understand along the way that *Ulysses* is not built of a language per se but a sort of all-consuming glossolalia that absorbs echoes of every kind with a seemingly endlessly vast lexicon.

Variously Irish, British, Gaelic, *Ulysses* can be as bizarre as Jonathan Swift's satires when it discusses English lords, calm as Pantagruel's wisdom, and clownish as our own macaronic heroes. In it appear fossilized lingos, authorial styles across time, literary echoes and antique voices – such as the peculiar mode of locution of *Ayenbyte of Inwyt*, a fourteenth-century Kentish treatise that appears only a few times in my edition, but memorably so (I translated it in Latin, *Morsua animi*, to keep some flavour of an ancient text).

I came to understand that I had to face up to similar dangers and embrace the disorder of the words, treating them as swerving miscellanies of fantasy. I realized that it was not as important to understand everything as it was to attune my ear to a resonance that becomes more recognizable just as it comes swooping down through ambiguous expressions, archaic idioms, pub chatter, linguistic outgrowths of various times.

Ulysses soon departs from a somewhat familiar mode of narration and dives into a chaotic array of words, driven by digressions of the mind only held together by the narrator's so-called stream of consciousness, a constant succession of thoughts and images that pass through his head, one dissolving into or invoking others, almost nonstop. A free-for-all in which inner and outer perceptions flow together, slipping over and under one another, from the panorama at hand to memory as a form of *rêverie* (dream or fantastication), which becomes the base of the constant wanderings of our ordinary heroes, Stephen Dedalus and Leopold Bloom.

This stream of consciousness radically transforms the concept of a coherent novelistic plot typically imposed on linear sequences. In those years only one figure stands out as perceiving in ways akin to Joyce a general sense of discontinuous yet collective motion located everywhere, along any given stretch of road, any place with a shop or factory:

the great filmmaker Dziga Vertov, who in his extraordinary 1929 film *Man with a Movie Camera* seems to share certain affinities with Joyce in this portrait of life in constant flux.

After Mr Bloom ventures into the city at the beginning of the book, there is something that gradually expands with a recognizable emotional tonality. This tonality continues to grow over the course of the digression during which Mr Bloom mulls at the cemetery over the fact that the dead all become food for worms. And in this mounting tonality, increasingly fragmentary insertions make their way into the text, the crippled soldier playing a tune in the street or the seagulls over the Liffey in search of food, or someone by the river who predicts the coming of Elijah, or the clusters of people toting billboards on street corners, or the trams slowly shunting around Nelson's pillar – all facets of the stream of consciousness that attracts and distracts Mr Bloom.

But as the episodes progress, always mutating, there arise new means of distraction, strange suggestions that lead to a diffused *rêverie*, as for example the reading of hangman Rumbold's letter arguing his case to be employed in the service of the city, a scholar of linguistics who interprets the growling of a dog as recalling 'intricate alliterative and isosyllabic rules of the Welsh englyn', or the oppressive fourteenth-century prose parodically honouring the evangelical maxim extolling the virtues of 'that exalted of reiteratedly procreating function', in other words, to 'increase and multiply', or the masses of specialized terms and myriads of pages from a nonsensical medical symposium in which there abound various solemn imitations of eighteenth-century prose. It is impossible to translate such acrobatics without taming or flattening them out, thanks to Joyce's ceaselessly mutating and expanding lexicon, vaster perhaps than any other known author.

Together with this wander scattered insertions that outstrip all respectable criteria, up to the night in the red-light district where the stream of consciousness seems invaded by phantasms (from the objects to the characters that suddenly appear) and where everything and everyone can speak and have its say, in a society of aliens akin to the lords targeted by Swift in his satires. And it is here in the brothel that Mr Bloom bears the punishment of the average sensual man.

Difficult chapters, always more contorted. But it seems to me that the difficulties of the text can be overcome provided you do not hurry and that you greet with fondness the disarray of words. For this reason, it is not so important to understand everything as it is to listen to a musical or songlike tonality, which becomes more familiar when we seem to plunge into a chaotic stream of words. *Ulysses* is a book in which musicality is a fundamental aspect for every deviation, doubling-back, surprise, iteration, monologue. It is a book felt and sustained by the special perceptive faculty of music, beyond an objective sense of things or an assertion of words, a book that takes part in resonances spreading out in all directions.

After all, *Ulysses* is a book written by someone who was to become a tenor (Joyce when living in Trieste) and who had learned how to transmit onto the page what musicians call the 'inner ear', beyond any definite sense of words. A tally of the songs that spring up in *Ulysses* every few pages would reveal myriad melodic references at the heart of Joyce's project, countless musical echoes that are pathways through the thickets of tangled discourses: from opera to obscene jingles, from Gregorian chants ('Gloria in excelsis Deo') to the sound of the viceroy's carriage as it passes along the river ('Clapclap. Clipclap. Clappyclap.'), from nursery rhymes to a German poem about the siren's song ('Von der Sirenen Listigkeit …'), from the song of the cuckoo ('Cuckoo! Cuckoo!') to *The Barber of Seville* (opera), from the clinking of glasses in the act of toasting ('Tschink. Tschunk.') to the banging of a tuning fork ('Tap. Tap. Tap. Tap.'), to certain lines from Mozart's *Don Giovanni* that resurface time and again in Mr Bloom's thoughts ('Vorrei e non vorrei, mi trema un poco il cor'), and so on.

The focal axis of Mr Bloom's wanderings is everyday life, life without particular allure, dreamlike life resembling a long chat with its various selves – the uninterrupted modern flux of life, with the meanings of words taking flight as soon they reach the ears along Grafton Street or as they appear on a watchmaker's shopfront window, yet again ordinary life that passes by every second, with modern sounds and jingles and operettic arias, and the adverts on human billboards wandering the streets.

This, too, in my translation posed a quandary, through which I sought a path, in part by re-evoking this everyday life, whose representative is Mr Bloom, but above all by bringing out the sense of an unending song, the song of the everyday, which traditionally is the simplest way of passing the time in everyday life. This leads me to believe (doubtfully) that the Irish may be (or were in Joyce's time) more melodic, closer to song in speech, than Italians (of today) – and the flowering of songs or snippets of opera on their lips was something out of which Joyce made a national phenomenon. This brings me back to the (hypothetical) fact that Joyce was unable to think of anything unless it were a musical phenomenon – beyond all the prevailing categories of logical truth or dialectical certainty that humanism has bequeathed to us.

Figure 31.1   Gianni Celati writing at the side of the road behind a green
Renault 4, unknown date. Reprinted by permission of Gillian Haley.

Bibliography of original source texts by Gianni Celati

Note: these original source texts are listed in the order in which they appear in the book, which, apart from the first piece, is also in the chronological order in which they were first published.

'Esercizio autobiografico in 2000 battute' ('One-page autobiography'), in *Riga 40: Gianni Celati*, ed. Marco Belpoliti, Marco Sironi and Anna Stefi (Macerata: Quodlibet, [2008] 2019), 20.

'Parlato come spettacolo' ('Speech as spectacle'), in *Animazioni e incantamenti*, ed. Nunzia Palmieri (Rome: L'Orma, [1968] 2017), 282–93.

'Gianni Celati e Italo Calvino, Corrispondenze (*Comiche*)' ('Gianni Celati and Italo Calvino, correspondence [*Comiche*]'), in *Riga 28: Gianni Celati* (Extra), ed. Marco Belpoliti and Marco Sironi (Milan: Marcos y Marcos, [circa early 1970s] 2008), http://rigabooks.it/extra.php?idlangua ge=1&id=404&idextra=539.

'Il racconto di superficie' ('Surface stories'), *Riga 14: Alì Babà*, ed. Mario Barenghi and Marco Belpoliti (Milan: Marcos y Marcos, [1973] 1998), 176–96.

'Le virtù del gorilla' ('The virtues of the gorilla'), *Animazioni e incantamenti*, ed. Nunzia Palmieri (Rome: L'Orma, [1974] 2017), 385–90.

'Il bazaar archeologico' ('The archaeological bazaar'), *Riga 14: Alì Babà*, ed. Mario Barenghi and Marco Belpoliti (Milan: Marcos y Marcos, [1975] 1998), 200–23.

'Il corpo comico nello spazio' ('The comic body in space'), *Animazioni e incantamenti*, ed. Nunzia Palmieri (Rome: L'Orma, [1976] 2017), 303–14.

'Contro-informazione sul potere. A proposito di *Sorvegliare e punire* di Foucault' ('Counter-information on power: on Foucault's *Discipline and Punish*'), *Riga 28: Gianni Celati*, ed. Marco Belpoliti and Marco Sironi (Milan: Marcos y Marcos, [1977] 2008), 191–3.

'Sull'epoca di questo libro' e 'Alice e l'avvenimento …' ('On the era of this book' and 'Alice and the occurrence …'), *Alice disambientata: Materiali collettivi (su Alice) per un manuale di soprav-vivenza* (Florence: Le Lettere, [1978] 2007), 5–11, 66–72.

'Oggetti soffici' ('Soft objects'), *Animazioni e incantamenti*, ed. Nunzia Palmieri (Rome: L'Orma, [1979] 2017), 329–42.

'L'avventura verso la fine del XX secolo' ('Adventure at the end of the twentieth century'), *Conversazioni del vento volatore* (Macerata: Quodlibet, [1982] 2011), 16–25.

'Un sistema di racconti sul mondo esterno' ('A system of stories about the external world') *Riga 28: Gianni Celati*, ed. Marco Belpoliti and Marco Sironi (Milan: Marcos y Marcos, [1986] 2008), 196–206.

'Traversate del deserto' ('Desert crossings'), *Conversazioni del vento volatore* (Macerata: Quodlibet, [1986] 2011), 13–15.

'Traducendo Jack London' ('Translating Jack London') *Narrative in fuga*, ed. Jean Talon (Macerata: Quodlibet, [1986] 2019), 57–64.

'La veduta frontale. Antonioni, *L'Avventura* e l'attesa' ('The frontal view: Antonioni, *L'Avventura* and waiting'), *Cinema & Cinema*, 49 (June 1987), 5–6.

'Finzioni a cui credere, un esempio' ('Fictions to believe in, an example'), *Paessagio italiano*, by Luigi Ghirri (Milan: Electa, 1989), 32–3.

'Commenti su un teatro naturale delle immagini' ('Comments on a natural theatre of images'), *Il profilo delle nuvole*, by Luigi Ghirri (Milan: Feltrinelli, 1989), n. p.

'Swift, profetico trattato sull'epoca moderna' ('Swift, prophetic treatise on the modern age'), *Narrative in fuga*, ed. Jean Talon (Macerata: Quodlibet, [1990] 2019), 277–96.

'Il sentimento dello spazio: Conversazione con Gianni Celati' ('The sentiment of space: conversation with Gianni Celati'), *Cinema & Cinema*, 18, no. 62 (1991), 25–8.

'Note d'avvio' ('Introductory note'), *Narratori delle riserve*, ed. Gianni Celati (Milan: Feltrinelli, 1992), 9–10.

'Soglia per Luigi Ghirri: Come pensare per immagini' ('Threshold for Luigi Ghirri: how to think through images'), *Animazioni e incantamenti*, ed. Nunzia Palmieri (Rome: L'Orma, [1992] 2017), 374–82.

'Elogio della novella' ('In praise of the tale'), *Conversazioni del vento volatore* (Macerata: Quodlibet, [1992] 2011), 35–42.

'Morte di Italo' ('Italo's Death'), *Riga 9: Italo Calvino*, ed. Marco Belpoliti (Milan: Riga, 1996), 204–8.

'Ultimi Contemplatori' ('Last contemplators'), *Riga 28: Gianni Celati* (Extra), ed. Marco Belpoliti and Marco Sironi (Milan: Marcos y Marcos, [1997] 2008), http://rigabooks.it/extra.php?idlanguage=1&id=404&idextra=559.

'Due anni di studio nella biblioteca del British Museum' ('Two years of study at the British Museum'), *Conversazioni del vento volatore* (Macerata: Quodlibet, [2001] 2011), 44–50.

'Riscrivere, riraccontare, tradurre' ('Rewriting, retelling, translating'), *Riga 28: Gianni Celati*, ed. Marco Belpoliti and Marco Sironi (Milan: Marcos y Marcos, [2007] 2008), 45–9.

'Andar verso la foce' ('Heading to the river's mouth'), *Riga 28: Gianni Celati* (Extra), ed. Marco Belpoliti and Marco Sironi (Milan: Marcos y Marcos, 2008), http://www.rigabooks.it/index.php?idlanguage=1&zone=9&id=404.

'A Zurigo con Joyce' ('In Zurich with Joyce'), *Riga 40: Gianni Celati*, ed. Marco Belpoliti, Marco Sironi and Anna Stefi (Macerata: Quodlibet, [2009] 2019), 151–9.

'Su Jonathan Swift e lo sviluppo degli alieni' ('On Jonathan Swift and the development of aliens'), *Conversazioni del vento volatore* (Macerata: Quodlibet, [2010] 2011), 148–53.

'Il disordine delle parole: Su una traduzione dell'*Ulisse* di Joyce' ('The disorder of words: on a translation of Joyce's *Ulysses*'), *Narrative in fuga*, ed. Jean Talon (Macerata: Quodlibet, [2013] 2019), 327–34.

Selected bibliography

Note: this bibliography contains selected primary and secondary sources cited by Celati in his writings collected in this book; it is not an exhaustive list of all references. I have provided English language versions where possible.

Arendt, Hannah. 'Introduction'. In *Illuminations: Essays and reflections*, by Walter Benjamin, ed. Hannah Arendt, trans. Harry Zohn, 1–58. New York: Schocken Books, 2007, 1–58.

Argan, Carlo Argan. *Stora d'Italia*, Vol. I. Turin: Einaudi, 1972.

Ariosto, Ludovico. *Orlando Furioso, Part I*, trans. Barbara Renolds. London: Penguin, 1973.

Ariosto, Ludovico. *Orlando Furioso, Part II*, trans. Barbara Renolds. London: Penguin, 1977.

Artaud, Antonin. *Selected Writings*, ed. Susan Sontag. Berkeley: University of California Press, 1988.

Bakhtin, Mikhail *Problems of Dostoevsky's Poetics*, ed. and trans. Caryl Emerson. Minneapolis: University of Minnesota Press, 1984.

Barthes, Roland. 'Drame, poème, roman'. In *Tel Quel: Théorie d'ensemble*. Paris: Seuil, 1968, 25–41.

Barthes, Roland. *Critical Essays*, trans. Richard Howard. Evanston: Northwestern University Press, 1972.

Barthes, Roland. *S/Z*, trans. Richard Miller. New York: Hill and Wang, 1975.

Beckett, Samuel. *Three Novels: Molloy, Malone dies, the unnamable*. New York: New Directions, 2009.

Benjamin, Walter. 'On the concept of history', trans. Andy Blunden, https://www.marxists.org/reference/archive/benjamin/1940/history.htm.

Benjamin, Walter. 'Paris, capital of the 19th century'. *Perspecta* 12 (1969): 163–72.

Benjamin, Walter. 'The work of art in the age of mechanical reproduction'. In Walter Benjamin, *Illuminations: Essays and Reflections*, ed. Hannah Arendt, trans. Harry Zohn. New York: Schocken Books, 2007, 217–52.

Benjamin, Walter. *Angelus Novus: Saggi e frammenti*, ed. Renato Solmi. Turin: Einaudi, 1962.

Benjamin, Walter. *One Way Street and Other Writings*, trans. Edmund Jephcott and Kingsley Shorter. London: NLB, 1979.

Benjamin, Walter. *The Arcades Project*, trans. Keven McLaughlin. Cambridge: Belknap Press, 2002.

Benjamin, Walter. *The Origin of German Tragic Drama*, trans. John Osborne. London: Verso, 2003.

Bergson, Henri. *Key Writings*, eds. Keith Ansell-Pearson and John Ó Maoilearca. New York: Bloomsbury, 2014.

Bertram, Joseph Lean. *Acting Shakespeare*. London: Theatre Art Books, 1960.

Blanchot, Maurice. *The Space of Literature*, trans. Ann Smock. Lincoln: University of Nebraska Press, 1982.

Boccaccio, Giovanni. *The Decameron*, ed. Jonathan Usher, trans. Guido Waldman. Oxford: Oxford University Press, 1993.

Boiardo, Matteo Maria. *Orlando innamorato*, ed. Andrea Canova. Milan: Rizzoli, 2011.

Borges, Jorge Luis. *Labyrinths*. New York: New Directions, 2007.

Brecht, George and Henry Martin. 'An interview with George Brecht'. In *An Introduction to George Brecht's Book of the Tumbler on Fire*, ed. Henry Martin, 74–82. Milan: Multipla Editions, 1978 (1967).

Breton, André. *Nadja*, trans. Richard Howard. New York: Grove Press, 1960.

Bruns, Gerald L. *Maurice Blanchot: The refusal of philosophy*. Baltimore: Johns Hopkins University Press, 2002.

Calvino, Italo. *T Zero*, trans. William Weaver. San Diego: Harcourt, 1969.

Calvino, Italo. *Invisible Cities*, trans. William Weaver. San Diego: Harcourt, 1974.

Calvino, Italo. *The Castle of Crossed Destinies*, trans. William Weaver. New York: Harcourt Brace Jovanovich, 1979.

Calvino, Italo. *Una pietra sopra*. Turin: Einaudi, 1980.

Carroll, Lewis. *Alice's Adventures in Wonderland* and *Through the Looking-Glass*. New York: Barnes and Noble Classics, 2004.

Céline, Louis-Ferdinand. *Entretiens avec le Professeur Y*. Paris: Gallimard, 1955.

Céline, Louis-Ferdinand. *Guignol's Band*, trans. Ralph Manheim. New York: New Directions, 1969.

Céline, Louis-Ferdinand. *Death on the Installment Plan*, trans. Ralph Manheim. New York: New Directions, 1971.

Céline, Louis-Ferdinand. *London Bridge*, trans. Dominic Di Bernardi. Dallas: Dalkey Archive Press, 1995.

Céline, Louis-Ferdinand. *North*, trans. Ralph Manheim. Dallas: Dalkey Archive Press, 1996.

Cervantes, Miguel de. *Don Quixote*, ed. and trans. John Rutherford. New York: Penguin, 2003.

Choay, François. *La città, utopie e realtà*. Turin: Einaudi, 1973.

Collodi, Carlo. *The Adventures of Pinocchio*, trans. Nicolas J. Perella. Berkeley: University of California Press, 1991.

Conrad Joseph. *Heart of Darkness*. London: Penguin, 2012.

Deleuze, Gilles and Felix Guattari. *Anti-Oedipus: Capitalism and Schizophrenia*, trans. Robert Hurley, Mark Seem and Helen R. Lane. Minneapolis: University of Minnesota Press, 1983.

Deleuze, Gilles. *The Logic of Sense*, trans. Mark Lester, with Charles Stivale. New York: Columbia University Press, 1990.

Deleuze, Gilles. *Difference and Repetition*, trans. Paul Patton. New York: Columbia University Press, 1994.

Delfini, Antonio. *Autore Ignoto Presenta*, ed. Gianni Celati. Turin: Einaudi, 2008.

Derrida, Jacques. *Writing and Difference*, trans. Alan Bass. Chicago: University of Chicago Press, 1979.

Dickens, Charles. *The Pickwick Papers*. Oxford: Oxford University Press, 2008.

Eliot, T. S. *On Poetry and Poets*. New York: Farrar Straus and Giroux, 2009.

Flaubert, Gustave. *Bouvard and Pécuchet*, trans. Mark Polizzotti. Dallas: Dalkey Archive Press, 2005.

Foakes, Reginald A. 'Elizabethan acting'. In *Essays and Studies Collected for the English Association, IV*. London: Murray, 1954.

Foucault, Michel. *Discipline and Punish: The birth of the prison*, trans. Alan Sheridan. New York: Vintage, 1979.

Frisch, Max. *I'm Not Stiller*, trans. Michael Bullock. San Diego: Harcourt Brace, 1994.

Gabellone, Lino. *L'oggetto surrealista*. Turin: Einaudi, 1977.

Gadda, Carlo Emilio. *That Awful Mess on the Via Merulana*, trans. William Weaver. New York: New York Books Classics, 2007.

Gardner, Martin. *The Annotated Alice*. New York: Bramhall, 1960.

Ghirri, Luigi, Gianni Leone, and Enzo Velati, eds. *Viaggio in Italia*. Alessandria: Il Quadrante, 1984.

Ghirri, Luigi. *Paessagio italiano*. Milan: Electa, 1989.

Ghirri, Luigi. *Kodachrome*. London: Mack Books, 2012.

Ginzburg, Carlo. 'Spie: Radici di un paradigma idiziario'. In *Crisi della ragione*, ed. by Aldo Gargani. Turin: Einaudi, 1979.

Ginzburg, Carlo. *Il formaggio e i vermi*. Turin: Einaudi, 1976.

Goffman, Erving. *Forms of talk*. Philadelphia: Pennsylvania University Press, 1981.

Izzo, Carlo. *Storia della letteratura inglese dalle origini ai nostri giorni*. Milan: Accademia, 1961.

Jacobs, Jane. *The Life and Death of Great American Cities*. New York: Vintage, 1961.

Kafka, Franz. 'The Great Wall of China', trans. Ian Johnston, *Franz Kafka Online*, http://www.kafka-online.info/the-great-wall-of-china.html.

Kafka, Franz. 'Unknown laws', trans. Michael Hofmann, *London Review of Books* 37, no. 14 (July 16, 2015), https://www.lrb.co.uk/v37/n14/franz-kafka/short-cuts.

Kaufmann, Pierre. *L'expérience émotionelle de l'espace*. Paris: Vrin, 1969.

Labov, William. *Sociolinguistic Patterns*. Philadelphia: Pennsylvania University Press, 1973.

Lear, Edward. *A Book of Nonsense*. London: David Campbell, 1992.

Lynch, Kevin. *The Image of the City*. Cambridge, MA: MIT Press, 1964.

Manganelli, Giorgio. *Nuovo commento*. Turin: Einaudi, 1969.

Melandri, Enzo. *La linea e il circolo*. Bologna: Il Mulino, 1968.

Merleau-Ponty, Maurice. *Phenomenology of Perception*, trans. Donald A. Landes. London: Routledge, 2013.

Moravia, Alberto. *Roman Tales*. New York: Farrar, Straus and Cudahy, 1957.

Morgenstern, Oskar and John von Neumann. *Theory of Games and Economic Behavior*. New York: Science Editions, 1964.

Mumford, Lewis. *The City in History: Its origins, its transformations, and its prospects*. New York: Harcourt, Brace & World, 1961.

Neri, Guido. *Aporie della realizzazione. Filosofia e ideologia nel socialismo reale*. Milan: Feltrinelli, 1980.

Nietzsche, Friedrich. *Untimely Meditations*, ed. Daniel Breazeale, trans. R. J. Hollingdale. Cambridge: Cambridge University Press, 1997.

Oldenburg, Claes. 'I am for …', in *Environments, Situations, Spaces*. New York: Martha Jackson Gallery, 1961; reprinted in an expanded version in: Oldenburg, Claes and Emmett Williams. *Store Days: Documents from The Store (1961) and Ray Gun Theatre (1962)*, 39–42. New York: Something Else Press, 1967.

Palandri, Enrico. *Boccalone*. Milan: Bompiani, 2017.

Palmieri, Nunzia, ed. *Documentari imprevedibili come i sogni: Il cinema di Gianni Celati*. Rome: Fandango, 2011.

Pirandello, Luigi. *Stories for the Years*, trans. Virginia Jewiss. New Haven, CT: Yale University Press, 2020.

Pirandello, Luigi. *The Late Mattia Pascal*, trans. William Weaver. New York: New York Review of Books Classics, 2004.

Polanyi, Livia. *Telling the American Story: A structural and cultural analysis of conversational storytelling*. Cambridge, MA: The MIT Press, 1989.

Queneau, Raymond. *Letters, Numbers, Forms: Essays 1928–70*, trans. Jordan Stump. Champaign: University of Illinois Press, 2007.

Rimbaud, Arthur. *Complete Works*, trans. Paul Schmidt. New York: Harper Colophon, 1976.

Rimbaud, Arthur. *Complete Works*, trans. Wallace Fowlie. Chicago: University of Chicago Press, 2005.

Rimbaud, Arthur. 'Cities (I)', trans. John Ashbery. *The New Yorker* (January 30, 2011), https://www.newyorker.com/magazine/2011/02/07/cities-i.

Rosenquist, James. 'What Is Pop Art?' *ARTnews* (February 1964), http://www.artnews.com/2017/04/03/from-the-archives-james-rosenquist-defines-pop-art-in-1964/.

Russell, John and Suzi Gablik. *Pop Art Redefined*. London: Thames & Hudson, 1969.

Sacks, Harvey. 'Lectures 1964–1965'. *Human Studies* 12 (1989): 185–209.

Sanguineti, Edoardo. *Capriccio italiano*. Milan: Feltrinelli, 1963.

Sanguineti, Edoardo. *Giuoco dell'Oca*. Milan: Feltrinelli, 1967.

Segalen, Victor. *Stèles. Peintures. Équipée*. Paris: Le Club du Meilleur livre, 1952.

Sewell, Elizabeth. *The Field of Nonsense*. London: Chatto and Windus, 1952.

Shillan, David. *Spoken English: A short guide to English speech*. London: Longmans, Green, 1954.

Stendhal. *The Charterhouse of Parma*, trans. John Sturrock. London: Penguin, 2007.

Stevenson, Robert Louis. *Kidnapped*. London: Penguin, 1946.

Stevenson, Robert Louis. *The Master of Ballantrae: A winter's tale*. New York: The Modern Library, 2002.

Verga, Giovanni. *Mastro-don Gesualdo*, trans. Giovanni Cecchetti. Berkeley: University of California Press, 1979.

Vittorini, Elio. 'Parlato e metafora'. In *Il menabò 1*, 125–7. Turin: Einaudi, 1959.

Watt, Ian. *The Rise of the Novel*. London: Chatto & Windus, 1957.

Wittgenstein, Ludwig, *Tractatus Logico-Philosophicus*, trans. F. P. Ramsey, *The Ludwig Wittgenstein Project*, https://www.wittgensteinproject.org.

Index

place (*cont.*)
  displacement in 99–109
  dwelling in 148
  empty 131
  familiar 87, 251
  of hiding 163
  and identity 77
  lingering in 157, 159
  lived 244
  molecular 74
  names of 124
  picturesque 216
  representations of 145
  sense of 242
  timeless 124
  urban 76
photography 1, 6, 15, 132–2, 148,
  158–60, 161–74, 201–7, 241–5
Piacenza 216–19
Pirandello, Luigi 209, 211, 213–14
Pop Art 35, 74, 79
Po River Valley 1–2, 6, 15, 159, 165,
  167, 172–3, 191, 215, 216–19,
  221, 241–6, 260

Queneau, Raymond 18–19

Reggio Emilia 5, 51, 171, 217,
  219–20
retelling 4, 7, 235, 238
rewriting 4, 7, 11, 35, 108, 213,
  235–9, 254
Rimbaud, Arthur 57–8, 74, 76–8
Rivière, Pierre 68, 72
Rossi, Aldo 166
ruins 45, 57, 59, 189, 211, 220,
  229, 231

Sabbioneta 167
Sanguineti, Edoardo 4, 31, 35, 47,
  n. 239
Sassetta 164, 192, 203
Scabia, Giuliano 5, 51–3, n. 148
space 5, 7, 145, 169, 219, 245
  of ambiguity 212
  in cinema 193, 242
  closed 192
  collagelike 121

of the comic body 83–92
delimiting of 4, 31, 216
diffuse 172
of discourse 32
and dreams 79
edenic 124
empty 33, 119, 131, 133, 146,
  147
external 95
flat, 215–16
flux in 10
of games 40
indefinable 179
internal 95
lived 163, 203–4
marginalized 75
of memory 43
of metamorphosis 38
open 155–6, 168, 173, 206, 216
orientation in 133, 205
perspectival 132
prescribed 138
public 167
referential 44
regulated 218
sentiment of 191, 193
soft 119–20
textual 34, 41, 143
and time 61, 142
urban 77
Stendhal 3, 11, 123, 170
Sterne, Laurence 21
Stevenson, Robert Louis 124
surrealism 57, 79, 80
Swift, Jonathan 11, 177–89,
  253–6

tales 1, 7, 39, 42, 44–5, 47, 58, 152,
  155, 177–8, 209–14, 235, 238,
  245; *see also* narration
temporality 5, 47, 75–6, 80, 211
threshold 73, 132–3, 147, 158, 163,
  165, 173, 201–7, 216, 219
tourism 77, 104, 147, 202, 206,
  224, 227, 241, 250
translation 2–4, 7–8, 10–12, 15, 34,
  124, 127, 235–9
  and Jack London 151–5

Milton Keynes UK
Ingram Content Group UK Ltd.
UKHW050230230324
440007UK00006B/108

9 781800 086418